Congressional Abdication on War and Spending

Congressional Abdication on War and Spending

Louis Fisher

TEXAS A&M UNIVERSITY PRESS : COLLEGE STATION

Texas A&M University Press
expresses its appreciation
for support in publishing works
on the presidency and leadership to
The Center for Presidential Studies
George Bush School of Government and Public Service
Texas A&M University

For a complete list of books in print in this series,
see the back of the book.

Library of Congress Cataloging-in-Publication Data

Fisher, Louis.
    Congressional abdication on war and spending / Louis Fisher.
        p.   cm.—(The Joseph V. Hughes, Jr., and Holly O. Hughes series in the presi-
dency and leadership studies ; no. 7)
    Includes bibliographical references and index.
    ISBN 0-89096-950-7 (cloth)—ISBN 0-89096-951-5 (paper)
        1. Separation of powers—United States.   2. United States—Appropriations and
expenditures.   3. War and emergency powers—United States.   4. United States
Congress—Powers and duties.   5. Executive power—United States.   I. Title.
II. Series.
    JK305.F53   2000
    328.73'074—dc21   00-027191

To

LEONARD W. LEVY,

dear friend, richly blessed
with intellect and spirit

Contents

Preface

The Vietnam War and the Watergate crisis stimulated many books that decried the "Imperial" presidency and urged Congress to reassert its constitutional powers.[1] Out of this ferment came such landmark statutes as the War Powers Resolution of 1973 and the Congressional Budget and Impoundment Control Act of 1974. Both measures were widely billed as efforts by Congress to recapture its powers over war and spending. By the 1980s, the belief in a reinvigorated Congress had produced many books that warned of an "Imperial Congress" and objected to statutory restraints that "fettered" the president.[2]

As is often the case, political rhetoric outran reality. Instead of reasserting congressional power, the War Powers Resolution marked an abject surrender of legislative prerogatives to the president. The budget reform statute of 1974 played into the hands of President Ronald Reagan in 1981, helping to generate a five-fold increase in the national debt. The Gramm-Rudman-Hollings Act of 1985, supposedly a bold effort to control deficits, was another surrender of legislative power. Over the last decade Congress has stayed on the sidelines, passively watching Presidents George Bush and Bill Clinton engage in military activities in Panama, Somalia, Haiti, Bosnia, Yugoslavia, Afghanistan, Sudan, and Iraq. In 1996, Congress transferred to the president new spending authorities in the form of the Line Item Veto Act. This is an "imperial" Congress?

Although Congress remains a formidable legislative body—capable in many areas of controlling executive agencies and the president—the legislative decline in war and spending powers has been stunning. My judgments about the failure of Congress to protect these key legislative prerogatives do not lessen my appreciation and respect for much of the good that Congress does, day in and day out. In three decades with the Congressional Research Service (CRS), I have worked closely with lawmakers and congressional staff and watched them discharge their duties with thoughtfulness, dedication, and hard work. They do a remarkable job with scarce resources. I only wish they could act with greater confidence on matters of war and spending and fight for the institutional powers entrusted to them by the Constitution.

Developments over the past half century do little to support the framers' expectation that each branch of government would protect itself by repulsing usurpations and transgressions by other branches. From 1789 to 1945, the framers' constitutional design worked fairly well. Yet from World War II to the present, Congress has repeatedly abdicated fundamental war and spending powers to the president. What explains this collapse? What, if anything, might be done about it?

I use the word *abdication* deliberately to distinguish these congressional failings from conventional and understandable delegations. Abdication means to relinquish a right or power, which is what Congress has been doing with the war power and—to a lesser extent—with the spending power. Abdication means giving someone else something that belongs to you. More seriously, something that has been *entrusted* to you.

With delegation, the transfer of legislative authority to the president is not meant to be complete or irreversible. There may be an element of legislative irresponsibility with both abdication and delegation, but there are crucial differences. Delegation of power to agencies is necessary; we debate only the scope and extent of the delegation and the quality of legislative oversight. Abdication is not necessary; in fact, it undermines Congress as a separate and coequal institution and violates constitutional principles. Another difference: the subject matter. Delegation runs the gamut of governmental programs from environmental policy to housing policy. The abdication of authority discussed in this book concerns rock-bottom, nondelegable legislative prerogatives: war and the power of the purse.

My work with CRS involved me in many of these issues. In the early 1970s I helped Senator Sam Ervin on the impoundment of funds controversy during the Nixon years. That led to staff work on the initial impoundment bill and, later, on the Congressional Budget and Impoundment Control Act of 1974. I testified on the Gramm-Rudman-Hollings Act of 1985, served as research director of the House Iran-Contra Committee in 1987, and was heavily involved at all stages of the Line Item Veto Act of 1996. Many of my thirty-seven appearances to testify before congressional committees have dealt with these executive-legislative disputes. Some of those experiences are reflected in this book.

Portions of this book were presented at a symposium held October 16–17, 1998, at the Saint Louis University Law School on "The Presidency: Twenty Five Years After Watergate." My paper was published in the *Saint Louis University Law Journal* (summer, 1999). I want to thank Neal Devins, Joel Goldstein, Walter Oleszek, and Doug Williams for their comments on the paper. On October 22, 1999, I returned to the law school to participate in another conference, this one devoted solely to the issue of congressional abdication of its war and spending powers. I learned much on this return trip. My paper will be published in the *Saint Louis University Public Law Review*.

Peri Arnold and Fred Greenstein offered many thoughtful ideas on converting these papers to a book. Nancy Kassop and Bob Spitzer were model reviewers of the book manuscript, offering detailed and constructive suggestions. Dave Adler, Richard Kogan, Jim Pfiffner, and Jim Thurber also read portions of the manuscript and offered sound and valued advice. Over the years, many other colleagues and friends have helped sharpen and deepen my understanding of war and spending: Dave Ackerman, Stan Bach, Bill Banks, Dave Davis, Sandy Davis, John Hart Ely, Jim English, Roger Garcia, Mike Glennon, Dick Grimmett, Sue Hardesty, Lou Henkin, Bill Hoagland, Fred Kaiser, Bob Keith, Harold Koh, Leonard Levy, Jim Lindsay, Jules Lobel, Ginger McMurtry, Ron Moe, Peter Raven-Hansen, Harold Relyca, Don Robinson, Mort Rosenberg, Allen Schick, Wendy Selig, Gordon Silverstein, Jane Stromseth, Charles Tiefer, Bob Turner, Lawrence Velvel, and John Yoo. My thanks to all.

Congressional Abdication on War and Spending

I

The Framers' Design

The contemporary shift of war and spending powers from Congress to the president belies a core belief by the framers that each branch of government would protect its own prerogatives. They believed that a powerful dynamic of institutional self-defense would safeguard the structure of separation of powers and give life and energy to the system of checks and balances. They expected Congress to be especially vigilant in protecting powers that formed the heart of representative government: the power to go to war and the power of the purse. Their model worked for about 160 years, but the record since 1950 reveals an alarming decline in congressional confidence and institutional self-esteem. What the framers had in mind clearly isn't working today. Citizens need to understand what has happened, and why, and debate whether the original constitutional principles are worth preserving.

James Madison argued in *Federalist 51* that "the great security against a gradual concentration of the several powers in the same department, consists in giving to those who administer each department the necessary constitutional means and personal motives to resist encroachments of the others. The provision for defence must in this, as in all other cases, be made commensurate to the danger of attack. Ambition must be made to counter ambition. The interest of the man must be connected with the constitutional rights of the place."[1] The core principle: each branch would defend its prerogatives. Madison asked how the partition of power among the three branches would be maintained. Acknowledging that other systems had been inadequate, "the defect must be supplied, by so contriving the interior structure of the government as that its several constituent parts may, by their mutual relations, be the means of keeping each other in their proper places."[2]

The framers depended on a written constitution, representative government, and democratic pressures, but they wanted more. Madison agreed that a "dependence on the people is, no doubt, the primary control on the government; but experience has taught mankind the necessity of auxiliary precautions."[3] The auxiliary precautions: separation of powers, checks and balances, and each branch looking out for its own interests.

The American framers did not borrow the separation doctrine from Montesquieu, who presented a tidy, uncomplicated model of separate branches, free of partisan battles and the evolving cabinet system in England. Montesquieu promoted an idealized form of government, corresponding more to his conceptions—or misconceptions—than to the reality of British politics.[4] Justice Holmes spoke bluntly of this contrivance: "His England—the England of the three-fold division of power into legislative, executive and judicial—was a fiction invented by him, a fiction which misled Blackstone and Delolme."[5]

For the most part, Montesquieu adhered to a strict separation of powers. He maintained that the legislative body should not impeach the executive, for the "moment he is accused or tried there is an end to liberty."[6] He gave his "senate" (the house of nobles) the power to reject bills relating to supplies (funding), but no authority to amend them.[7] He allowed the executive a veto to reject legislation, but opposed any other participation in the legislative process.[8] On all those points, and others, the framers rejected Montesquieu. Yet they agreed on his fundamental premise that power must check power: *"il faut que, par la disposition des choses, le pouvoir arrête le pouvoir."*[9]

Lessons from Home

Colonial governments in America accumulated their own insights into the problem of checks and balances. During this period, complaints about institutional encroachments were common. After achieving their independence from England, many of the states wrote into their constitutions explicit guarantees for a separation between the branches of government, but the meaning of separation varied from state to state and became a source of continual misunderstanding. Despite the strong language in the Massachusetts Constitution, forbidding one department from exercising the powers of another, the executive possessed a qualified veto over the legislature; the senate acted as a court of impeachment; members of the judiciary were appointed by the governor; and the legislature appointed the major generals of the militia, an advisory council for the governor, and appointed several officers of the administration.[10]

Other state constitutions announced separation in strict terms but departed from the maxim when necessary. New Hampshire, the last of the thirteen states to form a constitution, prudently acknowledged the gap between a literal interpretation of separated powers and the demands of workable government. The three departments were to be kept "as separate from and independent of each other, as the nature of a free government will admit, or as is consistent with that chain of connection that binds the whole fabric of the constitution in one indissoluble bond of union and amity."[11]

In the months just before the Philadelphia Convention, Madison identified for Thomas Jefferson the essential elements of the new national government, including a reorganization to provide for separate branches. Madison's interest in three branches was drawn more from administrative necessities than from the writings of Montesquieu. The Continental Congress had mismanaged its power during the Articles of Confederation, he told Jefferson, and administrative duties under the new government would be even more demanding.[12] At the convention, Madison reminded the delegates that experience with the states had proved "a tendency in our government to throw all power into the Legislative vortex. The Executives of the States are in general little more than Cyphers; the legislatures omnipotent."[13] The separation set up in the state constitutions had turned out to be a matter of mere "parchment barriers" incapable of preventing legislatures from drawing other branches into their orbit.[14]

After the convention had adjourned, Madison confided to Jefferson that the boundaries between the executive, legislative, and judicial powers, "though in general so strongly marked in themselves, consist in many instances of mere shades of difference."[15] He set out in the *Federalist Papers* to contrast the overlapping of powers in the Constitution with the abstract and impracticable partitioning of powers advocated by some of the critics. Few writers can compete with Madison for lucidity and precision of expression, yet he paused in *Federalist 37* to reflect on the inherent shortcomings of our language. Just as naturalists had difficulty in defining the exact line between vegetable life and the animal world, so was it an even greater task to draw the boundary between the departments of government, or "even the privileges and powers of the different legislative branches. Questions daily occur in the course of practice, which prove the obscurity which reigns in these subjects, and which puzzle the greatest adepts in political science."[16]

The bulk of Madison's analysis of the separation doctrine appears in *Federalist 47*. He upheld the basic principle of the maxim that tyranny results whenever three branches are concentrated in the same hands, but he charged that the maxim had been "totally misconceived and misapplied."[17] Montesquieu, he said, could not possibly have meant that the three powers of the British government were actually kept separate. The executive magistrate formed a part of the legislative power by making treaties with foreign sovereigns, and he had a share in the judicial power by appointing the members of the judiciary, as well as having the power to remove them. Moreover, one house of the legislature formed a constitutional council for the executive, had judicial power in the impeachment process, and was invested with the supreme appellate jurisdiction in all other cases. The judges could not vote in legislative actions but were permitted to participate in the deliberations.[18]

Madison then turned to the state constitutions for further guidance, pointing out that in no instance were the several departments of power kept absolutely separate and distinct. The intent of Montesquieu, Madison concluded, could be no more than this: "that where the *whole* power of one department is exercised by the same hands which possess the *whole* power of another department, the fundamental principles of a free constitution are subverted."[19]

Checks and Balances

By the late 1780s, the concept of checks and balances had gained dominance over the doctrine of separated powers, which one contemporary pamphleteer called a "hackneyed principle" and a "trite maxim."[20] Yet several delegates at the state ratifying conventions expressed shock at the degree to which the Constitution had mingled the departments.

"How is the executive?" cried one delegate at the Virginia ratifying convention. "Contrary to the opinion of all the best writers, blended with the legislative. We have asked for bread, and they have given us a stone."[21] The draft Constitution was attacked at the North Carolina ratifying convention for violating the maxim whereby the three branches "ought to be forever separate and distinct from each other."[22] Overlapping of departments also provoked criticism in Pennsylvania. Opponents of the Constitution insisted that the Senate's judicial power in impeachment, as well as the executive's power in making treaties, constituted an "undue and dangerous mixture of the powers of government." A lengthy quotation from Montesquieu was introduced to demonstrate the dependence of freedom and liberty on a separation of powers.[23]

These three states recommended that a separation clause be added to the national bill of rights. Virginia offered draft language: "legislative, executive, and judiciary powers of Government should be separate and distinct." North Carolina and Pennsylvania submitted their own versions of a separation clause.[24] Congress compiled a tentative list of restrictions on the national government, among which was the following: "The powers delegated by this constitution are appropriated to the departments to which they are respectively distributed:

so that the legislative department shall never exercise the powers vested in the executive or judicial[,] nor the executive exercise the powers vested in the legislative or judicial, nor the judicial exercise the powers vested in the legislative or executive departments."[25]

This language was among seventeen constitutional amendments sent to the Senate, which struck it from the list. A substitute amendment (to make the three departments "separate and distinct," and to assure that the legislative and executive departments would be restrained from oppression by "feeling and participating the public burthens" through regular elections) was also voted down.[26] The list of seventeen amendments was whittled down to twelve. Among the deleted amendments was the separation clause.

The framers did not object to a sharing or partial intermixture of powers. They were not doctrinaire advocates of a pure separation of powers between branches. Some overlapping was necessary to assure a vigorous system of checks and balances. They knew that the "danger of tyranny or injustice lurks in unchecked power, not in blended power."[27]

War and Spending Prerogatives

The framers were particularly intent on vesting the power of the purse and the power of initiating war in the Congress, as the people's representative. They were well aware of the efforts of English kings to rely on extra-parliamentary sources of revenue for their military expeditions and other activities. Some of the payments came from foreign governments; others came from private citizens. Because of these transgressions and encroachments of legislative prerogatives, England lurched into a bloody civil war and Charles I lost both his head and his office.[28] Joseph Story, who served on the Supreme Court from 1811 to 1845, wrote about the essential republican principle of vesting in the representative branch the decision to go to war (see box 1).

The U.S. Constitution attempted to avoid the British history of civil war and bloodshed by vesting the power of the purse squarely in Congress. Under Article I, section 9, "No Money shall be drawn from the Treasury, but in Consequence of Appropriations made by Law." In *Federalist 48*, Madison explained that "the legislative department alone has access to the pockets of the people."[29] In Article I, section 8, Congress is empowered to lay and collect taxes, duties, imposts and excises; to borrow money on the credit of the United States; and to coin money and regulate its value. The power of the purse, said Madison in *Federalist 58*, represents the "most complete and effectual weapon with which any constitution can arm the immediate representatives of the people, for obtaining a redress of every grievance, and for carrying into effect every just and salutary measure."[30]

The framers did more than place the power of the purse with Congress. They deliberately divided government by making the president the commander in chief and reserving to Congress the power to finance military expeditions. The framers rejected a government in which a single branch could both make war and fund it. In *Federalist 69,* Alexander Hamilton argued that the American president was far less threatening than the king of England. He explained that the power of the king "extends to the *declaring* of war and to the *raising* and *regulating* of fleets and armies."[31] In contrast, the Constitution placed those powers expressly with Congress. Jefferson praised this transfer of the war power "from the executive to the Legislative body, from those who are to spend to those who are to pay."[32] Madison warned against placing the power of commander in chief in the same hands as the power to go to war: "Those who are to *conduct a war* cannot in the nature of things, be proper or safe judges, whether *a war ought* to be *commenced, continued,* or *concluded.* They are barred from the latter functions by a great principle in free government, analogous to that which separates the sword from the purse, or the power of executing from the power of enacting laws."[33] George Mason advised his colleagues at the Philadelphia Convention in 1787 that the "purse & the sword ought never to get into the same hands <whether Legislative or Executive.>"[34]

The framers were aware that British models placed the power to initiate war with the monarch. John Locke's *Second Treatise on Civil Government* (1690) spoke of three branches of government: legislative, executive, and "federative." The last consisted of "the power of war and peace, leagues and alliances, and all the transactions with all persons and communities without the commonwealth." The federative power (or what we would call foreign policy today) was "always almost united" with the executive.

Similarly, Sir William Blackstone, the great eighteenth-century jurist, vested foreign policy and the war power exclusively with the monarch. In his *Commentaries,* he defined the king's prerogative broadly to include the right to send and receive ambassadors, to make war or peace, to make treaties, to issue letters of marque and reprisal (authorizing private citizens to undertake military actions), and to raise and regulate fleets and armies.

Steeped in these models and theories, the framers nonetheless vested in Congress many of Locke's federative powers and Blackstone's royal prerogatives. At the Philadelphia Convention, Charles Pinckney said he was for "a vigorous Executive but was afraid the Executive powers of <the existing> Congress might extend to peace & war &c which would render the Executive a

BOX 1

Story's View of the War Power

. . . the power of declaring war is not only the highest sovereign prerogative; . . . it is in its own nature and effects so critical and calami-
tous, that it requires the utmost deliberation, and the successive review
of all the councils of the nations. War, in its best estate, never fails to
impose upon the people the most burthensome taxes, and personal
sufferings. It is always injurious, and sometimes subversive of the great
commercial, manufacturing, and agricultural interests. Nay, it always
involves the prosperity, and not infrequently the existence, of a nation.
It is sometimes fatal to public liberty itself, by introducing a spirit of
military glory, which is ready to follow, wherever a successful commander will lead; . . . It should therefore be difficult in a republic to
declare war; but not to make peace. . . . The co-operation of all the
branches of the legislative power ought, upon principle, to be required
in this the highest act of legislation. . . .

Source: Joseph Story, *Commentaries on the Constitution of the United States*, vol. 3, pp.
60–61.

Monarchy, of the worst kind, towit an elective one."[35] James Wilson supported
a single executive but "did not consider the Prerogatives of the British Monarch as a proper guide in defining the Executive powers. Some of these prerogatives were of a Legislative nature. Among others that of war & peace &c."[36]

Edmund Randolph worried about executive power, calling it "the foetus of
monarchy." The delegates to the Philadelphia Convention, he said, had "no
motive to be governed by the British Governmt. as our prototype." Wilson
agreed that the British model "was inapplicable to the situation of this Country; the extent of which was so great, and the manners so republican, that nothing
but a great confederated Republic would do for it."[37] The powers over foreign
affairs and war that Locke and Blackstone had given to the monarch were allo-
cated either exclusively to Congress or shared between the president and the
Senate (as with the treaty and appointment powers).

The one exception to this pattern of legislative control was the discretion
left to the president to take certain defensive actions. The early draft empowered Congress to "make war." Charles Pinckney objected that legislative pro-

ceedings "were too slow" for the safety of the country in an emergency, because he expected Congress to meet but once a year. Madison and Elbridge Gerry moved to insert "declare" for "make," leaving the president with "the power to repel sudden attacks." Their motion carried. The duty to repel sudden attacks represented an emergency measure that permitted the president to take actions necessary to resist sudden attacks either against the mainland of the United States or against American troops abroad. This discretionary authority did not extend to taking the country into full-scale war or to mount an offensive attack against other nations. As John Bassett Moore, a noted scholar of international law, remarked: "There can hardly be room for doubt that the framers of the constitution, when they vested in Congress the power to declare war, never imagined that they were leaving it to the executive to use the military and naval forces of the United States all over the world for the purpose of actually coercing other nations, occupying their territory, and killing their soldiers and citizens, all according to his own notions of the fitness of things, as long as he refrained from calling his action war or persisted in calling it peace."[38]

Responses to the Madison-Gerry amendment reinforce the narrow grant of authority to the president. Pierce Butler wanted to give the president the power to make war, but other delegates strongly objected. They were for "clogging rather than facilitating war" (see box 2).

The framers gave Congress the power to initiate war because they believed that presidents, in their search for fame and personal glory, would have an appetite for war.[39] John Jay warned in Federalist No. 4 that "absolute monarchs will often make war when their nations are to get nothing by it, but for purposes and objects merely personal, such as a thirst for military glory, revenge for personal affronts, ambition, or private compacts to aggrandize or support their particular families or partisans. These and a variety of other motives, which affect only the mind of the sovereign, often lead him to engage in wars not sanctified by justice or the voice and interests of his people."[40] Writing in 1793, Madison called war "the true nurse of executive aggrandizement. . . . In war, the honours and emoluments of office are to be multiplied; and it is the executive patronage under which they are to be enjoyed. It is in war, finally, that laurels are to be gathered; and it is the executive brow they are to encircle. The strongest passions and most dangerous weaknesses of the human breast; ambition, avarice, vanity, the honourable or venial love of fame, are all in conspiracy against the desire and duty of peace."[41]

At the Pennsylvania ratifying convention, James Wilson expressed the prevailing sentiment that the system of checks and balances "will not hurry us into war; it is calculated to guard against it. It will not be in the power of a single

---

BOX 2

Debate on the Madison-Gerry Amendment

Mr [Pierce] Butler. . . . He was for vesting the [war] power in the President, who will have all the requisite qualities, and will not make war but when the Nation will support it. . . .

Mr Sharmen [Sherman] thought it stood very well. The Executive shd. be able to repel and not to commence war. "Make" better than "declare" the latter narrowing the power too much.

Mr Gerry never expected to hear in a republic a motion to empower the Executive alone to declare war.

Mr. [Oliver] Elseworth [Ellsworth]. there is a material difference between the cases of making *war,* and making *peace.* It shd. be more easy to get out of war, than into it. . . .

Mr. Mason was agst giving the power of war to the Executive, because not <safely> to be trusted with it; or to the Senate, because not so constructed as to be entitled to it. He was for clogging rather than facilitating war; but for facilitating peace. He preferred *"declare"* to *"make."*

Source: Max Farrand, ed., *The Records of the Federal Convention of 1787,* vol. 2, at pp. 318–19.

---

man, or a single body of men, to involve us in such distress; for the important power of declaring war is vested in the legislature at large."[42] Similar comments were made by delegates to the North Carolina and South Carolina ratifying conventions.[43]

Letters of Marque and Reprisal

Through the granting of letters of marque and reprisal, sovereigns were able to authorize private citizens to wage war on other countries. By turning to citizens (or privateers), nations could augment their armies and navies and respond more swiftly and with greater force to emergencies and threats. Privately owned vessels were authorized to prey on foreign vessels and take plunder, or "prizes." The phrase "letters of marque and reprisal" came to refer to any use of force short of a declared war.

Unlike Blackstone, who recognized that the king had the power to issue letters of marque and reprisal, the framers transferred that responsibility solely to Congress and associated it with the power to declare war. Congress is given the power "To declare war, grant letters of Marque and Reprisal, and make rules concerning Captures on Land and Water." Any initiation of war, whether by declaration or by marque and reprisal, was reserved to Congress. Thus, both general and limited wars were left to the decision of the representative branch. At a time when the United States lacked a standing army and a strong navy, reliance on private citizens was important.

In 1793, Secretary of State Thomas Jefferson related marque and reprisal to the power to wage war. The making of a reprisal on a nation, he said, "is a very serious thing. . . . when reprisal follows, it is considered an act of war, & never yet failed to produce it in the case of a nation able to make war." If it became necessary to invoke this power, "Congress must be called on to take it; the right of reprisal being expressly lodged with them by the constitution, & not with the executive."[44]

During the Quasi War against France, from 1798 to 1800, Congress authorized private citizens to provide vessels and other military assistance. Alexander Hamilton, always protective of executive power, recognized that the Constitution vested in Congress exclusive power over reprisals. In the midst of hostilities, the president could repel force by force, but any actions beyond those measures "must fall under the idea of *reprisals* & requires the sanction of that Department which is to declare or make war."[45] Congress also authorized letters of marque during the War of 1812, but has not done so since that time. Signatories to the Declaration of Paris, after the Crimean War in 1856, renounced the use of letters of marque.

The Law of Nations

Seven clauses of the Constitution vest war powers in Congress. Clause 11 empowers Congress to declare war, grant letters of marque and reprisal, and make rules concerning captures on land and water. Clauses 12 and 13 empower Congress to raise and support armies and provide and maintain a navy. Clauses 14, 15, and 16 authorize Congress to make rules for the government and regulations of the land and naval forces, to call forth the militia, and to provide for the organizing, arming, and disciplining of the militia. At the top of the list stands Clause 10, which empowers Congress "to define and punish Piracies and Felonies committed on the high Seas, and Offences against the Law of Nations."

This cluster of powers broke with prevailing theories that placed war powers, foreign affairs, and judgments on the law of nations with the executive. Blackstone, for example, regarded the law of nations as part of the king's power. The law of nations consisted of "mutual compacts, treaties, leagues, and agreements" between various countries.[46] It was the king's prerogative to make treaties, leagues, and alliances with foreign states.

At the Philadelphia Convention, Madison emphasized the importance of drafting a constitution that would "prevent those violations of the law of nations & of Treaties which if not prevented must involve us in the calamities of foreign wars."[47] One of the early statutes Congress passed was legislation in 1790, setting forth punishments for certain crimes against the United States. One provision established fines and imprisonment for any person who attempted to prosecute or bring legal action against an ambassador or other public minister from another country. Persons who took such actions were deemed "violators of the laws of nations" who "infract the law of nations."[48] Actions against ambassadors and public ministers "tends to provoke the resentment of the sovereign whom the ambassador represents, and to bring upon the state the calamities of war."[49]

The Neutrality Act of 1794 gave the Washington administration the legal footing it needed to fine and imprison American citizens whose actions might have embroiled the United States in the war between France and England. Almost two centuries later, a district judge noted that one of the major purposes of the Neutrality Act "was to protect the constitutional power of Congress to declare war or authorize private reprisal against foreign states."[50]

Scholarly Consensus

Questions about framers' intent invariably cause scholars to scatter and divide. Not so with the war power. There is remarkable agreement among experts on the war power that the framers broke with available monarchical precedents and vested in Congress the sole power to initiate hostilities against other nations. Taylor Reveley wrote that if you could ask a man in the state of nature to read the war-power provisions in the Constitution and compare them to war-power practices after 1789, "he would marvel at how much Presidents have spun out of so little. On its face, the text tilts decisively toward Congress."[51] To Charles Lofgren, the grants of power to Congress to declare war and to issue letters of marque and reprisal "likely convinced contemporaries even further that the new Congress would have nearly complete authority over the commencement of war."[52] He concluded that the years following ratification of the Constitution helped reinforce the view that Americans "originally understood Congress to have at least a coordinate, and probably the dominant, role in initiating all but the most obviously defensive wars, whether declared or not."[53]

John Hart Ely noted that when academics try to divine the "original understanding" of the Constitution, the results can be "obscure to the point of inscrutability." But when the focus turns on the war power, the issue isn't that complicated. All wars, big or small, declared or undeclared, "had to be legislatively authorized."[54] David Gray Adler writes that the Constitution "makes Congress the sole and exclusive repository of the ultimate foreign relations power—the authority to initiate war."[55]

Michael Glennon said that it "is clear that the Constitution's textual grants of war-making power to the President are paltry in comparison with, and are subordinate to, its grants to Congress."[56] He further noted that there "is no evidence that the Framers intended to confer upon the President any independent authority to commit the armed forces to combat, except in order to repel sudden attacks."[57] Harold Koh writes in a similar fashion. The first three articles of the Constitution "expressly divided foreign affairs powers among the three branches of government, with *Congress,* not the president, being granted the dominant role."[58] The framers "pointedly denied" the president other grants of power, such as the power to declare war, "thereby rejecting the English model of a king who possessed both the power to declare war and the authority to command troops."[59]

The major exception to these studies is an article written in 1996 by John Yoo, who argues that the framers designed a system that encouraged presidential initiative in war.[60] Yoo never distinguishes between the president's *defensive* powers as opposed to initiating *offensive* actions against another country. Taking the United States from a state of peace to a state of war was a prerogative assigned exclusively to Congress. Yoo makes no mention of the many statements by President Washington, Secretary of War John Knox, President Jefferson, and others that recognized that presidents were limited to defensive actions. According to Yoo, the Constitution's provisions on the war power did not break with British precedents, but that argument is contradicted not only by statements made at the Philadelphia Convention and the state ratification debates but by express language in Articles I and II of the Constitution.

It was only with a comparatively recent event—Truman's intervention in Korea in 1950—that presidential power began to veer from what the framers intended. What could have been categorized as a momentary aberration is now the norm, helped along by the Vietnam War, the War Powers Resolution, and military initiatives by Presidents Reagan, Bush, and Clinton. These shifts of legislative power to the president were accompanied by the Budget Act of 1974, the Gramm-Rudman-Hollings Act of 1985, and the Line Item Veto Act of 1996, representing other institutional failures by Congress.

2

The Record from 1789 to 1945

The framers' model for constitutional government and democratic control worked well for about 160 years. Of course the balance of power between Congress and the president varied from decade to decade, depending on who served in the White House and what kind of political conditions temporarily upset the distribution of power. But Congress was fairly consistent in protecting its war and spending powers. There was no wholesale delegation or abdication.

Military Initiatives

For all of the major military actions, Congress either declared war or authorized it. A declaration of war was used for the War of 1812 against England, the War of 1846 against Mexico, the Spanish-American War of 1898, World War I, and World War II. On other occasions Congress used the statutory process to authorize war, as with the "Quasi War" with France from 1798 to 1800 and the Barbary wars during the Jefferson and Madison administrations. Similarly, Congress passed legislation authorizing military action in the Indian wars and the Whiskey Rebellion.[1]

During these early decades, presidents and executive officials uniformly acknowledged the need to come to Congress for authority to support anything other than purely defensive operations. President Washington understood that existing statutory authority, giving him access to the militia to protect inhabitants of the frontiers, permitted only defensive actions against hostile Indian forces. Secretary of War Henry Knox told territorial governors that until Congress decided otherwise, military operations were to be confined to "defensive measures."[2] The direction of offensive operations had to await the decision of

Congress, which was "solely . . . vested with the powers of War."[3] Washington knew that any step beyond defensive actions required authority from Congress.[4] Knox stated that Congress was "alone . . . competent to decide upon an offensive war."[5]

Even for domestic insurrections, like the Whiskey Rebellion of 1794, Washington adhered to procedures set forth by Congress. Under statutory law, the president could call forth the state militias to suppress insurrections, but only after complying with a novel check on executive power. An associate justice of the Supreme Court or a federal district judge would have to first notify the president that the ordinary governmental institutions within a state were unable to meet the danger.[6] In putting down the Whiskey Rebellion, President Washington received from Justice James Wilson a certification that ordinary legal means were insufficient to execute national law.[7] After Washington called forth the militias of four states to put down the rebellion, District Judge Richard Peters joined Alexander Hamilton and District Attorney William Rawle in accompanying the troops.[8]

In proposing military action against France in the Quasi War, 1798–1800, President John Adams never argued that he could act unilaterally. He knew he had to seek authority from Congress, which enacted several dozen statutes increasing the size of the military and reinforcing the defense of ports and harbors.[9]

President Thomas Jefferson—never shy about invoking executive power—recognized the difference between defensive and offensive military operations. On December 8, 1801, he told Congress that he had sent a small squadron of frigates to the Mediterranean to protect against attacks by the Barbary pirates, but sought further legislative guidance because he was "unauthorized by the Constitution, without the sanction of Congress, to go beyond the line of defense." It was up to Congress to authorize "measures of offense also."[10] In at least ten statutes, Congress authorized Presidents Jefferson and Madison to take military actions against the Barbary powers.[11]

No doubt Jefferson's message to Congress omits many details of what happened in the Mediterranean.[12] However, the essential legal point is that he went to Congress to seek statutory authority. He did not claim an independent and exclusive power to go to war. In 1805, when conflicts arose between the United States and Spain, Jefferson reported to Congress about the situation and spoke plainly about constitutional principles: "Congress alone is constitutionally invested with the power of changing our condition from peace to war."[13]

Certainly presidential powers expanded in ways unexpected by the framers, particularly after presidents had a standing army and could move troops into disputed areas to provoke war, as President James K. Polk did with Mexico. Polk was intent on gaining from Mexico the territories known as Upper California and New Mexico. Through a series of diplomatic and military initiatives, he was able to bring about a military clash between American and Mexican troops and tell Congress that "war exists." Although some legislators objected to Polk's tactics, Congress declared war by recognizing that "a state of war exists."[14]

Even under the crisis period of the Civil War, when President Lincoln exercised extraordinary power while Congress was in recess, he recognized that some of his actions (particularly suspending the writ of habeas corpus) were probably in excess of his constitutional authority. Lincoln operated under what John Locke called the "prerogative": the executive power to act "according to discretion for the public good, without the prescription of the law and sometimes even against it."[15] In the hands of an indiscriminate and unprincipled executive this formula can lead to autocracy, but Lincoln was not inclined to be a dictator.

When Congress returned he explained that his actions, "whether strictly legal or not, were ventured upon under what appeared to be a popular demand and a public necessity, trusting then, as now, that Congress would readily ratify them."[16] He conceded that he had acted not only under his Article II powers but the Article I powers of Congress as well. He believed that suspending the writ of habeas corpus was not "beyond the constitutional competency of Congress."[17] Congress debated at length his request for retroactive authority. Legislators ended up supporting the president on the explicit assumption that his actions were illegal.[18] Legislation was passed "approving, legalizing, and making valid all the acts, proclamations, and orders of the President, etc., as if they had been issued and done under the previous express authority and direction of the Congress of the United States."[19] Furthermore, Lincoln based his actions partly on statutes enacted in 1795 and 1807 that authorized the president to use military force to suppress insurrections.[20] The turn of the twentieth century led to other wars, but they were all declared by Congress: the Spanish-American War of 1898, World War I, and World War II.

Early Court Decisions

A recent study on judicial cases affecting the war power concludes that courts are reluctant to rule on these matters but "when they are forced to rule, they usually uphold presidential action."[21] There are many cases, however, that restrict presidential power and recognize that the warmaking power resides in Congress. Certainly that is true of the early nineteenth century.

Although the constitutional text only empowers Congress to declare war, it was well recognized by the framers that governments can make war without a formal declaration. The first major war—the Quasi War against France from 1798 to 1800—was not declared. Yet it was authorized by a number of statutes. The war against France came to the Supreme Court in two cases decided in 1800 and 1801, both of which acknowledged that Congress can resort to authorization rather than declaration. In the first case, Justice Washington said that war could be of two forms: (1) "declared in form, . . . *solemn,* and . . . of the perfect kind" and (2) "imperfect" (undeclared but authorized).[22] To Justice Chase, Congress "is empowered to declare a general war, or congress may wage a limited war; limited in place, in objects, and in time." In his judgment, the war against France was "a limited partial war. Congress has not declared war in general terms; but congress has authorized hostilities on the high seas by certain persons and in certain cases. There is no authority to commit hostilities on land."[23] Justice William Paterson spoke of an "imperfect war."[24] A year later, Chief Justice John Marshall decided the second case on the undeclared war with France. The "whole powers of war," he said, were vested in Congress (see box 3).

These cases reject the proposition that the power of Congress over war is confined to declared wars and that presidents may use independent authority to engage in military actions for undeclared wars. Congress has jurisdiction over both declared and undeclared (authorized) wars. Legislative acts were the sole guides to judicial inquiry.

A third case from the war against France raised another issue: When Congress has legislated military policy, can presidents exceed those boundaries by issuing proclamations and other executive decrees? Part of the legislation enacted from 1798 to 1800 authorized the president to seize vessels sailing *to* French ports. President John Adams issued an order directing American ships to capture vessels sailing *to* or *from* French ports. Captain George Little followed Adams's order by seizing a Danish ship sailing from a French port. He was subsequently sued for damages.

When Chief Justice Marshall received this case, his "first bias" was to support Captain Little. Although the instructions from President Adams "could not give a right, they might yet excuse [a military officer] from damages." Military men were expected to follow the orders of their superiors. Upon further reflection, Marshall decided that Captain Little was liable for damages: "I have been convinced that I was mistaken, and I have receded from this first opinion. I acquiesce in that of my brethren, which is, that the instructions [by Adams] cannot change the nature of the transaction, or legalize an act which, without

---

BOX 3

Chief Justice Marshall on the War Power

The whole powers of war being, by the constitution of the United States, vested in congress, the acts of that body can alone be resorted to as our guides in this inquiry. It is not denied, that congress may authorize general hostilities, in which case the general laws of war apply to our situation; or partial hostilities, in which case the laws of war, so far as they actually apply to our situation, must be noticed.

To determine the real situation of America in regard to France, the acts of congress are to be inspected.

Source: *Talbot v. Seeman*, 5 U.S. (1 Cr.) 1, 28 (1801).

---

those instructions, would have been a plain trespass."[25] In short, when Congress establishes national policy for military operations, the president, in his capacity as commander in chief, must execute statutory policy, not independent and inconsistent executive initiatives.

Two years later a circuit court, dealing with a case growing out of neutrality act prosecutions, again rejected the notion that the president could exercise war powers independent of and in conflict with legislative policy. President George Washington had issued his Proclamation of Neutrality in 1793 to prevent private citizens from engaging in military initiatives that might embroil the United States in war between France and England. When the administration tried to prosecute citizens who violated the proclamation, jurors rebelled and refused to convict someone for a crime established by a proclamation.[26] If the administration wanted to punish citizens for committing a crime, they would need a statute from Congress. After President Washington asked for legislative authority, Congress passed the Neutrality Act of 1794.

In one of the significant cases defining the power of Congress to restrict presidential action, a circuit court in 1806 reviewed the indictment of Colonel William S. Smith for engaging in military actions against Spain. He claimed that his military enterprise "was begun, prepared, and set on foot with the knowledge and approbation of the executive department of our government."[27] The court repudiated the argument that a president or his assistants could somehow authorize military adventures that violated congressional policy. Executive officials, including the president, could not waive statutory provisions: "if a private individual, even with the knowledge and approbation of this high and preeminent officer of our government [the president], should set on foot such a military expedition, how can he expect to be exonerated from the obligation of the law?"[28]

The circuit court hammered home the point. Even if the president had known about the expedition and approved of it, "it would not justify the defendant in a court of law, nor discharge him from the binding force of the act of congress." Reaching to a core value, the court asked: "Does [the president] possess the power of making war? That power is exclusively vested in congress." It was "the exclusive province of congress to change a state of peace into a state of war."[29]

In *The Prize Cases* of 1863, the Supreme Court spoke clearly about the president's authority to conduct defensive but not offensive actions. Justice Grier said that President Lincoln had authority to take military action in a civil war "without waiting for Congress to baptize it with a name," but carefully stated that the president "has no power to initiate or declare a war either against a foreign nation or a domestic State."[30] The executive branch took exactly the same position. During oral argument Richard Henry Dana, Jr., representing the United States, said that Lincoln's action in responding to the civil war had nothing to do with "the right *to initiate a war, as a voluntary act of sovereignty. That is vested only in Congress.*"[31]

Unauthorized Presidential Actions

From 1789 to 1950, presidents used military force unilaterally a number of times without seeking or obtaining the authority of Congress. Those ventures, however, were relatively modest in scope and limited in duration. As Edward S. Corwin noted, these presidential initiatives consisted largely of "fights with pirates, landings of small naval contingents on barbarous or semi-barbarous costs, the dispatch of small bodies of troops to chase bandits or cattle rustlers across the Mexican border, and the like."[32] They are in no sense a precedent for singlehanded presidential actions after World War II, such as Truman's war against North Korea, Bush's claim in 1990 that he could go to war against Iraq without congressional authority, and Clinton's repeated use of military force in Bosnia, Yugoslavia, Iraq, Haiti, Sudan, and Afghanistan without ever seeking authority from Congress.

Lists have been compiled to show that presidents have resorted to force against other countries hundreds of times without Congress declaring or authorizing military action.[33] Many of these operations were minor, such as American forces building a fort on the Marquesas Islands in 1813–14 to protect three prize ships captured from the British, brief landings in Cuba in 1823 in pursuit of pirates, an 1840 landing on the Fiji Islands to punish natives for attacking American exploring and surveying parties, a display of naval force in Japan in 1853–54, another display of naval force off Turkey in 1858–59, the landing of a naval party in Buenos Aires in 1890 to protect the U.S. consulate and legation, the landing of U.S. forces in Beirut in 1903 to protect the American consulate, and the sending of troops to Panama in 1912 to supervise elections outside the Canal Zone.

Some of the military interventions were much more significant but would hardly serve as a model for U.S. policy today. For example, in 1854 an American ship was ordered to the Nicaraguan port of Greytown (now San Juan del Norte) to compel local authorities to make appropriate amends for an affront to an American diplomat. When U.S. officials considered the apology to be inadequate, the ship bombarded the town and sent forces ashore to destroy by fire whatever remained of the town.[34] A number of other military operations, including the occupation and bombardment of Veracruz in 1914, the intervention and occupation of Haiti from 1915 to 1934, an eight-year occupation of the Dominican Republic, beginning in 1916, and repeated interventions in Nicaragua from 1909 to 1933 would be condemned today, both under the non-intervention policy of the Organization of American States (OAS) and Article 2(4) of the UN Charter, proscribing "the threat or use of force against the territorial integrity or political independence of any state."

Power of the Purse

For the first 160 years, the spending power remained largely in the hands of Congress. During the early decades, the House Ways and Means Committee and the Senate Finance Committee exercised broad control over the budget; they were responsible not only for taxes and tariffs but also for appropriations and banking and currency. The committees retained those jurisdictions until reforms in the 1860s, when control over appropriations and banking and currency were parceled out to new committees.[35]

President Andrew Jackson and Congress clashed over the status of the secretary of the treasury. Some legislators regarded the secretary as the agent of Congress. By statute, Congress had delegated to the secretary—not the president—the responsibility for placing government funds either in the national bank or state banks. Jackson directed Secretary of the Treasury William Duane to place the funds in state banks. When Duane refused, Jackson removed him and picked a successor willing to carry out his orders. The Senate responded with a resolution of censure, claiming that Jackson had assumed "authority and power not conferred by the Constitution and laws, but in derogation of both."

Outraged that the Senate would censure him on the basis of unspecified charges and without an opportunity to be heard, Jackson prepared a lengthy and impassioned protest. Arguing that the secretary of the treasury was "wholly an executive officer," subject to the president's control, Jackson said that the Senate had itself violated the Constitution by charging him with an impeachable offense without first waiting for the House to act.[36] Three years later, after the Democrats regained control of the Senate, the censure resolution was expunged.[37]

Throughout the nineteenth century, Congress monitored with great care any discretionary spending power left to executive officials. Annual estimates of expenditures originated in the various bureaus and agencies of the executive branch, but the president had no formal or statutory duty to prepare a national budget. At an informal level, presidents intervened as best they could to influence agency estimates.[38]

Many of the executive-legislative budgetary disputes during the nineteenth century concerned the degree to which presidents and executive officials could move funds from one appropriations account to another account (transfers between accounts) or from one fiscal year to the next (transfers between years). Congress regularly went back and forth in prohibiting such transfers altogether while allowing them under certain conditions and exigencies.[39]

The President as Fiscal Guardian

In the years following the Civil War, some presidents gained the reputation as "guardian of the purse." The image was simplistic, of course, in the sense that special interests could (and did) exert influence on executive decisions. Yet Congress came in for heavy criticism during this period.

Part of the attack focused on the way Congress handled rivers and harbors bills. Increased expenditures for these projects reflected a number of changes, including a shift in committee jurisdiction. In 1865, the House created an Appropriations Committee to handle all of the funding bills. Two years later the Senate adopted the same reform. Gradually, the appropriations power was stripped away from the Appropriations Committees and parceled out to authorizing committees. For example, in 1878 the House Commerce Committee gained the privilege of reporting bills to fund the improvement of rivers and harbors.[40] Other authorizing committees gained similar privileges.

The breakup of the Appropriations Committees came from the rank-and-file who wanted greater spending for their districts. They believed that the committees had emphasized economy at the expense of constituent needs. When it was pointed out that the splintering of the appropriations process might lead to greater spending, Charles Lore of Delaware asked: would a legislator "come here and wear his boy's roundabout which he has outgrown and when he has come to man's stature? Would he take his old coat split up the back like a locust?"[41] Speaker Thomas Reed also emphasized the growing needs that pressed upon the country in the years after the Civil War.[42]

Several presidents won public support for resisting these expenditures by Congress. President Chester A. Arthur explained that the rivers and harbors bills—through the process of log-rolling—secured additional support as they became more objectionable. Although Congress in 1882 overrode his veto of one of these bills, he received favorable publicity for his effort. A cartoon by Thomas Nast shows Arthur, armed with a rifle, watching an oversized vulture perched on the Capitol consume his veto message. At the bottom of the cartoon are these words of encouragement: "President Arthur, hit him again! Don't let the vulture become our national bird."[43]

Another heavy drain on the Treasury came from the military pension system, sanctified by an aura of patriotism and self-sacrifice. Frauds had followed the Revolutionary War and the War of 1812, but the full measure of chicanery by pension claimants and their agents was not felt until after the Civil War. Federal outlays for military pensions reached record heights from one decade to the next: $29 million in 1870, $57 million in 1880, $106 million in 1890, and $139 million at the turn of the century. The last veteran's benefit for the Revolutionary War was paid in 1906: 123 years after that war had ended.[44]

Congress was widely considered to be incapable of intelligently considering the thousands of private pension bills introduced each year.[45] The number of deserters during the Civil War was officially estimated at over a half million soldiers, prompting Charles Francis Adams to call the soldiers "far more battle-scared than battle-scarred." He marveled at the amount of "cant and fustian—nauseating twaddle, perhaps, would not be too strong a term," that had been used by members of Congress in praise of veterans.[46]

Veterans met slight resistance from Congress, while President Grover Cleveland stands as the only determined counterforce among the presidents. In his first term he issued 304 regular vetoes—almost three times as many as all regular vetoes before him. A full 241 of the Cleveland vetoes were leveled at private and general pension bills.[47] Even those statistics do not capture the poor quality of pension legislation. Forty-two pension bills were killed by pocket vetoes.

Other bills became law without Cleveland's signature because he lacked time to study them.

On a single day in 1886 he was handed nearly 240 private bills—granting new pensions, increasing their benefits, or restoring old names to the list. A check by the Pension Bureau revealed that most of the claims had been there before and had been rejected. Some disabilities existed before the claimant's enlistment; others were not incurred in the line of military duty; still others had their origin after discharge. Denied relief by the bureau, individuals turned to their congressman for assistance through private bills.[48]

Cleveland's vetoes of pension bills earned a well-deserved reputation for their sarcastic quality. One claimant, who enrolled in the Army on March 25, 1865, entered a post hospital a week later with the measles. He returned to duty on May 8 and was mustered out of the service three days later. Cleveland observed that fifteen years after this "brilliant service and this terrific encounter with the measles," the claimant discovered that the measles had somehow affected his eyes and spinal column. Cleveland found no merit to the claim. He bristled at another pension request from a widow whose husband had joined the service and deserted several days later. "Those who prosecute claims for pension," said Cleveland, "have grown very bold when cases of this description are presented for consideration."[49]

Within the space of three days, in June, 1886, he turned out forty-three pension bills. Another Thomas Nast cartoon captures the president exercising his role as protector of the purse. Cleveland manfully blocks the door to the U.S. Treasury while thwarted pension agents slink from his presence.[50]

The Budget and Accounting Act

Proposals to shift budgetary prerogatives to the president, by adopting the British parliamentary system, were regularly rejected. This lesson is drawn from the struggles from the William Howard Taft to the Warren G. Harding administrations, eventually resulting in the Budget and Accounting Act of 1921. As a result of this battle, the president gained statutory authority to prepare a national budget, but Congress remained fully empowered to change the president's budget in any manner it saw fit.

Early in the twentieth century, several top officials and academic experts recommended that Congress surrender a substantial part of the power of the purse to the president. When John J. Fitzgerald, chairman of the House Appropriations Committee, met with the New York constitutional convention in 1915, he supported a procedure that would make it as difficult as possible for

Congress to increase the spending estimates submitted by the president. He believed that Congress should be prohibited from appropriating any money "unless it had been requested by the head of the department, unless by a two-thirds vote, or unless it was to pay a claim against the government or for its own expenses."[51]

Charles Wallace Collins, a prominent scholar of budget reform, published an article in 1916 that argued for a form of parliamentary government. "Our institutions," he wrote, "being more nearly akin to those of England, it is to the English budget system that we more naturally look for the purpose of illustration." He pointed out that Parliament had long ago yielded the initiative in financial legislation to the Cabinet. The budget was prepared and introduced by the executive and approved without change by Parliament. According to Collins, a prerequisite for budget reform in America would be "the relinquishing of the initiative in financial legislation to the executive by the Congress." The president would possess the functions of "a Prime Minister in relation to public finance" by taking responsibility for preparing a budget. Congress would then yield its power to increase any item in the budget or to introduce any bill making a charge upon the Treasury unless the executive consented.[52]

Collins had other ideas for subordinating Congress to the president. He would have granted members of the cabinet a seat in the House and a voice (but not a vote) in all legislative proceedings involving the budget. The committee system of making appropriations "would cease." Congress would have no right to add an item, increase an item, or consider any measure that would impose a burden upon the Treasury without first obtaining executive approval.[53]

In 1918, Representative Medill McCormick (strongly influenced by Collins) introduced a number of bills and resolutions calling for budget reform. A new House budget committee, created to replace the Committee on Ways and Means, would have power to reduce presidential estimates but not to add to them, unless requested by the secretary of the treasury upon the authority of the president or unless the committee could muster a two-thirds majority. Members of the House would be prohibited from adding to the budget bill when it reached the floor, except to restore what the president had originally requested.[54]

Cabinet members endorsed this approach. William McAdoo, the first secretary of the treasury under President Woodrow Wilson, recommended that legislators have no power to increase the president's budgetary requests: "Let us be honest with ourselves and honest with the American people. A budget which does not cover the initiation or increase of appropriations by Congress will be a semblance of the real thing."[55] When the next secretary of the treasury, Carter

Glass, submitted budget estimates in 1919, he said that the budget "as thus prepared for the President and on his responsibility should not, as such, be increased by the Congress."[56] David Houston, the following secretary of the treasury, asked lawmakers in 1920 not to add to the president's budget unless they received the recommendation of the secretary of the treasury or approved the increase by a two-thirds vote.[57]

Congress considered, and rejected, these proposals. "Uncle Joe" Cannon, Speaker of the House from 1903 to 1911, warned in 1919 that an executive budget along the lines of the British parliamentary system would signify the surrender of the most important element of representative government: "I think we had better stick pretty close to the Constitution with its division of powers well defined and the taxing power close to the people."[58] Edward Fitzpatrick, author of a budget study in 1918, characterized the executive budget proposal as a step toward autocracy and a Prussian-style military state.[59]

The House Select Committee on the Budget supported the president's right to submit a budget and be responsible for the estimates in it. The budget was "executive" in that sense. Thereafter it became a "legislative budget" because Congress would have full power to increase or reduce the president's estimates. Increases could be made in committee or on the floor, and in either place by simple majority vote. The act did not contemplate in any fashion the surrender of congressional power. It did not make Congress subordinate to the president's plan (see box 4).

The Budget and Accounting Act of 1921 followed this principle of protecting legislative prerogatives. A Bureau of the Budget, located in the Treasury Department, was created to help the president prepare the budget. To protect its interests, Congress created a General Accounting Office and empowered the head of that agency, the comptroller general, to investigate all matters relating to revenues, appropriations, and expenditures.[60] In 1939, President Franklin D. Roosevelt used his reorganization authority to transfer the Budget Bureau from the Treasury to the newly formed Executive Office of the President.[61]

Some Slippage in the 1930s

Although Congress generally protected its war and spending prerogatives from 1789 to 1945, there were disturbing signs in the 1930s of legislative abdication in the areas of tariff policy and executive reorganization.

Throughout the nineteenth century, Congress had delegated to the president a number of discretionary powers over tariffs, including the power to impose embargoes, suspend duty-free arrangements, and the ability to admin-

---

BOX 4

Both an Executive and *Legislative Budget*

It will doubtless be claimed by some that this is an Executive budget and that the duty of making appropriations is a legislative rather than Executive prerogative. The plan outlined does provide for an Executive initiation of the budget, but the President's responsibility ends when he has prepared the budget and transmitted it to Congress. To that extent, and to that extent alone, does the plan provide for an Executive budget, but the proposed law does not change in the slightest degree the duty of Congress to make the minutest examination of the budget and to adopt the budget only to the extent that it is found to be economical. If the estimates contained in the President's budget are too large, it will be the duty of Congress to reduce them. If in the opinion of Congress the estimates of expenditures are not sufficient, it will be within the power of Congress to increase them. The bill does not in the slightest degree give the Executive any greater power than he now has over the consideration of appropriations by Congress.

Source: H. Report No. 14, 67th Cong., 1st sess., 6–7 (1921).

---

ister a set of flexible tariffs.[62] Tariff bills, such as the Smoot-Hawley Tariff Act of 1930, became so protectionist that the public turned against Congress for enacting high tariffs to satisfy the needs of lobbyists. So discredited was the legislative attempt at general tariff-making that Congress, within a few years, delegated to the president and the Tariff Commission (later the International Trade Commission) the power to negotiate with other countries for the reciprocal reduction of duties. Legislators, clobbered in the press, learned a painful lesson: "Every favor which can be conferred is also a danger, because it must sometimes be refused. Responsibility involves blame. And, if the demands exceed what the congressman can effectively handle, then he may happily yield up a significant portion of his power. That is what happened with the tariff."[63]

The big step came in 1934, when Congress passed the Reciprocal Trade Act. The statute authorized the president to adjust duties by up to fifty percent by entering into reciprocal agreements with other nations. For the first time, the president possessed advance authority to enter into trade agreements without the advice and consent of the Senate or the approval of Congress in a regular

bill. Over the next few decades, Congress periodically reauthorized the reciprocal trade legislation and helped create new international organizations to do
what had been done in Congress.

These statutes may appear to be standard delegations (and thus beyond the
scope of my book), but the transfer of tariff-reduction power to the president
had a motivation closer to abdication. This was not the customary case of leg-
islating broad policy and leaving to the executive branch the responsibility to
"fill in the details." The actions in the 1930s revealed that Congress was willing,
out of institutional embarrassment and self-doubt, to kick some functions permanently to the president and his assistants.

This pattern of acquiescence was reinforced by other actions. Until 1932,
executive agencies were reorganized through the regular legislative process. Presidents proposed changes and Congress enacted them, with whatever amendments it decided were necessary. In 1929, President Herbert Hoover offered a
new model by asking Congress to delegate reorganization authority to him,
subject to the approval of a joint committee of Congress.[64] That type of authority was enacted in 1932. Instead of approval by a joint committee, Congress allowed the president to submit reorganization plans that would become
law within sixty days unless either House disapproved.[65]

In other words, a presidential proposal would automatically become law
within a fixed number of days unless one House voted against it. The president
could make law without Congress. There were other benefits for the executive
branch. Unlike other legislative proposals from the White House, a reorganization plan could not be buried in committee, filibustered, or amended by Congress, either in committee or on the floor. Congress was limited to an up or
down vote, and had to act within a specified number of days. In delegating this
extraordinary authority, legislators were clearly disillusioned by their inability
to enact necessary legislation in the face of strong interest groups. Congressional sentiment is reflected in a statement by Senator David Reed, Republican
from Pennsylvania (see box 5).

Other broad delegations during the 1930s involved emergency relief programs, setting aside billions to be spent at the president's discretion. An act of
1934 appropriated $950 million for emergency relief programs and the Civil
Works Program, making the money available "for such projects and/or purposes and under such rules and regulations as the President in his discretion
may prescribe."[66] The Emergency Relief Appropriations Act of 1935 appropriated $4.880 billion to be used "in the discretion and under the direction of the
President."[67] When legislators debated vague phrases ("alleviating distress") to
guide the president, Senator Arthur Vandenberg suggested it would be simpler

to strike the text and substitute two brief sections: "SECTION 1. Congress hereby appropriates $4,880,000,000 to the President of the United States to use as he pleases. SEC. 2. Anybody who does not like it is fined $1,000."[68]

The Mischief of *Curtiss-Wright*

A Supreme Court decision in 1936 has been pivotal in transferring greater power to the presidency. Had the Court limited itself to the issue presented in the lawsuit, no such transfer would have resulted. Instead, the author of the opinion, Justice George Sutherland, went beyond the issue and indulged in dicta to magnify executive power. Although his opinion is deficient legally and historically, it has nonetheless had a powerful effect in helping to justify the existence of an independent, executive prerogative.

The issue in *United States v. Curtiss-Wright Corporation* was quite simple and limited: Had Congress delegated too broadly when it empowered the president to declare an arms embargo in South America? The statute allowed the president to prohibit the shipment of arms to the area whenever he found that it "may contribute to the reestablishment of peace" between belligerents. In 1935, in two cases, the Court struck down the delegation of *domestic* power to the president.[69] Was the delegation in the arms embargo case similarly invalid?

All the Court had to do was announce that Congress could delegate more broadly in international affairs than in domestic affairs. Certainly a reasonable

---

BOX 5

Time for a Mussolini?

Senator David Reed (R-Pa.):

Mr. President, I do not often envy other countries their governments, but I say that if this country ever needed a Mussolini it needs one now. I am not proposing that we make Mr. Hoover our Mussolini, I am not proposing that we should abdicate the authority that is in us, but if we are to get economies made they have to be made by someone who has the power to make the order and stand by it. Leave it to Congress and we will fiddle around here all summer trying to satisfy every lobbyist, and we will get nowhere. The country does not want that. The country wants stern action, and action taken quickly, . . .

Source: 75 *Cong. Rec.* 9644 (1932).

case could be made that shifting, unpredictable conditions in world affairs justified greater discretion for the president. The issue was never the existence of some kind of independent presidential power. The Court was asked whether *Congress,* in determining the extent of *its* power, could delegate *legislative* power to the president in this manner. The question decided by the district court, and appealed to the Supreme Court, was a narrow one: did the congressional statute constitute an unconstitutional delegation of legislative power?[70] The brief by the Justice Department, arguing in support of the statute, was limited to that question.[71] The administration did not claim an independent power for the president.

Despite the limited nature of this case, Justice Sutherland decided to uphold the statute by advancing a far-reaching theory of presidential power. In so doing, he could shoehorn into the decision material he had earlier developed as a senator from Utah and a member of the Senate Foreign Relations Committee. His decision in *Curtiss-Wright* draws heavily from his article, "The Internal and External Powers of the National Government" (printed as a Senate document in 1910), and his book, *Constitutional Power and World Affairs* (1919).[72] As noted by his biographer, Sutherland advocated "a vigorous diplomacy which strongly, even belligerently, called always for an assertion of American rights."[73]

In *Curtiss-Wright,* Sutherland argued that foreign and domestic affairs were different "both in respect of their origin and their nature" because the powers of external sovereignty "passed from the Crown not to the colonies severally, but to the colonies in their collective and corporate capacity as the United States of America."[74] By so arguing, Sutherland implied that the power of external sovereignty somehow bypassed the colonies, or states, and went directly to the president. But of course the president did not exist in 1776. Moreover, the historical record is clear that the states in 1776 operated as sovereign entities and exercised the power to make treaties, borrow money, solicit arms, lay embargoes, collect tariff duties, and conduct separate military campaigns.[75]

Even if the power of external sovereignty had somehow passed intact from the Crown to the "United States," the Constitution allocates that power both to Congress and the president. The president and the Senate share the power of treaties and appointments, including the appointment of ambassadors. Congress as a whole is given express powers to declare war, to raise and support the military forces, to make rules for their regulation, to provide for the calling up of the militia to suppress insurrections and to repel invasions, and to provide for the organization and disciplining of the militia. Congress also has the power to lay and collect duties on foreign trade, to regulate commerce with foreign nations, and to establish a uniform rule of naturalization. Nothing in the text of the Constitution or its history gives the president exclusive control over external sovereignty.

Sutherland wrote eloquently about "this vast external realm, with its important, complicated, delicate and manifold problems." As a consequence, he said, legislation over the international field must often accord to the president "a degree of discretion and freedom from statutory restrictions which would not be admissible were domestic affairs alone involved."[76] Note the jump. Sutherland goes from statutory grants of power from Congress to the president, as with the arms embargo, to "freedom from statutory restrictions." Through this analysis, the president has gained the ability to operate on his own, unrestricted by Congress or the Constitution. Sutherland reaches this result by identifying the "very delicate, plenary and exclusive power of the President as the sole organ of the federal government in the field of international relations."[77]

Here is another Sutherland misconception: the power of the president to operate as the "sole organ" in foreign affairs. The phrase implies that the power of sovereignty centers in the president as an exclusive quality. The phrase carries added weight because John Marshall used it in a speech in 1800 while serving in the House of Representatives. Given Marshall's elevation a year later to become chief justice of the Supreme Court, Sutherland seems to be drawing from an impeccable, authoritative source. But Sutherland badly distorts the record. At no time did Marshall suggest that the president could act unilaterally to make foreign policy.

Why did Marshall make that statement in 1800? Some members of the House wanted to impeach President John Adams because he had agreed to turn over to England someone charged with murder in an American court. By their reasoning, the president had encroached upon the judiciary and violated the doctrine of separation of powers. It was at that point that Marshall took the floor, denying that there was any basis for impeachment. Adams was merely carrying out an extradition treaty entered into between England and the United States. As president, Adams had a constitutional duty to carry out legislative policy, either in the form of a statute or a treaty. Adams never argued that he was the "sole organ" in *making* national policy, which requires joint action by the president and Congress. Only after Congress had enacted a law, or after the Senate had approved a treaty, did the president become "sole organ" in *implementing* national policy (see box 6).

Nothing in Marshall's public service argues for inherent and independent power. His decisions as chief justice reinforce the point that he never regarded the president as sole organ in making foreign policy. When a presidential ac-

BOX 6

The President As "Sole Organ"

[Congressman John Marshall]. The [dispute] was in its nature a national demand made upon the nation. The parties were the two nations. They cannot come into court to litigate their claims, nor can a court decide them. Of consequence, the demand is not a case for judicial cognizance.

The President is the sole organ of the nation in its external relations, and its sole representative with foreign nations. Of consequence, the demands of a foreign nation can only be made on him.

He possesses the whole Executive power. He holds and directs the force of the nation. Of consequence, any act to be performed by the force of the Nation is to be performed through him.

He is charged to execute the laws. A treaty is declared to be a law. He must then execute a treaty, where he, and he alone, possesses the means of executing it.

The treaty, which is a law, enjoins the performance of a particular object. The person who is to perform this object is marked out by the Constitution, since the person is named who conducts the foreign intercourse, and is to take care that the laws be faithfully executed. The means by which it is to be performed, the force of the nation, are in the hands of this person. Ought not this person to perform the object, although the particular mode of using the means has not been prescribed? Congress, unquestionably, may prescribe the mode, and Congress may devolve on others the whole execution of the contract; but, till this be done, it seems the duty of the Executive department to execute the contract by any means it possesses.

Source: *Annals of Congress,* 6th Cong., 613–14 (1800).

tion in national security conflicted with a statute passed by Congress, the legislative will prevailed.[78]

Justice Robert Jackson, in 1952, noted that "much of the [Sutherland] opinion is dictum."[79] In 1981, a federal appellate court cautioned against placing undue reliance on "certain dicta" in Sutherland's opinion: "To the extent that denominating the president as the 'sole organ' of the United States in international affairs constitutes a blanket endorsement of plenary Presidential power over any matter extending beyond the borders of this country, we reject that characterization."[80] Nevertheless, *Curtiss-Wright* is frequently cited to support not only broad delegations of legislative power to the president but also the existence of independent, implied, and inherent powers for the president.[81]

For more than a century and a half—from 1789 to 1945—Congress and the president followed the general constitutional principle that the initiation of war against foreign nations lay with the representative branch, Congress. That understanding was recognized in several court decisions, some of them authored by Chief Justice Marshall. A number of presidential military initiatives were taken during this period, but those actions were relatively modest in scope and limited in time. During this period, no president claimed the right to take the country to war against another country without first seeking the authority of Congress. In the one major military conflict where the president acted first— Lincoln and the Civil War—the dispute was domestic, not foreign. Even here Lincoln acknowledged that he lacked full constitutional authority for what he had done and asked Congress to enact legislation that would provide the necessary legitimacy.

The same pattern applies to the spending power. Although in 1921 presidents gained the statutory authority to submit a national budget, Congress stated clearly that this form of an "executive budget" did not change in any sense the power of Congress to alter the president's budget estimates in any way that legislators deemed appropriate. However, in the 1930s there were several warning signs that the traditional war and spending powers assigned to Congress might be in danger of slipping to the president. This shift of legislative power to the president accelerated after World War II.

3

War Powers after World War II

World War II had the customary effect of pushing power to the president. Toward the end of the war, Congress reviewed what had happened to its dwindling prerogatives over the previous decade. The decline of parliamentary institutions throughout the world prompted some of the stocktaking, but there was a growing awareness that Congress was no longer able to compete effectively with the executive branch. Congress was rapidly becoming a second-class, second-rate institution. The Joint Committee on the Organization of Congress, established in 1944, voiced its apprehension:

> [T]he decline of Congress in relation to the executive branch of our Federal Government has caused increased legislative concern. Under the Constitution, Congress is the policy-making branch of government. There are manifest growing tendencies in recent times toward the shift of policy-making to the Executive, partly because of the comparative lack of effective instrumentalities and the less adequate facilities of the legislative branch. To redress the balance and recover its rightful position in our governmental structure, Congress, many Members feel, must modernize its machinery, coordinate its various parts, and establish the research facilities that can provide it with the knowledge that is power.[1]

The committee explained that it was created "in response to a widespread congressional and public belief that a grave constitutional crisis exists in which the fate of representative government itself is at stake."[2] Of particular concern to the committee was the large number of administrative agencies headed by nonelected officials, with insufficient oversight by Congress. The result of the committee's effort was the Legislative Reorganization Act of 1946, which restructured congressional committees and strengthened the analytical ability of Congress. To assist Congress in maintaining control over the executive branch, standing committees were directed to exercise "continuous watchfulness" over executive agencies.[3]

However, unlike in the periods following previous wars and domestic crises, power did not flow back to Congress. Instead of the pendulum automatically swinging back to legislators, it remained stuck on the executive side. On May 8, 1945, President Truman announced the end of the war in Europe. On August 14 he reported the surrender of Japan. Yet emergency executive powers did not cease. The following May, Truman seized some bituminous coal mines under the authority of the War Labor Disputes Act of 1943, which empowered the president to take possession of any plant, mine, or facility as may be required for the "war effort." Such authority remained in force until the president proclaimed the "termination of hostilities," a step Truman did not take until December 31, 1946—more than sixteen months after Japan's surrender. By proclaiming that hostilities had terminated, Truman relinquished some wartime powers but retained others that remained in force during "a state of war" or "a state of emergency." His December 31 announcement stressed that "a state of war still exists."[4]

On July 25, 1947, Congress terminated a number of temporary emergency and war powers. About 175 statutory provisions were involved, many dating back to World War I. Even after taking that action, 103 war or emergency statutes remained in effect. Not until April 28, 1952, did President Truman sign a statement terminating the state of war with Japan, as well as the national emergencies proclaimed by President Roosevelt in 1939 and 1941. Thus, even though actual hostilities between the United States and enemy forces lasted for less than four years, Presidents Roosevelt and Truman together exercised emergency and war powers for more than twelve years.

International and Regional Bodies

In 1950, President Truman singlehandedly intervened in Korea without ever seeking authority from Congress. This was the first time that a president used independent power to intervene in a major war, and Congress failed to protect its prerogatives. A powerful precedent had been established to allow presidents to fight "police actions" under the "aegis" of the United Nations. The Truman precedent would later be used by President George Bush to wage war against Iraq and by President Bill Clinton to initiate military actions in Haiti, Bosnia, and Iraq. Much of this presidential latitude can be traced to misuse of the United Nations Charter of 1945 and the mutual security pacts (especially NATO) created after World War II.

United Nations Charter

The UN Charter of 1945 was drafted against the backdrop of the disasters of the Versailles Treaty and President Woodrow Wilson's determination to make foreign policy without Congress. When he submitted the treaty to the Senate on July 10, 1919, he attached to it the Covenant of the League of Nations. The covenant provided for an assembly (giving each member nation an equal voice) and a council (consisting of representatives from the United States, Great Britain, France, Italy, Japan, and four other nations elected by the assembly). Members pledged to submit to the league all disputes threatening war and to use military and economic sanctions against nations that threatened war.

Senator Henry Cabot Lodge (R-Mass.) offered a number of "reservations" to the covenant to protect American interests. The second of the fourteen reservations stated that nothing in the league could take from Congress its "sole power" under the Constitution to declare or authorize the use of military force against other nations (see box 7). Wilson opposed the Lodge reservations, claiming that they "cut out the heart of this Covenant" and represented "nullification" of the treaty.[5]

Wilson's strategy of tossing the treaty to the Senate as a *fait accompli,* over which the Senate had no right of amendment, marked an abysmal failure. The Senate rejected the treaty in November, 1919, and again in March, 1920. Decades later, in the midst of World War II, allied nations took steps to create a world organization. Wilson's dismal experience remained part of the collective conscience. In the meetings that led to the United Nations, the predominant view was that any commitment of U.S. forces to a world body would require prior authorization by both Houses of Congress. That attitude is reflected in the debates over the UN Charter, the UN Participation Act of 1945, and the 1949 amendments to the UN Participation Act.

In 1943, both Houses of Congress passed resolutions supporting the concept of a United Nations, on the condition that participation by the United States be "through its constitutional processes."[6] The United States, the United Kingdom, the Soviet Union, and China met at Dumbarton Oaks, in Washington, D.C., to give further definition to an international organization. Negotiations over the United Nations continued at the conference in San Francisco in 1945, which was attended by fifty nations and lasted nine weeks.

Procedures were developed to permit the United Nations to employ military force to deal with threats to peace, breaches of the peace, and acts of aggression. All UN members would make available to the Security Council, "on its call and in accordance with a special agreement," armed forces and other

BOX 7

Lodge's Reservation on War

The United States assumes no obligation to preserve the territorial integrity or political independence of any other country or to interfere in controversies between nations—whether members of the league or not—under the provisions of article 10, or to employ the military or naval forces of the United States under any article of the treaty for any purpose, unless in any particular case the Congress, which, under the Constitution, has the sole power to declare war or authorize the deployment of the military or naval forces of the United States, shall by act or joint resolution so provide.

Source: 58 *Cong. Rec.* 8777 (1919).

assistance for the purpose of maintaining international peace and security. The special agreements reached between the Security Council and member states "shall be subject to ratification by the signatory states in accordance with their respective constitutional processes." Given the variety of governmental systems among the member states, each nation would have to determine for itself the meaning of "constitutional processes." For the United States, would approval have to be granted by Congress, the president, or the two branches acting jointly?

From Potsdam, President Truman sent a cable to the Senate stating that all agreements involving U.S. troop commitments to the United Nations would first have to be approved by both Houses of Congress. He pledged without any equivocation: "When any such agreement or agreements are negotiated it will be my purpose to ask the Congress for appropriate legislation to approve them."[7] Backed by this assurance from Truman, the Senate supported the UN Charter by a vote of 89 to 2.[8]

With the charter approved, Congress had to decide the meaning of "constitutional processes." What procedure was required under the U.S. Constitution to bring into effect the special agreements needed to contribute American troops to UN military actions? That question was answered by the UN Participation Act of 1945. Without the slightest ambiguity, Section 6 of that statute provided that the agreements "shall" be subject to the approval of Congress by bill or joint resolution (see box 8).

In appearances before congressional committees, Under Secretary of State

Dean Acheson assured legislators that the constitutional balance would be preserved. He testified that only after the president received the approval of Congress was he "bound to furnish that contingent of troops to the Security Council; and the President is not authorized to furnish any more than you have approved of in that agreement."[9] When Congresswoman Edith Rogers (R-Mass.) remarked that Congress "can easily control the [Security] Council," Acheson was quick to agree: "It is entirely within the wisdom of Congress to approve or disapprove whatever special agreement the President negotiates."[10] Other parts of the legislative history reinforce the understanding of a shared, coequal relationship between the president and the Congress.[11]

The restrictions on the president's power to use armed force under a UN action are clarified by amendments adopted in 1949, allowing the president on his own initiative to provide military forces to the United Nations for "cooperative action." However, executive power is tightly constrained. These forces may serve only as observers and guards, may perform only in a noncombatant capacity, and may not exceed one thousand.[12]

The NATO Treaty

In addition to citing the UN Charter and Security Council resolutions as grounds for using American troops in military operations, presidents regard mutual security treaties as another source of authority. The same problem of defining "constitutional processes" under Article 43 of the UN Charter applies to language in mutual security treaties. For example, the NATO treaty of 1949 provides that an armed attack against one or more of the parties in Europe or North America "shall be considered an attack against them all."[13] The treaty further provides that, in the event of an attack, the member states may exercise the right of individual or collective self-defense recognized by Article 51 of the UN Charter and assist the country or countries attacked by taking "such action as it deems necessary, including the use of armed force." Article 11 of the treaty states that it shall be ratified "and its provisions carried out by the Parties in accordance with their respective constitutional processes."[14]

First, it is well recognized that the concept in mutual security treaties of an attack on one nation being an attack on all does not require an immediate response from any nation. Each country maintains the sovereign right to decide such matters by itself. As noted in the Rio Treaty of 1947, "no State shall be required to use armed force without its consent."[15] That same principle applies to NATO. During hearings in 1949, Secretary of State Dean Acheson told the Senate Foreign Relations Committee that it "does not mean that the United

BOX 8

Prior Approval by Congress Required

The President is authorized to negotiate a special agreement or agreements with the Security Council which shall be subject to the approval of the Congress by appropriate Act or joint resolution, providing for the numbers and types of armed forces, their degree of readiness and general location, and the nature of facilities and assistance, including rights of passage, to be made available to the Security Council on its call for the purpose of maintaining international peace and security in accordance with article 43 of said Charter. The President shall not be deemed to require the authorization of the Congress to make available to the Security Council on its call in order to take action under article 42 of said Charter [providing for blockades and other non-military, non-combatant measures] and pursuant to such special agreement or agreements the armed forces, facilities, or assistance provided therein: *Provided,* that nothing herein contained shall be construed as an authorization to the President by the Congress to make available to the Security Council for such purpose armed forces, facilities, or assistance in addition to the forces, facilities, and assistance provided for in such special agreement or agreements.

Source: UN Participation Act of 1945, 59 Stat. 621, sec. 6.

States would automatically be at war if one of the other signatory nations were the victim of an armed attack. Under our Constitution, the Congress alone has the power to declare war."[16] He and Senator Tom Connally (D-Tex.), chairman of the Foreign Relations Committee, engaged in this exchange:

THE CHAIRMAN: [I]t is up to each country to determine for itself, is it not, what action it deems necessary to restore the security of the Atlantic Pact area?

SECRETARY ACHESON: There is no question about that, Senator. That is true.[17]

These parts of the legislative history establish that NATO does not give the president any type of unilateral authority in the event of an attack. But what does the treaty mean when it says that its provisions shall be "carried out by the Parties in accordance with their respective constitutional processes"? How is Congress involved in implementing the treaty?

To some extent, NATO is tied to understandings of presidential power under the UN Charter. In reporting the NATO treaty, the Senate Foreign Relations Committee pointed out that the provisions of the defense pact "are expressly subordinated to the purposes, principles, and provisions of the United Nations Charter."[18] If the president lacks unilateral powers under the UN Charter, he lacks those powers under NATO and other mutual security treaties. Furthermore, the president and the Senate could not use the treaty procedure to strip the House of Representatives of its prerogatives over the use of military force.

NATO did not authorize offensive actions or general peacekeeping operations. The North Atlantic Treaty was a *defensive* pact, intended to contain the Soviet Union. The treaty's parties were "resolved to unite their efforts for collective defense" and "resist armed attack." In 1999, Secretary of State Madeleine Albright spoke with approval these words of Prime Minister Paul Henri Spaak of Belgium, offered five decades earlier: "The new NATO pact is purely defensive; it threatens no one."[19] Yet, under Clinton, NATO would expand its mission to justify offensive operations in Yugoslavia.

At the time NATO was established, one scholar argued that the provisions of the treaty that it be carried out according to constitutional processes was "intended to ensure that the Executive Branch of the Government should come back to the Congress when decisions were required in which the Congress has a constitutional responsibility."[20] The NATO treaty "does not transfer to the President the Congressional power to make war."[21] Yet decades later, under the Clinton administration, it would become clear that the NATO treaty had in fact shifted war power from Congress to the president.

The Korean War

Given these statutory safeguards, supposedly enacted to protect constitutional principles and congressional prerogatives, and given Truman's assurances from Potsdam, how could he send U.S. troops to Korea without ever seeking or obtaining congressional approval? Answer: Truman simply ignored the procedure for special agreements that was designed to safeguard congressional control. No special agreement was entered into in 1950, nor has any special agreement ever been entered into, by any nation, in the years since 1950. The procedure for special agreements had been made a nullity by the executive branch.

President Truman was able to exploit the UN machinery because of a fluke: the Soviet Union had absented itself from the Security Council when it twice passed resolutions concerning military action in Korea. Had the Soviet Union been present, it would likely have exercised a veto over the resolutions. Still, it is difficult to argue that the president's constitutional powers vary with the presence or absence of Soviet delegates to the Security Council. As Robert Bork noted in 1971, "the approval of the United Nations was obtained only because the Soviet Union happened to be boycotting the Security Council at the time, and the President's Constitutional powers can hardly be said to ebb and flow with the veto of the Soviet Union in the Security Council."[22]

The Truman administration pretended that it was acting pursuant to UN authority. On June 29, 1950, Secretary of State Acheson claimed that all U.S. actions taken in Korea "have been under the aegis of the United Nations."[23] Aegis is a fudge word, meaning shield or protection. Acheson used the word to suggest that the United States was acting under the legal banner of the United Nations, which was never the case. He said that President Truman had done his "utmost to uphold the sanctity of the Charter of the United Nations and the rule of law," and that the administration was in "conformity with the resolutions of the Security Council of June 25 and 27, giving air and sea support to the troops of the Korean government."[24]

The fact is that President Truman committed U.S. forces to Korea before the council called for military action. General Douglas MacArthur was immediately authorized to send supplies of ammunition to the South Korean defenders. On June 26, Truman ordered U.S. air and sea forces to give South Koreans cover and support.[25] After Acheson had summarized the military situation for some members of Congress at noon on June 27, Truman exclaimed: "But Dean, you didn't even mention the U.N.!"[26] Later that evening the Security Council passed the second resolution, which gave the go-ahead for military action. In his memoirs, Acheson admitted that "some American action, said to be in support of the resolution of June 27, was in fact ordered, and possibly taken, prior to the resolution."[27] After he left the presidency, Truman was asked whether he had been willing to use military force in Korea without UN backing. He replied, with customary bluntness, "No question about it."[28]

President Truman did not seek the approval of members of Congress for his military actions in Korea. As Acheson suggested, Truman might have wished only to "tell them what had been decided."[29] Truman met with congressional leaders at 11:30 A.M. on June 27, after the administration's policy had been established and implementing orders issued.[30] He later met with congressional leaders to give them briefings on developments in Korea without ever asking for authority.[31] Some consideration was given to presenting a joint resolution to Congress to permit legislators to voice their approval, but the draft resolution never left the administration.[32]

Congressional Response

Floor statements in Congress were generally supportive of Truman's decision to commit U.S. armed forces to Korea. Legislative deference is remarkable in view of the lengthy debates in 1945 about creating the United Nations and assuring congressional control (through the UN Participation Act) over any U.S. commitment of troops to UN military actions. Yet few members of Congress took Truman to task for failing to come to Congress to seek approval of a special agreement. Senator Herbert Lehman (D-N.Y.), relying on leadership and expertise from the administration, supported U.S. intervention in Korea. "Let us continue to act," he said, "under the United Nations Charter, and within the framework of that Organization."[33] He made no mention of the role of Congress in approving special agreements.

After Truman dispatched U.S. forces to Korea, Senator James P. Kem (R-Mo.) asked: "Does that mean that he has arrogated to himself the authority of declaring war?" Senate Majority Leader Scott Lucas responded: "I do not care to debate that question. . . . I do not believe that it means war but the Senator can place his own interpretation on it." When Kem pressed the issue, asking under what authority the president could authorize an armed attack, Lucas replied that "history will show that on more than 100 occasions in the life of this Republic the President as Commander in Chief has ordered the fleet or the troops to do certain things which involved the risk of war."[34] Of the hundred incidents referred to by Lucas, not one approached the magnitude of the Korean War.

Senator Leverett Saltonstall (R-Mass.), the minority whip, approved of Truman's action, concluding that "it seems to me the responsibility of the President of the United States to protect the security of the United States."[35] Senator Arthur Watkins (R-Utah) asked whether the president should not have notified Congress before ordering military forces to Korea. Lucas responded: "I am willing to leave what has been done in the hands of the Commander in Chief."[36] A purer form of abdication could not be imagined. Watkins, without making specific reference to the UN procedure for special agreements, said that during debate on the UN Charter "we were told time and time again . . . that nothing would take us into war under that pact without action by the Congress. The President could not do it." He thought the president should have advised Congress of developments in Korea and asked for authority "to go ahead and do whatever was necessary to protect the situation."[37]

Senator Hubert H. Humphrey (D-Minn.) praised the president for exercising "the leadership and the statesmanship which the people require of the President."[38] Senator Estes Kefauver (D-Tenn.) advised that "this is a time to close our ranks, to forget political considerations, and to stand behind the President in the vital decision he has made."[39] Senator Connally urged the legislators "to stand behind the President. . . . We cannot hesitate; we cannot divide. Any division here, by a speech or by any other expression of sentiment would be placarded all over the world as evidence that the United States is cautious or is afraid or is quaking in its boots."[40]

Senator George Malone (R-Nev.) spoke deferentially about the president's authority in foreign affairs: "Congress cannot determine policy. Congress can only debate the foreign policy determined by the executive department. . . . The Constitution of the United States leaves determinations of foreign policy to the President."[41] Malone acknowledged that the Constitution expressly vests foreign trade and foreign commerce in Congress, but argued that "in 1934 the Congress, just as stupidly, transferred that authority to the executive branch of the Government through the 1934 Trade Agreements Act."[42] He spoke as though Congress, when it decided to delegate some of its trade authority, had somehow permanently rewritten the Constitution to place all of foreign affairs in the executive. The Trade Agreements Act of 1934 delegated *legislative* authority; it remains legislative authority unless and until the Constitution is changed to transfer foreign trade to the president.

One of the few challenges to Truman's action came from Representative Vito Marcantonio, a member of the American Labor Party from New York. He specifically objected to the reliance on the Security Council resolution: " . . . when we agreed to the United Nations Charter we never agreed to supplant our Constitution with the United Nations Charter. The power to declare and make war is vested in the representatives of the people, in the Congress of the United States. That power has today been usurped from us with the reading of this short statement by the President to the people of the world. We here in Congress are asked to supinely accept this usurpation of our right as representatives of the American people. We have abdicated it for I have heard no protest, I have heard not a single word against it."[43]

It has been argued that President Truman consulted in good faith with Congress and was told that he could act without legislative authority. He reached Senator Connally by phone and asked whether he would have to ask Congress for a declaration of war if he decided to send American forces to Korea. Connally offered this advice: "If a burglar breaks into your house, you can shoot at him without going down to the police station and getting permission. You might run into a long debate by Congress, which would tie your hands completely. You have a right to do it as commander-in-chief and under the U.N. Charter."[44]

It cannot be reasonably argued that the president may satisfy statutory, treaty, and constitutional obligations by touching base with a senator and getting a green light, especially from someone like Connally, whose positions on the war power were repeatedly repudiated by the Senate and Congress.[45] Independent of interesting phone conversations, we have to analyze statutes, treaties, the Constitution, and the structure of government to determine the legality of presidential actions.

Similarly, it is argued that President Truman acted properly because Senator Lucas, who served on the Foreign Relations Committee and played an active role during the 1945 debates on the UN Charter and the UN Participation Act, saw no need for Congress to authorize the intervention in Korea.[46] When President Truman asked congressional leaders on July 3, 1950, whether he should present to Congress a joint resolution expressing approval of his action in Korea, Lucas acquiesced to the executive (see box 9).

Again, certainly an interesting comment by the Senate majority leader, but nothing Lucas could say in private or in public could alter the text and intent of the Constitution, the UN Charter, and the UN Participation Act. Truman had no authority to alter those documents and neither did Lucas. Even if a case could be made that the emergency facing Truman in June, 1950, was so fast-moving and perilous that it was incumbent upon him to act promptly without first seeking and obtaining legislative authority, nothing prevented him from returning to Congress at the earliest opportunity to ask for a supporting statute or retroactive authority, as Lincoln had done. In a genuine (not a contrived) emergency, a president may have to act without congressional authority, trusting that the circumstances are so urgent and compelling that Congress will endorse his actions and confer a legitimacy that only Congress, as the people's representatives, can provide.

The "Great Debate" in 1951

Having involved the country in war in Korea, Truman announced in 1951 that he intended to send ground troops to Europe. Asked whether he believed that he needed congressional approval before sending troops abroad, he replied: "No, I do not."[47] A week later, Truman said he had constitutional power as commander in chief to send troops "anywhere in the world," and that he intended

BOX 9

Lucas Defers to Truman

SENATOR LUCAS said that he frankly questioned the desirability of [asking Congress to pass a joint resolution of approval]. He said that things were now going along well. . . . He said that the President had very properly done what he had to without consulting the Congress. He said that the resolution itself was satisfactory and that it could pass. He suggested as an alternative that the President might deliver this message as a fireside chat with the people of the country. . . .

SENATOR LUCAS said that to go up and give such a message to Congress might sound as if the President were asking for a declaration of war. . . . On the other hand a fireside chat with the people would be good. . . .

SENATOR LUCAS stated that Senator [Kenneth] Wherry was complaining because the President didn't go to Congress before he acted. Regarding the resolution he said he was just thinking out loud but it occurred to him that if the President should call the same group together we might get their reaction and then would have no trouble getting it through. He thought they would be unanimous. . . .

SENATOR LUCAS said that he felt he knew the reactions of Congress. He thought that only Senator Wherry had voiced the view that Congress should be consulted. Many members of Congress had suggested to him that the President should keep away from Congress and avoid debate. He thought a debate on the resolution might last at least a week. . . .

. . . SENATOR LUCAS said if there should be a row in Congress that would not help abroad. He did not think that Congress was going to stir things up.

Source: *Foreign Relations of the United States,* 1950, vol. 7, Korea, H. Doc. No. 82-264, vol. 7, 82d Cong., 1st sess., 287–88, 289–90, 291 (1976).

to live up to U.S. obligations under the UN Charter and mutual security trea-ties.[48] If consultations with Congress were necessary regarding military com-mitments abroad, he would contact only the Senate Committees on Foreign Relations and Armed Services, apparently on the theory that treaty obligations concerned only the Senate, not Congress as a whole. That meant the House would be excluded, except for whatever funds had to be appropriated.[49]

When Secretary of State Dean Acheson appeared before the Senate Com-mittees on Foreign Relations and Armed Services on February 16, he found the issues of congressional prerogatives and separation of powers plainly annoying. Although in the past he had gone out of his way to assure Congress that its constitutional powers would be respected, he now bristled at the mention of legislative involvement: "It seems to me that perhaps a little more is involved here, and that we are in a position in the world today where the argument as to who has the power to do this, that, or the other thing, is not exactly what is called for from America in this very critical hour, and if we could all agree on the fact that something should be done, we will perform a much greater role in the world, than by quarreling about who ought to do it."[50]

These haughty lectures from the Truman administration provoked mem-bers of Congress to take another look at the scope of presidential power. For three months in 1951 the Senate debated the principles of constitutional gov-ernment and the prerogatives of Congress. The major address was a 10,000-word speech delivered by Senator Taft, who urged his colleagues to defend their powers and challenge executive overreaching. With great force he rejected the idea that critiques of an administration's foreign policy were a threat to the nation and an aid and comfort to the enemy (see box 10).

The 1951 debate prompted both Houses of Congress to rethink the congres-sional role in foreign affairs and the war power. A report for the House Foreign Affairs Committee in 1951 correctly spotlighted the significance of the Korean War: "The action of the United States in Korea is in one sense unprecedented. For the first time the United States has committed large military forces in a foreign country in response to the action of an international organization. United States forces were committed in Korea by Presidential action."[51]

Judicial Checks

President Truman tried to justify his actions in Korea by calling it a "police action" rather than a war. That argument, suspect from the start, deteriorated as casualties climbed. On June 29, 1950, at a news conference, he was asked whether the country was at war. He responded: "We are not at war."[52] Asked

BOX 10

Taft Appeals for Constitutional Checks

During recent years a theory has developed that there shall be no criticism of the foreign policy of the administration, that any such criticism is an attack on the unity of the Nation, that it gives aid and comfort to the enemy, and that it sabotages any idea of a bipartisan foreign policy for the national benefit. I venture to state that this proposition is a fallacy and a very dangerous fallacy threatening the very existence of the Nation.

. . . As a see it, Members of Congress, and particularly Members of the Senate, have a constitutional obligation to reexamine constantly and discuss the foreign policy of the United States. If we permit appeals to unity to bring an end to that criticism, we endanger not only the constitutional liberties of the country, but even its future existence.

. . . unity carried to unreasonable extremes can destroy a country. The Kaiser achieved unity in Germany. Hitler again achieved the same unity at the cost of freedom many years later. Mussolini achieved unity in Italy. The leaders of Japan through a method of so-called thought control achieved unity in Japan. In every case, policies adopted by these enforcers of unity led to the destruction of their own country. . . .

The result of a general practice of secrecy in all the initial steps of foreign policy has been to deprive the Senate and Congress of the substance of the powers conferred on them by the Constitution.

. . . [President Truman] had no authority whatever to commit American troops to Korea without consulting Congress and without congressional approval. He could not commit our Armed Forces to support the United Nations under the very terms and provisions of the act which was passed by Congress to implement the United Nations Charter, for that act only recognized the commitment of troops in the event of the negotiation of a special military agreement with the Security Council "which shall be subject to the approval of the Congress by an appropriate act or joint resolution." . . .

Source: 97 *Cong. Rec.* 55, 57 (1951).

whether it would be more correct to call the conflict "a police action under the United Nations," he agreed with this softball question by saying that that "is exactly what it amounts to."[53] On July 13, at another news conference, he again called the Korean War a "police action."[54]

Efforts by Truman and Acheson to characterize the Korean War as some sort of a police action taken pursuant to a Security Council resolution would never wash. The United Nations exercised no real authority over the conduct of the war. Other than token support from a few nations, it remained an American war—measured by troops, money, casualties, and deaths—from start to finish. Although Truman and Acheson continued to avoid the designation of war for the fighting in Korea, federal courts had no difficulty in calling a spade a spade. A federal court noted in 1953: "We doubt very much if there is any question in the minds of the majority of the people of this country that the conflict now raging in Korea can be anything but war."[55]

In 1952, with public opposition mounting to the war in Korea, President Truman faced a nationwide strike of steelworkers. Calling steel "indispensable" for producing weapons and war materials, he issued an executive order to take possession of the plants and facilities of eighty-seven major steel companies.[56] His action was immediately challenged by some members of Congress, who pointed out that in 1951 Congress had specifically considered granting a president seizure authority and had rejected that course.[57] Newspapers around the country published editorials that condemned Truman's theory of inherent and emergency power. They ripped him for acting in a manner they regarded as arbitrary, dictatorial, dangerous, destructive, high-handed, and unauthorized by law.[58]

The steel companies went to court to challenge the constitutionality of Truman's action. Although he had based his executive order on authority under "the Constitution and laws of the United States, and as President of the United States and Commander-in-Chief of the armed forces of the United States," these purely constitutional and statutory sources were set aside by the Justice Department in court. It now argued that Truman had acted solely on inherent executive power without any statutory support. Assistant Attorney General Homer Baldridge told David A. Pine, a federal district judge, that courts were powerless to control the exercise of presidential power when directed toward emergency conditions:

> THE COURT: So you contend the Executive had unlimited power in time of an emergency?

MR. BALDRIDGE: He has the power to take such action as is necessary to meet the emergency.

THE COURT: If the emergency is great, it is unlimited, is it?

MR. BALDRIDGE: I suppose if you carry it to its logical conclusion, that is true. But I do want to point out that there are two limitations on the Executive power. One is the ballot box and the other is impeachment.

THE COURT: Then, as I understand it, you claim that in time of emergency the Executive has this great power.

MR. BALDRIDGE: That is correct.

THE COURT: And that the Executive determines the emergencies and the Courts cannot even review whether it is an emergency.

MR. BALDRIDGE: That is correct.[59]

Judge Pine wrote a blistering opinion that repudiated this theory of inherent and unchecked presidential power. In holding Truman's executive order to be unconstitutional, Pine acknowledged that a nationwide strike could do extensive damage to the country. Yet he believed that a strike "would be less injurious to the public than the injury which would flow from a timorous judicial recognition that there is some basis for this claim to unlimited and unrestrained Executive power, which would be implicit in a failure to grant the injunction."[60] The Supreme Court, split six to three, sustained Judge Pine's decision.[61] Each of the five concurring justices wrote separate opinions, advancing different views on the president's emergency power.

The Academic Community

Truman's cavalier handling of the Constitution, the UN Charter, and the UN Participation Act might have been checked earlier had leading academic figures exposed his illegalities. Instead, they rushed to his defense, preferring partisan advocacy over constitutional principles. Henry Steele Commager, a prominent historian, wrote in the *New York Times* that objections to Truman's actions in Korea "have no support in law or in history."[62] His own analysis, however, was shallow. With regard to Korea, Commager said that "it is an elementary fact that must never be lost sight of that treaties are laws and carry with them the same obligation as laws. When the Congress passed the United Nations Participation Act it made the obligations of the Charter of the United Nations law, binding on the President. When the Senate ratified the North Atlantic Treaty it made the obligations of that treaty law, binding on the President."[63] Of course treaties are laws and must be carried out, but the Constitution commands the president to "take Care that the Laws be faithfully executed." Truman's unilateral exercise of power was not faithful to the UN Charter and certainly not to the UN Participation Act.

Arthur S. Schlesinger, Jr., also came to Truman's defense. In a letter to the *New York Times,* he rejected Senator Robert Taft's argument that Truman "had no authority whatever to commit American troops to Korea without consulting Congress and without Congressional approval," and that by sending troops to Korea he "simply usurped authority, in violation of the laws and the Constitution." Schlesinger, calling Taft's position "demonstrably irresponsible," cited Jefferson's use of ships to repel the Barbary pirates and claimed that American presidents "have repeatedly committed American armed forces abroad without prior Congressional consultation or approval."[64]

Jefferson's action was not a precedent for Truman's. Jefferson took limited defensive actions and came to Congress because he was "unauthorized by the Constitution, without the sanction of Congress, to go beyond the line of defense." Jefferson acknowledged that it was the prerogative of Congress to authorize "measures of offense."[65] Congress enacted ten statutes authorizing action by Presidents Jefferson and Madison in the Barbary wars. Truman arrogated to himself the full warmaking power, both defensive and offensive, and never came to Congress for authority, either in advance or after the fact. Jefferson respected congressional prerogatives and constitutional limits; Truman ignored both. As for the numerous examples in which presidents "repeatedly committed American armed forces abroad without prior Congressional consultation or approval," of course not a single precedent was of the magnitude to justify or legalize what Truman had done in Korea.

Edward S. Corwin took Commager and Schlesinger to task by labeling them the "high-flying prerogative men."[66] Corwin himself had been careless in using loose language to describe presidential war power. In 1949 he argued that the original understanding that the president would "repel sudden attacks" had evolved into an "undefined power—almost unchallenged from the first and occasionally sanctified judicially—to employ without Congressional authorization the armed forces in the protection of American rights and interests abroad whenever necessary."[67] Those earlier life-and-property actions were minuscule in comparison to the Korean War. Nor can one find in the judicial record any decision that would come close to justifying Truman's war. Corwin did note, in his 1949 article, that the UN Participation Act was based on the theory that American participation in the United Nations "is a matter for Congressional collaboration."[68]

In the late 1960s, with the nation mired in a bitter and divisive war in Vietnam, both Commager and Schlesinger apologized for acting as indiscriminate cheerleaders of presidential power. By 1966 Schlesinger was counseling that "something must be done to assure the Congress a more authoritative and continuing voice in fundamental decisions in foreign policy."[69] In 1973, he published a book with the ironic title *The Imperial Presidency.* More than any other scholar, Schlesinger had built the imperial presidency, attributing to it every imaginable virtue and strength, elevating it to heroic and sublime heights. In his book, largely aimed at the excesses of Richard Nixon, Schlesinger said that the "idea of prerogative was *not* part of presidential powers as defined by the Constitution," although it "remained in the back of [the framers'] mind."[70] Some waffling there. The idea of prerogative—allowing executives to act in the absence of law and sometimes against it—was not in the Constitution but somewhere in the back of the framers' minds? Lots of things were in the back of their minds. So what?

Schlesinger expressed regret for calling Taft's position "demonstrably irresponsible." He explained that he had responded with "a flourish of historical documentation and, alas, hyperbole."[71] In other words, Schlesinger had set his hat as historian and scholar to the side and used partisan and exaggerated rhetoric to defend a president he admired and supported.

Commager also issued his apologies. During hearings before the Senate Foreign Relations Committee in 1967, he recommended that there should be a reconsideration of executive-legislative relations in the conduct of foreign relations.[72] When he returned to this committee in 1971, he testified that "it is very dangerous to allow the President to, in effect, commit us to a war from which we cannot withdraw, because the warmaking power is lodged and was intended to be lodged in the Congress."[73] Expressions of regret and new wisdom are always welcome, but independent scholarly checks are needed at the time of constitutional violations, not two decades later. Moreover, Schlesinger and Commager awoke to presidential abuse because they disliked a particular occupant: Lyndon Johnson and Richard Nixon. Scholars need to weigh in against executive wrongdoing at the time it appears, including offenses committed by presidents they like.

Vietnam: A Wake-up Call

During the Eisenhower years, from 1953 to 1961, the executive and legislative branches worked more cooperatively. President Dwight D. Eisenhower, who thought Truman's initiative in Korea was mistaken both politically and legally, made a conscious effort to seek authority from Congress. One of Eisenhower's ideas was to have Congress pass "area resolutions" to cover such potential troublespots as the Formosa Straits and the Middle East.[74] When congressional leaders asked why he sought authority from Congress when others argued he could act unilaterally, Eisenhower replied that the Constitution "assumes that our two branches of government should get along together."[75]

Commitment to Southeast Asia

In 1954, Eisenhower was pressured to commit American troops to Indochina. Asked at a news conference on March 10 for his policy, he replied in a straightforward manner: "I will say this: there is going to be no involvement of America in war unless it is a result of the constitutional process that is placed upon Congress to declare it. Now, let us have that clear; and that is the answer."[76] In a phone conversation on April 5 with Secretary of State John Foster Dulles, Eisenhower was again adamant about using unilateral executive power to become involved in Indochina: "such move is impossible. In the absence of some kind of arrangement getting support of Congress, would be completely unconstitutional & indefensible."[77]

On April 3, eight members of Congress met with Secretary Dulles and other executive officials to discuss the possibility of providing air and naval support to the French in Indochina. The "unanimous reaction" of the legislators was that there should be no congressional action until the secretary of state had obtained commitments from allies to join the effort.[78] An article by Chalmers M. Roberts provides further details of this meeting. Senator Earle C. Clements (D-Ky.) asked Admiral Arthur W. Radford, chairman of the Joint Chiefs of Staff, whether the administration's military plan had the approval of the other members of the joint chiefs. Radford answered in the negative. Clements asked: "How many of the three agree with you?" The reply: "None." Senator Lyndon B. Johnson referred to the problem in Korea, where up to ninety percent of the soldiers and the money came from the United States. He asked Dulles whether he had consulted nations who might be allies in the intervention. Dulles said he had not. Dulles was asked why he had not gone to the United Nations, as the Truman administration had done with Korea. He said it would take too long. All eight members of Congress agreed that Dulles should obtain support from allies before coming to Congress for authority.[79]

Eisenhower's philosophy of acting jointly with Congress was rejected by President John F. Kennedy, who was prepared to act during the Cuban missile crisis solely on what he considered his constitutional authority. He saw no need to share power, or responsibility, with Congress.[80] In declining congressional authority for an emergency action, either before or after the fact, he parted company with the important precedent established by Lincoln. Kennedy also expanded the U.S. military commitment to Vietnam. Presidents Truman and Eisenhower had provided economic and military assistance to the French in Indochina. Under Kennedy, the number of American military advisers climbed from 700 to 16,000. Kennedy initiated the Strategic Hamlet Program in an unsuccessful attempt to build support among the peasants in Vietnam. He also involved military advisers in combat roles and supported South Vietnamese raids against North Vietnam.[81] Kennedy authorized the use of armed helicopters, piloted by Americans, in military strikes against the North Vietnamese.[82]

President Lyndon B. Johnson recognized the hazards of getting involved in Vietnam, but he worried that the Republicans would exploit any sign of weakness ("soft on communism") on his part, jeopardizing his reelection in 1964. On February 3, 1964, he shared his misgivings with John S. Knight, chairman of the board of *Miami Herald:*

LBJ: What do you think we ought to do in Vietnam?
KNIGHT: . . . I never thought we belonged there . . . .
LBJ: Well, I opposed it in '54. But we're there now, and there's one of three things you can do. One is run and let the dominoes start falling over. And God Almighty, what they said about us leaving China would just be warming up, compared to what they'd say now. I see Nixon is raising hell about it today. Goldwater too. You can run, or you can fight, as we are doing, or you can sit down and agree to neutralize all of it [negotiate a peace]. But nobody is going to neutralize North Vietnam, so that's totally impractical. And so it really boils down to one or two decisions—getting out or getting in. . . .
KNIGHT: Long-range over there, the odds are certainly against us.
LBJ: Yes, there is no question about that. Anytime you got that many people against you that far from your home base, it's bad.[83]

The instincts of Senator J. William Fulbright (D-Ark.) were also against any commitment of U.S. troops to Vietnam. In a conversation with Johnson on December 2, 1963, he made it plain that a military victory was out of the question: "I just think [Vietnam] is a *hell* of a situation. It involves a lot more talk, but I'll be goddamned if I don't think it is hopeless. . . . I think the whole general situation is against us, as far as a real victory goes. . . . you don't want to send a whole lot more men in there, I don't think."[84] Despite their foreboding and reservations, both Johnson and Fulbright would take the lead in making a major commitment to Vietnam.

The Gulf of Tonkin Resolution

President Johnson asked Congress in August, 1964, to pass the Tonkin Gulf Resolution to authorize military action against North Vietnam. The subsequent escalation of the war and evidence of repeated stealth and deception by the Johnson administration convinced Congress that it had to take steps to restore congressional prerogatives. In foreign affairs, Congress had been increasingly marginalized since World War II.

This pattern was evident in the alacrity with which Congress passed the Tonkin Gulf Resolution. Johnson reported two attacks on U.S. ships by North Vietnam: one attack on August 2, the other on August 4. Although Senator Fulbright, chairman of the Foreign Relations Committee, said that the "facts of the immediate situation are clear," the second incident may never have occurred.[85] In a book published in 1996, Edwin E. Moïse studied documents and interviews to conclude that the second attack never took place but attributes the mistaken report to error rather than to an intentional lie by the administration.[86] In 1964, Secretary of Defense Robert S. McNamara was convinced that the second attack occurred. However, after a trip to Vietnam in 1995, he announced that "I am absolutely positive" the second attack never took place, and was prepared to say, "without a doubt, there was no second attack."[87]

Based solely on President Johnson's information, with no independent investigation by Congress or its committees, the House of Representatives passed the Tonkin Gulf Resolution by a unanimous vote, and there were only two votes of opposition in the Senate. Senator Gaylord Nelson (D-Wis.) offered an amendment to limit Johnson's authority under the resolution:

> The Congress also approves and supports the efforts of the President to bring the problem of peace in southeast Asia to the Security Council of the United Nations, and the President's declaration that the United States, seeking no extension of the present military conflict, will respond to provocation in a manner that is "limiting and fitting." Our continuing policy is to limit our role to the provision of aid, training assistance, and military advice, and it is the sense of Congress that, except when provoked to a greater response, we should continue to attempt to avoid a direct military involvement in the southeast Asian conflict.[88]

Senator Fulbright said that the amendment "states fairly accurately what the President has said would be our policy, and what I stated my understanding was as to our policy; also what other Senators have stated." Although Nelson stated a policy that "is unobjectionable," Fulbright said he could not accept the amendment because it would send the resolution to conference and delay enactment.[89] Two years later, after a massive escalation of the war in Vietnam, Fulbright expressed regret that he had not accepted Nelson's amendment.[90]

During the debate in 1964, senators quickly fell into line. Frank Church (D-Idaho) argued that although it was important to conduct legislative oversight and examination, the crisis in Southeast Asia did not permit independent inquiry by Congress. There is a time, he said, "to question the route of the flag, and there is a time to rally around it, lest it be routed. This is the time for the latter course, and in our pursuit of it, a time for all of us to unify."[91] Hubert H. Humphrey (D-Minn.) agreed. On many occasions there was an obligation on the part of Congress to question policy and hold committee hearings and receive testimony to assess the merits of an administration's course of action. But he said there comes a time, as with the Tonkin Gulf incident, "when an aggressor may feel that because of our discussions, we are disunited, and he then could launch an attack."[92] If lawmakers believe they have no time to debate, the result is capitulation.

Senator Wayne Morse (D-Ore.) presented the major opposition to the Tonkin Gulf Resolution. He attacked his colleagues for ducking their responsibilities under the theory that foreign policy was somehow assigned to the executive branch, and that the administration possessed superior information to which lawmakers had no access. Legislators were forgetting about the system of checks and balances and the duty of Congress to behave as a coequal branch. Moreover, he charged that the administration was deceiving Congress and the country by presenting North Vietnam as the aggressor whereas it was the United States that had acted as provocateur. Finally, he predicted—accurately—that any president who sent U.S. troops to Vietnam would be repudiated by the American people (see box 11).

Morse's comment about the United States being a provocateur was sensational but well-grounded. President Johnson told the nation on August 4 that North Vietnam had committed "open aggression on the high seas against the United States of America."[93] Yet he knew (because he authorized it) of U.S. covert operations "in that area that we have been carrying on—blowing up some bridges and things of that kind, roads and so forth."[94] Whatever happened in the Gulf of Tonkin may have been North Vietnam's response to U.S. participation in covert actions on July 30 and 31.[95]

BOX 11

Morse Attacks the Administration

MR. MORSE: . . . there are many congressional politicians who would evade their responsibilities as to American foreign policy in Asia by use of the specious argument that "foreign policy is a matter for the executive branch of the Government. That branch has information no Congressman has access to." Of course, such an alibi for evading congressional responsibility in the field of foreign policy may be based on lack of understanding or a convenient forgetting of our system of checks and balances that exists and should be exercised in the relationships between and among our three coordinate and coequal branches of government.

. . . if we are to talk about provocation, [then] the United States was a provocateur by having any ships anywhere within striking distance or bombing distance; and the South Vietnamese did bomb those islands. We should have been completely out of the scene.

If Senators want my opinion, a "snowjob" is being done on us by the Pentagon and the State Department. Not only had we full knowledge of it, but it was being done with our tacit approval. . . .

Unpopular as it is, I am perfectly willing to make the statement for history that if we follow a course of action that bogs down thousands of American boys in Asia, the administration responsible for it will be rejected and repudiated by the American people. It should be.

Source: 110 *Cong. Rec.* 18136, 18425, 18427 (1964).

Senator George Aiken (R-Vt.), while expressing "apprehension" and "misgivings" about the decision to use military force in Vietnam, felt that he, "as an American citizen, can do no less than support the President in his capacity as leader of our Nation." He did not believe that a legislator could afford to oppose the president for exercising the power "which we, under our form of government and through our legislative bodies, have delegated to his office."[96] Aiken was not a mere "American citizen." He was a legislator from a coequal branch, sworn to support the Constitution. As to power that Congress had "delegated" to the president to conduct war, Aiken did not—and could not—identify the constitutional or statutory provisions that supposedly vested this power solely in the president. What was at stake was not delegation. It was abdication.

Several senators argued that the role of Congress was purely advisory in the commitment of U.S. forces. Senator Jacob K. Javits (R-N.Y.) asked Fulbright whether the Foreign Relations Committee would "continue to play an active role in respect of the question. I believe an affirmative answer would be a real assurance to all of us." Fulbright replied that "our role is one of an advisory nature. . . . We have an opportunity to advise them, and that is all. We cannot direct or force them."[97] Senator Everett Dirksen (R-Ill.), one of the legislators who attended a White House briefing on the issue, made a similar point:

> We have constantly emphasized that all we ask, when a decision is pending or a crisis is upon us, is to be consulted, to have an opportunity to offer alternative proposals and substitutes. When we have had our day in court and the decision has been made, we are prepared to abide by the decision and to demonstrate to the whole wide world that there is no division between the Executive and Congress in repelling aggression aimed at our forces wherever we are under protocol or treaty obligations. . . .
>
> The President could have taken this action in his own right as the Commander in Chief. He does not have to ask Congress about the deployment of troops, submarines, bombers, and fighter planes.[98]

Did Dirksen mean that in moments of crisis, when "there is no division between the Executive and Congress," that emergencies suspend the principle of separation of powers and the system of checks and balances? Fulbright complimented Dirksen on his remarks, pointing out that while on certain matters Dirksen was "a great partisan leader," on all matters affecting the security of the country he "rises above partisanship." Such behavior, said Fulbright, was "normal and demonstrates the distinction between foreign relations and domestic relations."[99] According to this view, the legislative scrutiny that is fundamental to constitutional safeguards would be replaced by nonpartisan or bipartisan acquiescence to presidential decisions.

During House debate on the Tonkin Gulf Resolution, no one spoke in opposition to the legislation or to presidential initiatives. Representative Carl Albert (D-Okla.), the House majority leader, urged legislators to set aside party differences and unite behind the president:

> . . . this bipartisan congressional support has had the same effect—to let both friend and foe know that in time of crisis the American people will not permit party differences to divide them in meeting their responsibilities in the world.

. . . It is now time for all of us to join together as a nation firmly united behind our Commander in Chief and to express our complete confidence in him and in his leadership.[100]

The House minority leader, Charles Halleck (R-Ind.), offered similar reasons for supporting the president: "particularly when those matters involve armed aggression against the property and people of the United States and our flag, I stand with the President of the United States."[101] Representative Edwin Adair (R-Ind.) responded to the concern that passage of the Tonkin Gulf Resolution would signal that legislators are "abdicating our congressional rights and our congressional responsibilities with respect to the declaration of war and with respect to foreign affairs generally." He said that issue was raised in committee "and we were given assurance that it was the attitude of the Executive that such was not the case, that we are not impairing our congressional prerogatives."[102]

Quite a dialogue! Legislators asked executive officials if there had been abdication of congressional duties and were assured that everything was OK. Not to worry. Instead of legislators making an independent judgment about their constitutional rights and powers, they deferred to the word and analysis of executive officials.

The Vietnam commitment continued to expand because many lawmakers who strongly opposed the war refused to say anything in public. The prime example is Senator Richard Russell, powerful chairman of the Senate Armed Services Committee and an influential adviser to President Johnson. Russell had warned about American involvement in Vietnam from Eisenhower through Johnson but rarely spoke out about his misgivings.[103] Public opposition from Russell would have been pivotal in ending America's commitment to Southeast Asia, yet he kept silent. One scholar suggested two reasons: "First, he had a misguided sense of what was respect for the president, and of the need to support the flag once committed. More important was his total lack of understanding of congressional responsibility in exercising power over the executive under Article I, §8, of the Constitution."[104]

The National Commitments Resolution

Hearings in 1968 by the Senate Foreign Relations Committee raised substantial questions about whether the second attack in the Tonkin Gulf ever took place and whether the Johnson administration had helped provoke the incidents in the Tonkin Gulf. Senator Fulbright reviewed some of the new information, including telegrams, that cast doubt on what the administration had told Congress in 1964. In speaking about one telegram, Fulbright said that "if that had been put before me on the 6th of August, I certainly don't believe I would have rushed into action." However, instead of taking additional time to review the merits of the resolution, Fulbright accepted the accuracy of what he had been told by executive officials. He said he had "no independent evidence, and now I think I did a great disservice to the Senate. I feel very guilty for not having enough sense at that time to have raised these questions and asked for evidence. I regret it."[105]

On April 16, 1969, the Senate Foreign Relations Committee reported Senate Resolution 85, called the National Commitments Resolution. The measure provided that a national commitment by the United States to a foreign power "necessarily and exclusively results from affirmative action taken by the executive and legislative branches of the United States Government through means of a treaty, convention, or other legislative instrumentality specifically intended to give effect to such a commitment." Although the resolution was designed to respond to a number of secret agreements uncovered by Congress—such as agreements to provide economic, military, and other assistance to foreign governments—the committee report attempted to explain why Congress in recent decades had acquiesced to the president.

Part of the decline of congressional control, the report said, was that "crisis has been chronic" since 1940, producing a real or seeming need for independent executive action. Executive initiatives were important, but the fact that Congress had acquiesced in, or failed to challenge, the transfer of the war power to the executive, "is probably the most important single fact accounting for the speed and virtual completeness of the transfer." The atmosphere of urgency or contrived urgency put pressure on legislators to suspend doubts and rally to the president. The report also said that legislators were "overawed by the cult of executive expertise" (see box 12).

The report stated that overshadowing this attitude was a form of collective guilt by legislators that their past performance disqualified them from exercising coequal power. The Senate, for example, "acted with disastrous irresponsibility" in rejecting the Covenant of the League of Nations in 1919. Congress had done "a kind of penance" for its prewar isolationism, and that penance had sometimes resulted in "overly hasty acquiescence" to proposals submitted by the executive branch.[106]

Why this "collective guilt" and appetite for "penance"? The Senate's rejection of the covenant was not "disastrous irresponsibility." All of President Wilson's advisers in Paris—Herbert Hoover, Bernard Baruch, Secretary of State Robert

BOX 12

Senate Report on National Commitments

Our country has come far toward the concentration in its national executive of unchecked power over foreign relations, particularly over the disposition and use of the Armed Forces. So far has this process advanced that, in the committee's view, it is no longer accurate to characterize our government, in matters of foreign relations, as one of separated powers checked and balanced against each other. For causes to be detailed in the following pages, the executive has acquired virtual supremacy over the making as well as the conduct of the foreign relations of the United States.

The principal cause of the constitutional imbalance has been the circumstance of American involvement and responsibility in a violent and unstable world. Since its entry into World War II the United States has been deeply, and to a great extent involuntarily, involved in a series of crises. . . .

. . . If blame is to be apportioned, a fair share belongs to the Congress. It is understandable, though not acceptable, that in times of real or seeming emergency the executive will be tempted to take shortcuts around constitutional procedure. It is less understandable that the Congress should acquiesce in these shortcuts, giving away that which is not its to give, notably the war power, which the framers of the Constitution vested not in the executive but, deliberately and almost exclusively, in the Congress. . . .

The fact that Congress has acquiesced in, or at the very least has failed to challenge, the transfer of the war power from itself to the executive, is probably the most important single fact accounting for the speed and virtual completeness of the transfer. Why has Congress agreed to this rearrangement of powers which is without constitutional justification, and at its own expense?

To some degree, it seems to be the result of the unfamiliarity of the United States with its new role as a world power. . . . the fact that so many of the great policy decisions of the postwar era have been made in an atmosphere of real or contrived urgency has put tremendous pressure on Members of Congress to set aside apprehensions as to the exercise of power by the executive lest they cause some fatal delay or omission in the nation's foreign policy.

Another possible factor in congressional passivity is that Congress may have permitted itself to be overawed by the cult of executive expertise. . . . A veritable army of foreign policy experts has sprung up in government and in the universities in recent years, contributing greatly to our knowledge and skill in foreign relations but also purveying the belief that foreign policy is an occult science which ordinary citizens, including Members of Congress, are simply too stupid to grasp. . . .

Source: S. Report No. 129, 91st Cong., 1st sess., 7–8, 15–16 (1969).

Lansing, and Wilson's closest adviser, Col. Edward House—urged him to accept the Lodge reservations.[107] The Senate had a right to protect legislative prerogatives. What was the main reason the treaty fell? It was Wilson's intransigence, refusing to abide a "single further amendment."[108]

The committee report said that the Tonkin Gulf Resolution represented "the extreme point in the process of constitutional erosion that began in the first years of this century." In adopting a resolution with such sweeping language, however, Congress committed the error of "making a *personal* judgment as to how President Johnson would implement the resolution when it had a responsibility to make an *institutional* judgment, first, as to what any President would do with so great an acknowledgment of power, and, second, as to whether, under the Constitution, Congress had the right to grant or concede the authority in question."[109]

The report concluded with this advice. Should the president find himself confronted with a situation that is complex and ambiguous, leaving him without guidelines to decide what is constitutional, "it would be far better for him to take the action he saw fit without attempting to justify it in advance and leave it to Congress or the courts to evaluate his action in retrospect." A single unconstitutional act by the president would be preferable to an act "dressed up in some spurious, precedent-setting claim of legitimacy." The report quoted Representative Alexander White in 1789: "It would be better for the President to extend his powers on some extraordinary occasions, even where he is not strictly justified by the Constitution, than the legislature should grant an improper power to be exercised at all times."[110]

When the commitments resolution reached the floor, Senator Sam J. Ervin, Jr. (D-N.C.) noted that in the years since World War II the power to make foreign policy had shifted almost entirely to the president. A theory had developed that foreign policy was solely a presidential prerogative. That view was shared "by much of the public and, needless to say, it is forcefully espoused by the executive branch as well." Under this theory, Congress was "little more than a rubber-stamp of the executive branch," with a duty simply to approve what the president did in foreign affairs and to appropriate whatever he needed, "without question or cavil." The State Department had made it plain that foreign policy "is much too important and much too complicated to be left to the untutored mercies of mere Senators and Representatives." Ervin said that the State Department made the "common mistake of confusing information for knowledge, and knowledge for wisdom."[111] The resolution passed by a vote of 70 to 16. The final language:

> *Resolved,* That (1) a national commitment for the purpose of this resolution means the use of the armed forces of the United States on foreign territory, or a promise to assist a foreign country, government, or people by the use of the armed forces or financial resources of the United States, either immediately or upon the happening of certain events, and (2) it is the sense of the Senate that a national commitment by the United States results only from affirmative action taken by the executive and legislative branches of the United States Government by means of a treaty, statute, or concurrent resolution of both Houses of Congress specifically providing for such commitment.[112]

Although a sense of the Senate resolution is not legally binding, the measure was important because it represented a clear statement of constitutional principles. It was designed to put the president on notice that the Senate understood its constitutional duties and intended to exercise them in the future. Unfortunately, the Senate failed to live up to the spirit and language of the National Commitments Resolution. Within a few years it joined with the House in passing the War Powers Resolution of 1973, ceding major new powers to the president to act unilaterally with military commitments.

The War Powers Resolution

The War Powers Resolution is usually described as a major effort to "reassert" congressional prerogatives. In fact, by recognizing that the president may use armed force for up to 90 days without seeking or obtaining legislative authority, the resolution sanctions a scope of independent presidential power that would have astonished the framers. The founding fathers vested in Congress the power to initiate hostilities against foreign nations.

According to Section 2(a) of the War Powers Resolution, the measure is intended "to fulfill the intent of the framers" and to "insure that the collective judgment of both the Congress and the President" will apply to the introduction of U.S. forces to foreign hostilities. The resolution has had no such effect. Instead, it violates the intent of the framers and does not in any sense insure collective judgment. Presidents Reagan, Bush, and Clinton have made repeated use of military force without either seeking or obtaining authority from Congress.

Given the institutionally humiliating lesson of the Tonkin Gulf Resolution and the thoughtful deliberations that led to the National Commitments Resolution, how could Congress pass such a botched measure as the War Powers Resolution? In part, it represents an effort to blend House and Senate versions that were incompatible in constitutional principle. As Senator Tom Eagleton (D-Mo.) remarked, the two chambers "marched down separate and distinct roads, almost irreconcilable roads."[113]

The House was willing to recognize that the president, in certain extraordinary and emergency conditions, could defend the United States and its citizens without prior authorization from Congress. Its bill provided that unless Congress declared war within 120 days or specifically authorized the use of force, the president had to terminate the commitment after that period and remove the troops. The House thereby blessed presidential military initiatives for up to four months.

Senators refused to give the president such blanket authority. Instead, they tried to spell out the conditions under which the president could act on his own without legislative approval. Armed force could be used in three situations: first, to repel an armed attack upon the United States and its territories and possessions, retaliate in the event of such an attack, and forestall the direct and imminent threat of an attack; second, to repel an armed attack against U.S. armed forces located outside the United States and its territories and possessions, and forestall the direct and imminent threat of such an attack; and third, to rescue endangered American citizens and nationals in foreign countries or at sea. The president would have to cease military action unless Congress within 30 days specifically authorized the president to continue.

Under great pressure to report a bill, House and Senate conferees fashioned a compromise product. Splitting the difference between the two chambers is common and acceptable practice for most bills. Shall we spend $10 billion (House version) or $8 billion (Senate version) for a housing program? Settling on $9 billion does not threaten the Constitution. What the War Powers Resolution did, however, was to compromise basic institutional and constitutional prerogatives. The president ended up with a green light to use force anywhere in the world, for whatever reason, without ever seeking congressional authority.

Section 2(c) attempted to tie presidential use of force to constitutional values. The president could introduce U.S. forces into hostilities only upon a congressional declaration of war, statutory authorization, or an attack upon the United States. But that language—consistent with the framers' document—is then contradicted by other provisions in Sections 4 and 5, allowing the president to act unilaterally for 60 to 90 days. [In deference to the Senate, the House had agreed to shorten the time period from 120 to 60 days. The president could take an additional 30 days to withdraw troops.]

After President Nixon vetoed the bill, both Houses voted to override, the House narrowly (284 to 135) and the Senate by a more comfortable margin (75 to 18). Some of the support in the House for the override had nothing to do with the merits of the legislation. Several members let immediate political and partisan interests outweigh long-term institutional and constitutional interests. Fifteen members of the House initially voted against the bill and the conference version, arguing that the legislation was inadequate, unsound, and too generous to presidential power. To be consistent, they should have voted to sustain Nixon's veto to prevent the bill from becoming law. Yet they switched sides and delivered the decisive votes for enactment.[114]

These members reversed course for a variety of reasons. Some feared that a vote to sustain would lend credence to the views of presidential power advanced in Nixon's veto message.[115] Others thought that an override might be a step toward impeaching Nixon. Representative Bella Abzug (D-N.Y.) voted against the House bill and the conference version because they expanded presidential war power. As she noted during debate on the conference report: "[It] gives the President 60 to 90 days to intervene in any crisis situation, on any pretext, while Congress merely asks that he tell us what he has done."[116] Yet she strongly supported a veto override: "This could be a turning point in the struggle to control an administration that has run amuck. It could accelerate the demand for the impeachment of the President."[117]

Democrats had an additional reason to override Nixon. Eight times during the Ninety-third Congress he had vetoed legislation; eight times the Democratic Congress came up short on the override effort. Some legislators regarded the override vote on the War Powers Resolution as an essential means of reasserting congressional power, particularly in the midst of the Watergate scandals.[118] The Saturday Night Massacre, which sent Special Prosecutor Archibald Cox, Attorney General Elliot Richardson, and Deputy Attorney General William Ruckelshaus out of the government, occurred just four days before Nixon's veto of the War Powers Resolution. Ten days before the Saturday Night Massacre, Vice President Spiro Agnew's resignation in disgrace heightened the cry for partisan and institutional blood.

Even operating under these intense political pressures, several Democrats in the House recognized that the conference report tilted power decisively toward the president. William Green, from Pennsylvania, remarked that the War Powers Resolution "has popularly been interpreted as limiting the President's power to engage our troops in a war." Because he had opposed such unilateral presidential action, he wanted to explain that a careful reading of the bill indicated that it "is actually an expansion of Presidential warmaking power, rather than a limitation."[119] Vernon Thomson of Wisconsin had no illusion about the bill: "The clear meaning of the words certainly points to a diminution rather than an enhancement of the role of Congress in the critical decisions whether the country will or will not go to war."[120] Bob Eckhardt of Texas condemned the abdication of congressional power. By allowing the president to engage U.S. troops for up to 90 days, "the Congress provides the color of authority to the President to exercise a warmaking power which I find the Constitution has exclusively assigned to the Congress."[121] Ronald Dellums of California, having opposed the House bill and the conference version, held firm and voted to sustain the veto: "Richard Nixon is not going to be President forever. Although many people will regard this as a victory against the incumbent President, because of his opposition, I am convinced that it will actually strengthen the position of future Presidents."[122]

There were fewer clear thinkers on the Senate side. Senator Eagleton, a principal sponsor of the War Powers Resolution, denounced the bill that emerged from conference as a "total, complete distortion of the war powers concept." Instead of the three exceptions specified in the Senate bill and the 30-day limit, the conference report gave the president "carte blanche" authority to use military force for up to 90 days. Although the media continued to describe the bill as a constraint on presidential war power, Eagleton punctured these misconceptions. The bill was a sell-out, a surrender (see box 13).

Even those who continued to support the bill and urged a veto override had to concede the broad sweep of presidential power conferred by Congress. Senators Jacob Javits and Ed Muskie (D-Maine), in a "Dear Colleague" letter distributed to other legislators, admitted that nothing in the bill would have prevented President Nixon from sending U.S. troops to the Middle East to assist Israel against Egyptian threats. The bill, they said, "would have required the President only to report to the Congress within 48 hours in writing with

BOX 13

Eagleton on War Powers Bill

Mr. President, I rise to speak in support of the President's veto of the so-called war powers bill, and therefore in opposition to the attempt to override it.

[After describing the basic elements of the Senate version, he says that was the form it was in] when it went to that mysterious conclave called the conference committee. The Senate bill disappeared in conference. What came out is a total, complete distortion of the war powers concept, because what came out has nothing to do with emergency authority of the President. It has nothing to do with the central point of contention over war powers.

. . . What the conference bill now says is this, and the country had better know it. The country does not know it yet, because the media coverage of the bill still says that this limits the President's war power. It does not. The bill gives the President of the United States unilateral authority to commit American troops anywhere in the world, under any conditions he decides, for 60 to 90 days. He gets a free 60 days and a self-executing option for an additional 30 days, making 90. . . .

What this bill says is that the President can send us to war wherever and whenever he wants to. Troops could be deployed tomorrow to the Mideast under this bill without our prior authority. All the President has to do is to make a telephone call to Senator MANSFIELD and Senator SCOTT and say, "The boys are on the way. I think you should know." Consultation. There they are; 60 to 90 days. Once those troops are committed the history of this country is replete with examples; that once committed they remain.

. . . Despite what has been written and said about [this bill], it does not limit the power of the President of the United States to wage war by himself.

Quite to the contrary. It attempts to emblazon into law, that unilateral decisionmaking process.

Source: 119 *Cong. Rec.* 36176–77 (1973).

respect to the deployment of U.S. Armed Forces in foreign territory, airspace and waters."[123] The president could commit U.S. troops to the volatile Middle East with no nod to Congress other than having aides prepare a written report.

This was the legislation being praised as "congressional reassertion." Eagleton confessed to being "dumbfounded." With memories so fresh about presidential extension of the war in Southeast Asia, "how can we give unbridled, unlimited total authority to the President to commit us to war?" He charged that the bill, after being nobly conceived, "has been horribly bastardized to the point of being a menace."[124]

During the remainder of the 1970s, Presidents Gerald Ford and Jimmy Carter acted with restraint on military operations. They reported only five uses of armed forces, and three of the actions under Ford involved military efforts to evacuate American citizens and foreign nationals from Southeast Asia. Ignoring those actions, in the six and a half years of Ford's and Carter's terms of office there were only two presidential initiatives to use armed forces: the rescue effort of the *Mayaguez* crew in 1975 and the attempt to rescue American hostages in Iran in 1980.[125] However, military activity accelerated during the Reagan, Bush, and Clinton administrations.

Reagan's Initiatives

The caution exercised by Ford and Carter was not matched by President Ronald Reagan. Repeatedly he used military force against other countries, never once asking Congress for authority in advance or afterward. Even these actions, however, were relatively restrained when compared to the military initiatives undertaken by Presidents Bush and Clinton.

Troops to Lebanon

Following Israel's invasion of Lebanon in 1982, President Reagan sent U.S. Marines to Lebanon in August as part of a three-nation peacekeeping force (including France and Italy). The announced goal was to assure the withdrawal of the PLO (Palestine Liberation Organization) in order to restore the sovereignty of the Lebanese government. Reagan explained that U.S. troops would play a "carefully limited, noncombatant role," remaining in Lebanon for no longer than 30 days.[126] The military deployment, he said, had been undertaken solely on his constitutional authority.[127]

Two weeks later, with the withdrawal of the PLO from Beirut, it appeared that U.S. forces would be sent home as scheduled. However, in mid-September President-elect Bashir Gemayel of Lebanon was assassinated. The Israelis moved into strategic positions throughout West Beirut, in violation of the cease-fire understanding. A few days later hundreds of Palestinian men, women, and children were murdered in the Sabra and Shatila refugee camps, south of Beirut.

On September 20, Reagan announced a new multinational force in Lebanon, working again with France and Italy. He said the troops would remain in Beirut "for a limited period of time."[128] When the American military presence continued into the next year, a terrorist bomb exploded at the U.S. embassy in Beirut on April 18, 1983, killing 16 Americans. On August 29, the administration announced the deaths of 2 U.S. Marines in Beirut. Two more Marines were killed on September 6.

With the level of hostilities increasing, members of Congress called on Reagan to invoke Section 4(a)(1) of the War Powers Resolution to trigger the 60–90 day clock. When he refused, lawmakers used a statute to activate Section 4(a)(1). Enacted on October 12, 1983, the law backdated the 4(a)(1) date to August 29, 1983, when the first two U.S. Marines were killed, but also authorized military action for eighteen months.[129] This is the only time that Congress has acted to trigger the clock in the War Powers Resolution, and its choice of eighteen months on this occasion was a deliberate effort to push the Lebanon issue beyond public debate in the 1984 elections. A few weeks after this bill was enacted, a truck carrying 2,000 pounds of explosives broke through barriers surrounding U.S. headquarters in Beirut and smashed through the doors of the headquarters building. The explosion killed 241 Marines. A separate suicide mission killed more than 50 French soldiers.

Hostilities continued to mount. President Reagan ordered the battleship *New Jersey,* with its sixteen-inch guns, to join U.S. naval forces offshore. American warships began lobbing shells into Druze, Shiite, and Syrian positions. Several U.S. planes were shot down. In February, 1984, Congress began consideration of a resolution to require Reagan to withdraw U.S. forces from Lebanon. Later that month, Reagan ordered the redeployment of Marines from the Beirut Airport to U.S. ships offshore, and on March 30 he terminated U.S. participation in the multinational force.[130] What began as a humanitarian, peacekeeping, noncombatant mission deteriorated into war, stretching from its initial 30-day commitment to almost two years.

Invasion of Grenada

Two days after the October, 1983, suicide bombing in Beirut, President Reagan ordered U.S. forces into the Caribbean island of Grenada. He offered three reasons to justify the invasion: to protect lives, including American medical students; to forestall further chaos; and to restore conditions of law and order and of governmental institutions on the island. A coup had resulted in the killing of Prime Minister Maurice Bishop, three cabinet members, two labor leaders, and other citizens. Reagan informed Congress that the military action was undertaken pursuant to his constitutional authority "with respect to the conduct of foreign relations and as Commander-in-Chief of the United States Armed Forces."[131]

The UN Security Council drafted a resolution "deeply deploring" the invasion of Grenada, eleven members voting in favor and the United States exercising its veto. Britain, Togo, and Zaire abstained on the vote. A number of U.S. allies, including France, the Netherlands, and Pakistan, voted for the resolution. On the key language on legality, the Security Council "DEEPLY DE-PLORES the armed intervention in Grenada, which constitutes a flagrant violation of international law and of the independence, sovereignty and territorial integrity of that state."[132]

Congress acted quickly to put a short leash on this military operation. The House of Representatives, with a 403 to 23 margin, passed legislation to trigger the 60-day clock of the War Powers Resolution. The Senate was about to pass the same type of legislation.[133] The administration announced that it expected to conclude military actions within 60 days.[134] President Reagan was able, by December 8, to inform Congress that U.S. Marines and U.S. Army Rangers had been withdrawn from the island.[135]

Air Strikes against Libya

In March, 1986, U.S. forces traded fire with Libya, sinking three Libyan patrol boats and damaging another. President Reagan notified Congress of these actions, defending the strikes as an act of self-defense and within his authority as commander in chief.[136] In April, the administration blamed the Libyan regime for the bombing of a discotheque in West Berlin, which killed an Army sergeant, a Turkish woman, and injured about 230, including 50 American military personnel. In response to that attack, President Reagan authorized additional air strikes against Libya. The strikes were directed against the headquarters, terrorist facilities, and military assets that support Colonel Mu'ammar Qadhafi.[137]

President Reagan went on to explain that whenever "our citizens are abused or attacked anywhere in the world on the direct orders of a hostile regime, we will respond so long as I'm in this Oval Office. Self-defense is not only our right, it is our duty."[138] In fact, military force is used only against countries that are isolated and weak. If American citizens had been abused or attacked in Russia, China, Syria, or other countries, Reagan would not have responded with air strikes. When Reagan reported to Congress on the military action, he explained that he acted solely under his constitutional authorities and the right of self-defense under Article 51 of the UN Charter.[139]

Following the March air strikes, Congressman Dante Fascell, chairman of the House Foreign Affairs Committee, wrote to President Reagan, objecting that the actions against Libya failed to satisfy the requirements of the War Powers Resolution. In particular, he said that the "distinct possibility" of imminent involvement in hostilities required a presidential report under Section 4(a)(1), triggering the 60-day clock, and that prior consultation with members of Congress was required. A White House official, responding to Fascell, denied that there had been any breach of the War Powers Resolution. The administration took the position that consultation was not required "before conducting naval maneuvers in international waters or airspace." The White House official also stated that conducting the operations against Libya "did not place U.S. forces into hostilities or into a situation in which imminent hostilities were clearly indicated by the circumstances."[140] Through such interpretations the War Powers Resolution would have little effect in protecting legislative prerogatives and assuring "collective judgment."

Iran-Contra

The Iran-Contra affair burst upon an incredulous nation in November, 1986. Within a matter of weeks the public learned that the Reagan administration had sold arms to Iran and sent weapons to the Contra rebels in Nicaragua despite a statutory ban on such assistance. New details appeared almost daily, providing fresh insights into the scope of activities conducted by executive officials and private citizens. To investigate the matter, President Reagan set up the Tower Commission and asked Attorney General Edwin Meese to go to the special panel of federal judges to have an independent counsel appointed. Congress established a joint House-Senate committee to conduct hearings, take depositions, and issue a final report.

Iran-Contra violated both administration policy and statutory law. The Reagan administration publicly urged other nations to be neutral on the war between Iran and Iraq, objected to sending weapons to either side, and was steadfastly opposed to giving any concessions to terrorists. Yet it found itself engaged in providing Iranian terrorists with arms in exchange for American hostages. On the statutory front, Congress had enacted the Boland Amendment to prohibit all executive branch assistance of any kind to provide military support to the Contras: "During fiscal year 1985, no funds available to the Central Intelligence Agency, the Department of Defense, or any other agency or entity of the United States involved in intelligence activities may be obligated or expended for the purpose or which would have the effect of supporting, directly or indirectly, military or paramilitary operations in Nicaragua by any nation, group, organization, movement, or individual."[141]

No one in the administration challenged the legality or constitutionality of this language, including President Reagan when he signed the bill, the attorney general, or the Office of Legal Counsel in the Justice Department. When the administration's spokesman appeared at hearings conducted by the Senate Foreign Relations Committee and the House Appropriations Committee, he assured the legislators that the administration understood the meaning of the amendment and would comply fully. There would be no attempt, he said, to solicit funds from outside sources, such as private parties or other countries.[142]

Nevertheless, at the very moment of this testimony, executive branch officials were actively soliciting funds from private parties and from foreign governments to assist the Contras. Working closely with the White House and the National Security Council, private citizens raised money from private contributors to provide military weapons and supplies to the Contras.[143] Administration officials also made repeated efforts to obtain funds from foreign governments, succeeding with some countries (as with Saudi Arabia) and failing with others.[144]

Of all the revelations emanating from the Iran-Contra hearings in 1987, the most startling constitutional claim was the assertion that Congress cannot control foreign affairs by withholding appropriations. Some Reagan administration officials argued that if Congress prohibits the use of appropriations for foreign policy objectives, as it did with the Boland Amendment, the president can nevertheless pursue his goals by soliciting funds from the private sector and from foreign countries.[145] If one well dries up, tap another.

Had President Reagan defied the Boland Amendment by seeking financial or other assistance from foreign countries or private individuals, at a minimum he would have subjected the United States to ridicule and humiliation. Having been rebuffed by Congress, he would go hat in hand to foreign governments and private citizens for assistance in implementing the administration's foreign policy. Such conduct would risk a major collision with Congress, with the president acting in the face of a congressional policy enacted into law. In such circumstances, a president would invite, and deserve, impeachment proceedings. He would fail in his constitutional duty to see that the laws are faithfully executed and would precipitate a constitutional crisis by merging the power of the sword with the power of the purse.

Moreover, soliciting funds from foreign governments to promote U.S. foreign policy opens the door to rampant compromise and corruption. Admiral John Poindexter testified that the administration could withhold information from Congress because the Contras were being assisted with nonappropriated funds: "we weren't using appropriated funds. They were private, third-country funds."[146] Accepting funds from foreign governments to sustain U.S. policy creates an implicit quid pro quo, requiring the United States to reciprocate by giving contributing countries extra consideration in the form of foreign assistance, military assistance, arms sales, and trade concessions.[147] In 1989, Congress enacted legislation to stop these quid pro quos.[148]

Members Turn to the Courts

One of the byproducts of the War Powers Resolution has been the tendency of legislators to turn not to their colleagues to challenge the president—through statutory restrictions and congressional hearings—but rather to the courts. Private parties have also litigated military issues. None of these efforts has been successful.

On four occasions during the 1980s, members of Congress went to court to charge President Reagan with violations of the War Powers Resolution and other statutes. President Reagan did not report under any provision of the resolution when he sent military advisers to El Salvador in 1981. The State Department claimed that no report was necessary, because the Americans were not being introduced into hostilities or imminent hostilities. Several legislators filed a suit claiming that Reagan had violated the resolution by sending the advisers. Eventually, twenty-nine members of the House joined the action against Reagan. Arrayed on the opposite side were sixteen senators and twelve representatives who supported Reagan and urged that the case be dismissed. The federal judge, confronted by two congressional factions, refused to do the fact-finding that would have been necessary to determine whether hostilities or imminent hostilities actually existed. The court stated that it lacked "the resources and expertise" necessary to "resolve the disputed questions of fact concerning the military situation in El Salvador" and dismissed the case on political question grounds, noting that Congress had failed legislatively to restrain Reagan.[149]

In a similar case, eleven members of Congress brought action against President Reagan for his invasion of Grenada in 1983, contending that he had violated the power of Congress to declare war. The judiciary declined to exercise its jurisdiction because of the relief available to members through the regular legislative process. The message was clear: If Congress wants to confront the president, it must do so by exerting legislative powers, not by turning to the courts.[150]

Another suit involving the Reagan administration's activities in Nicaragua was avoided by the courts on similar grounds. Twelve members of the House, relying on a number of statutes including the War Powers Resolution, challenged the legality of Reagan's actions. The district court referred to the "impossibility of our undertaking independent resolution without expressing a lack of the respect due coordinate branches of government."[151] When this opinion was affirmed by the appellate court, Judge Ruth Bader Ginsburg noted that Congress "has formidable weapons at its disposal—the power of the purse and investigative resources far beyond those available in the Third Branch. But no gauntlet has been thrown down here by a majority of the Members of Congress."[152]

Also unsuccessful was a case brought by members of Congress who claimed that President Reagan's use of military force in the Persian Gulf in 1987 had not followed the procedures of the War Powers Resolution. The advice from the court was familiar. If Congress failed to defend its prerogatives, it could not expect to be bailed out by the courts.[153]

In the years following World War II, Congress lost ground steadily with the war power. Of the postwar presidents, Dwight D. Eisenhower remained sensitive to the prerogatives of Congress, the system of checks and balances, and the need for both branches to act jointly in military operations. The Vietnam War so bitterly divided the nation that Presidents Ford and Carter were also cautious about making unilateral commitments of U.S. armed forces. Reagan pushed the envelope by engaging in several military engagements, but his record pales in comparison to Bush and Clinton. The Korean War had a devastating impact on constitutional relationships. It was the first time that a president had singlehandedly taken the country to war against another country, and it allowed a president to seek "authority" from Security Council resolutions. Presidents Bush and Clinton would use that same justification during their terms in office, and Clinton would circumvent Congress still further by relying on "authority" from NATO.

4

Military Operations by Bush and Clinton

The cold war with Soviet Russia ended during Reagan's administration, supposedly relaxing world tensions and enabling Congress to recapture its war powers. Yet Congress has been more supine that ever. President George Bush invaded Panama without coming to Congress for authority and claimed he could go to war against Iraq without legislative approval. At the eleventh hour Congress authorized the operation, but even at that point, in his signing statement, Bush denied that he needed authority from Congress. As a humanitarian gesture, Bush sent troops to Somalia. That commitment grew bloody during President Bill Clinton's term, provoking Congress to cut off funds. Clinton also used military force in Iraq, Haiti, Bosnia, Yugoslavia, Afghanistan, and Sudan, never once asking lawmakers for authority. Congress started to confront him a number of times but never followed through.

Invasion of Panama

In December, 1989, with Congress out of session, President Bush ordered 11,000 troops into Panama to join 13,000 American troops already present in the Canal Zone. The goal was to remove General Manuel Noriega from power and restore President Guillermo Endara and his two vice presidents, who had been elected in May, 1989, but driven from office by Noriega. At the end of January, 1990, Bush notified Congress that American troops would be out of Panama by the end of February.[1] It appeared that the administration had decided to restrict itself—politically if not legally—to the 60-to-90-day clock of the War Powers Resolution.

President Bush advanced a number of arguments to justify the invasion. He said that Noriega's threats and attacks upon American citizens in Panama created an "imminent danger" to the 35,000 American citizens there and that, as president, he had "no higher obligation than to safeguard the lives of American citizens."[2] Why weren't the 13,000 American troops already stationed in the Canal Zone adequate protection for U.S. citizens? Moreover, if the United States has an inherent and obligatory right to invade other countries whenever American citizens are abused or threatened, there are dozens of such opportunities. But such responses would be roundly condemned in most cases.

The Organization of American States (OAS) Charter, signed by the United States, Panama, and other countries, explicitly provides that the territory of a nation is inviolable and it "may not be the object, even temporarily, of military occupation or of other measures of force taken by another State, directly or indirectly, on any grounds whatsoever." The OAS condemned the invasion of Panama by a vote of twenty to one.

Bush also defended the invasion as a way "to combat drug trafficking." He called Noriega "an indicted drug trafficker."[3] A member of the administration, Ambassador Thomas R. Pickering, argued that drug operations in Panama were analogous to military attacks on the United States:

> Countries that provide safe haven and support for the international drug trafficking cartels menace the peace and security just as surely as if they were using their own conventional military forces to attack our societies. The truth is, and every one of us knows it, General Noriega turned Panama into a haven for drug traffickers and a center for money laundering and transshipment of cocaine. General Noriega could not be permitted falsely to wrap himself in the flag of Panamanian sovereignty while the drug cartels with which he is allied intervene throughout this hemisphere. That is aggression. It is aggression against us all, and now it is being brought to an end.[4]

Such a rationale would justify American military intervention in Mexico, Colombia, Turkey, and any other nation that is a source of drugs flowing to the United States. Obviously that is not U.S. policy.

Congress made no formal response to the invasion of Panama. On February 7, 1990, the House of Representatives passed a resolution stating that Bush had acted "decisively and appropriately" in ordering U.S. forces to intervene in Panama. At the same time, the resolution counseled against using this action as a precedent for intervening elsewhere in Central America, Mexico, and the Caribbean. The resolution stated that the U.S. action in Panama "was a response to a unique set of circumstances, and does not undermine the commitment of the government of the United States to the principle of non-intervention in the internal affairs of other countries."[5]

Bush Acts against Iraq

Building on Truman's decision to rely on a Security Council resolution as legal cover for military action in Korea, President George Bush in 1990 developed the same strategy to wage war against Iraq. One precedent set the stage for another. President Bill Clinton would later rely on a Security Council resolution to threaten an invasion of Haiti in 1994 and would use a combination of Security Council resolutions and NATO decisions to order air strikes in Bosnia.

After President Saddam Hussein's invasion of Kuwait on August 2, 1990, President Bush sent several hundred thousand troops to Saudi Arabia. Initial troop deployments served a defensive purpose, but as the size of the American force climbed to 500,000 soldiers, an offensive capability emerged. Instead of seeking authority from Congress, Bush created a multinational alliance and encouraged the Security Council to authorize the use of military force. The strategic calculations were later revealed by James A. Baker, III, who served as secretary of state in the Bush administration. Baker realized that military initiatives by Reagan in Grenada and by Bush in Panama had reinforced in the national community the impression that American foreign policy followed a "cowboy mentality." In response to these concerns, Bush wanted to assemble an international political coalition. Baker notes: "[F]rom the very beginning, the President recognized the importance of having the express approval of the international community if at all possible."[6] Neither Bush nor Baker felt a comparable need to obtain the express approval of Congress.

This international political coalition was willing to make major financial contributions to cover the cost of military intervention in the Middle East. Saudi Arabia, Kuwait, the United Arab Emirates, Japan, Germany, France, and Great Britain agreed to commit financial resources. The administration wanted these funds to go directly to the Defense Department as "gifts."[7] President Bush could then spend the money without coming to Congress for an appropriation. Senator Robert C. Byrd quickly intervened to scotch this proposal. Contributions from foreign governments would go first to the Treasury, subject to appropriation by Congress.[8]

On November 29, 1990, the Security Council passed Resolution 678, authorizing member states to use "all necessary means" to force Iraqi troops out of Kuwait. The phrase "all necessary means" is diplomatic talk for military force.

To avoid war, Iraq had to withdraw from Kuwait by January 15, 1991.[9] The Security Council resolution granted "the most sweeping authorization to engage in warfare under U.N. sponsorship since the 1950 Korean war."[10] Although the Security Council "authorized" each nation to act militarily against Iraq, the resolution did not *compel* or *obligate* member nations to participate. States agree to use force pursuant to their own constitutional systems and judgments about national interests.[11] The Security Council "has never required states to use force; it has simply authorized or recommended that they do so."[12]

Following the Security Council vote, Professor Thomas M. Franck of the New York University Law School published an article in *The New York Times,* arguing that a congressional declaration of war "is inapplicable to U.N. police actions."[13] He claimed that the UN Charter "does not leave room for each state, once the Council has acted, to defer compliance until it has authority from its own legislature." Yet the legislative histories of the UN Charter and the UN Participation Act clearly show that Congress was expected to approve the use of military commitments to the Security Council. There was no intention of surrendering congressional power to the United Nations.

Franck later acknowledged that the purpose of the war-declaring clause in the U.S. Constitution is "to ensure that this fateful decision did not rest with a single person."[14] Did that concession open the door to a congressional role? Not to Franck. The proscription against unilateral action by the president could be satisfied by vesting the responsibility in the Security Council, "a body where the most divergent interests and perspectives of humanity are represented and where five of fifteen members have a veto power." Through this reasoning he neatly substituted the Security Council for Congress. The system of collective decision making established by the framers was now fundamentally changed by eliminating Congress from the decision to go to war.

Administration officials were similarly comfortable with excluding Congress. Secretary of Defense Dick Cheney testified before the Senate Armed Services Committee on December 3, 1990, stating that President Bush did not require "any additional authorization from the Congress" before attacking Iraq.[15] The phrase "additional authorization" implied that Security Council approval was sufficient. Cheney's testimony provoked the House Democratic Caucus to adopt a resolution stating that the president must first seek authorization from Congress before going to war against Iraq, unless American lives were in danger. The resolution passed by a vote of 177 to 37.[16]

When Congressman Ron Dellums went to court to challenge the power of President Bush to act singlehandedly against Iraq, the Justice Department claimed that Bush could order offensive actions against Iraq without seeking advance authority from Congress. That sweeping interpretation of presidential war power was systematically rejected by a federal district judge on December 13 before holding that the case was not ripe for judicial determination (see box 14).

The lack of ripeness in this case resulted from several factors, but particularly the failure of Congress to confront Bush. It was not enough for several dozen members of Congress to take a claim to the court. The judge said that Congress had to act as an institution: "In short, unless the Congress as a whole, or by a majority, is heard from, the controversy here cannot be deemed ripe."[17]

On January 8, 1991, President Bush asked Congress to pass legislation "supporting" the UN position, particularly Security Council Resolution 678 authorizing the use of all necessary means.[18] The next day reporters asked whether he needed a resolution from Congress. His reply: "I don't think I need it. . . . I feel that I have the authority to fully implement the United Nations resolutions."[19] Bush later noted that the United States had "used military force about two hundred times in its history and there had been only five declarations of war. . . . I wanted to avoid asking for 'authorization,' which implied Congress had the final say in what I believed was an executive decision."[20]

The legal crisis was defused on January 12 when Congress authorized President Bush to take offensive actions against Iraq. The House majority was large (250 to 183), but the vote in the Senate was quite close (52 to 47). In a separate vote on a nonbinding resolution, the House voted 302 to 131 for this language: "The Congress finds that the Constitution of the United States vests all power to declare war in the Congress of the United States. Any offensive action taken against Iraq must be explicitly approved by the Congress of the United States before such action may be initiated."[21]

In signing the bill, Bush continued to insist that he could have acted without congressional authority: "As I made clear to congressional leaders at the outset, my request for congressional support did not, and my signing this resolution does not, constitute any change in the long-standing positions of the executive branch on either the President's constitutional authority to use the Armed Forces to defend vital U.S. interests or the constitutionality of the War Powers Resolution."[22]

Regardless of what Bush said in his signing statement, the bill he signed expressly authorized him to act. Law is determined by language in a signed bill, not by remarks in a signing statement. Years later, Bush would write: "even had Congress not passed the resolutions I would have acted and ordered our troops into combat. I know it would have caused an outcry, but it was the right thing to do. I was comfortable in my own mind that I had the constitutional authority. It had to be done."[23]

BOX 14

A Federal Judge Analyzes War Power Issue

Judge Harold H. Greene: . . . the [Justice] Department contends that there are no judicially discoverable and manageable standards to apply, claiming that only the political branches are able to determine whether or not this country is at war. Such a determination, it is said, is based upon "a political judgment" about the significance of those facts. Under that rationale, a court cannot make an independent determination on this issue because it cannot take adequate account of these political considerations.

This claim on behalf of the Executive is far too sweeping to be accepted by the courts. If the Executive had the sole power to determine that any particular offensive military operation, no matter how vast, does not constitute war-making but only an offensive military attack, the congressional power to declare war will be at the mercy of a semantic decision by the Executive. Such an "interpretation" would evade the plain language of the Constitution, and it cannot stand.

. . . the Department goes on to suggest that the issue in this case is still political rather than legal, because in order to resolve the dispute the Court would have to inject itself into foreign affairs, a subject which the Constitution commits to the political branches. That argument, too, must fail.

. . . the Court has no hesitation in concluding that any offensive entry into Iraq by several hundred thousand United States servicemen under the conditions described above would be described as a "war" within the meaning of Article I, Section 8, Clause 11, of the Constitution . . .

Source: *Dellums v. Bush,* 752 F.Supp., 1141, 1145–46 (D.D.C. 1990).

Here Bush promotes an autocratic or monarchical model. What mattered to him was not the Constitution or legal constraints, but simply doing the "right thing." President Clinton would use the same phrase in justifying military force against Haiti and Bosnia. But the "right thing" to do is to recognize, and adhere to, legal and constitutional limitations. Bush excoriated Saddam Hussein for violating international law by invading Kuwait but felt at liberty to violate the Constitution whenever he considered it necessary.

Initiatives by Clinton

The decision by President Bush to seek a Security Council resolution for military action in Iraq was followed by the Clinton administration in both Haiti and Bosnia. In addition, President Clinton relied on decisions by the North Atlantic Council of the North Atlantic Treaty Organization (NATO) to conduct air strikes in Bosnia and to make war against Serbia. Both Bush and Clinton used UN and NATO "authority" to circumvent the constitutional authority of Congress to initiate military action against other nations.

Throughout Clinton's 1992 presidential campaign, he spoke out forcefully for an activist, interventionist philosophy abroad. Repeatedly he expressed a willingness to use military force. His image as a credible commander in chief had been damaged by conflicting stories about his draft record during the Vietnam War. Various accounts surfaced on the techniques he used to avoid military service. Yet in an interview in June, 1992, he insisted that he could be trusted to be commander in chief and stated that he was prepared to use military force in Bosnia.[24]

Clinton's capacity to serve credibly as commander in chief came to a head soon after he took office and proposed that gays be allowed to serve in the military. The Joint Chiefs of Staff objected that they had not been properly consulted, and the Senate threatened to write the existing administration ban into law. At a news conference on March 23, 1993, Clinton was asked a searching question: "Mr. President, you seem to be having some difficulty with the Pentagon. When you went to the U.S.S. *Theodore Roosevelt*, the sailors there were mocking you before your arrival, even though you are Commander in Chief. The services have been undercutting your proposal for permitting gays to be in the military. . . . Do you have a problem, perhaps because of your lack of military service or perhaps because of issues such as gays in the military, in being effective in your role as Commander in Chief, and what do you propose to do about it?"[25] Clinton denied that he had a problem being commander in chief. Within a few months, he would have what White House officials considered an opportunity to demonstrate his military "toughness."

Launching Missiles against Baghdad

Clinton's first use of military force came on June 26, 1993, when he ordered air strikes against Iraq. In an address to the nation, he said that the Kuwaiti government in April had uncovered what they suspected was a car-bombing plot to assassinate former President Bush during a visit to Kuwait. Sixteen suspects, including two Iraqi nationals, had been arrested. Although the trial of those suspects was still underway in Kuwait, the CIA concluded that there was "compelling evidence" of a plot to assassinate Bush and that this plot, including the use of a powerful bomb made in Iraq, had been directed and pursued by the Iraqi intelligence service. Clinton called the action against Bush "an attack against our country and against all Americans."[26] In a message to Congress two days later, he said that the attack was ordered "in the exercise of our inherent right of self-defense as recognized in Article 51 of the United Nations Charter and pursuant to my constitutional authority with respect to the conduct of foreign relations and as Commander in Chief."[27]

Clinton did not consult with members of Congress before ordering the launching of twenty-three Tomahawk cruise missiles against the Iraqi intelligence service's principal command-and-control facility in Baghdad. The facility was badly damaged, but three of the missiles also destroyed homes in the surrounding neighborhood, killing eight people and wounding at least twelve others.

News analyses suggested that the White House appreciated that the use of force would help rebuild Clinton's image into that of a strong and decisive leader. After Clinton's difficult start as president, members of Congress and the public had questioned his ability to lead the nation. The cruise missile attack, a White House aide commented, would "serve notice to one and all that Americans are prepared first of all to exercise leadership and to remain engaged and to act with military forces as appropriate." A senior administration official remarked: "We were showing that Bill Clinton can take the challenge." Aides disclosed to the press that Clinton, shortly after making an address from the Oval Office on the bombing, returned to the White House residence to watch a movie with his wife and slept "a solid eight hours."[28] The word was out: Clinton could make the tough military calls and not be bothered by them.

Clinton explained that the attack on Baghdad "was essential to protect our sovereignty, to send a message to those who engage in state-sponsored terrorism, to deter further violence against our people, and to affirm the expectation of civilized behavior among nations." He further noted that there should be no mistake about the message being sent to Iraq and to other nations: "We will combat terrorism. We will deter aggression. We will protect our people."[29] That argument was not credible. As two attorneys of constitutional law pointed out, "calling the U.S. bombing of Iraq an act of self-defense for an assassination plot that had been averted two months previously is quite a stretch."[30] Moreover, what Clinton did to Iraq he would not have done to other countries suspected of terrorist activity. For example, in response to evidence that Syria was behind a terrorist action, he would not have launched cruise missiles at intelligence facilities in Damascus. Other responses, less confrontational, would have been used. Iraq was attacked because—like Cambodia and Libya—it fell into the category of a weak and isolated nation that could be punished militarily with little fear of retaliation.

Combat Operations in Somalia

Shortly before leaving office, President Bush dispatched U.S. troops to Somalia as part of a multinational relief effort. Bush said that there were no plans "to dictate political outcomes" and no intent to become "involved in hostilities."[31] Yet in President Clinton's first year, the humanitarian venture turned bloody and shifted focus to hunt down and arrest a Somali political figure, Mohamed Farah Aideed. Congress used its power of the purse to bring this operation to a halt the following year.

Bloodshed first occurred in June, 1993, when twenty-three Pakistani peacekeepers were killed. U.S. airplanes launched a retaliatory attack, hitting a radio station and four weapons-storage sites. Clinton explained that military force was needed "to undermine the capacity of Aideed to wreak military havoc in Mogadishu. He murdered 23 U.N. peacekeepers."[32] Two months later, four U.S. soldiers were killed when a land mine blasted apart their Humvee vehicle in Mogadishu. Aideed was again blamed for the deaths. Earlier conflicts had killed four other American soldiers. Officials in the Clinton administration began to talk of "nation building": rebuilding political structures in Somalia to form a stable order.

Congressman Lee Hamilton, chairman of the House Foreign Affairs Committee, objected to this new mission: "I do not believe that the United States should be engaged in nation building in Somalia. That is the task of the United Nations."[33] Congressman Ron Dellums (D-Calif.) asked: "who gave us the right—as peacekeepers—to determine which political figure or faction deserves to emerge victorious in Somalia?"[34] On October 3, about a week after this debate, eighteen Army soldiers were killed. Aideed's forces captured an American pilot and displayed him, battered and dazed, to TV cameras. The body of a dead U.S. soldier was dragged through the streets of Mogadishu by an angry mob.

Congress began to draft legislation to require Clinton to remove the troops from Somalia by a certain date unless he obtained statutory authority. Under this pressure, Clinton announced on October 7 that all American troops would be out of Somalia no later than March 31, 1994, except for a few hundred support personnel in noncombatant roles.[35] A week later he repeated that

---

BOX 15

Congress Cuts Off Funds for Somalia

. . . funds appropriated, or otherwise made available, in this or any other Act to the Department of Defense may be obligated for expenses incurred only through March 31, 1994, for the operations of United States Armed Forces in Somalia: *Provided further,* That such date may be extended if so requested by the President and authorized by the Congress: *Provided further,* That funds may be obligated beyond March 31, 1994, to support a limited number of United States military personnel sufficient only to protect American diplomatic facilities and American citizens, and noncombat personnel to advise the United Nations commander in Somalia: . . .

Source: 107 Stat. 1476, sec. 8151(b)(2)(B) (1993).

---

pledge, noting that the U.S. mission "is not now nor was it ever one of 'nation building.'"[36]

Congress used its power of the purse to bring the military operation to a halt. Legislation prohibited the use of any funds after March 31, 1994, for the operations of U.S. armed forces in Somalia unless the president requested an extension and received authority from Congress. The legislation permitted the use of funds after the cutoff date to protect American diplomatic facilities and American citizens (see box 15).

Invasion of Haiti

President Clinton put pressure on the military regime in Haiti to resign and allow the return of the democratically elected president, Jean-Bertrand Aristide, who had been ousted on September 30, 1991. On June 16, 1993, the UN Security Council adopted an oil, arms, and financial embargo against Haiti to force the military regime to step down. On July 3, at Governors Island in New York, the coup's leader, Lieutenant General Raoul Cedras, signed an agreement promising Aristide's return by October 30.

In October, Clinton sent about 600 U.S. military construction troops to Haiti to prepare the way for Aristide. The troops were largely military engineers sent to work on roads, bridges, and water supplies. When the ships arrived, a group of armed civilians prevented the troops from landing.

On October 15, Clinton implied that he might have to use military force against Haiti, ticking off the telltale signs of an impending U.S. intervention: a thousand American citizens lived in Haiti or worked there, Americans helped to operate the U.S. embassy, and the United States had "an interest in promoting democracy in this hemisphere." He also ordered six destroyers to patrol the waters off Haiti and ordered an infantry company to be on standby at Guantanamo Naval Base in Cuba.[37] Madeleine Albright, U.S. ambassador to the United Nations, said that the administration had "not ruled out" a unilateral use of force in Haiti.[38]

An amendment in the Senate, to require prior congressional authority to send U.S. forces to Haiti except to protect and evacuate U.S. citizens, was rejected decisively, 81 to 19.[39] On October 21, the Senate adopted (98 to 2) nonbinding language that expressed the sense of Congress that Congress should authorize U.S. military operations in Haiti unless U.S. citizens were in imminent need of protection and evacuation or the president determined that deployment was vital to national security interests.[40] The essential decisions to use force were left to the president.

In the enacted bill, Congress settled for nonbinding statutory language, stating that it was the "sense of Congress" that funds in the defense appropriations bill should not be obligated or expended for U.S. military operations in Haiti unless (1) authorized in advance by Congress, (2) it was necessary to protect or evacuate U.S. citizens, or (3) the president determined that the deployment was "vital" to U.S. national security interests and there was insufficient time to seek and obtain congressional authorization. Even those elastic guidelines could be set aside if the president reported in advance that the deployment was justified by U.S. national security interests (see box 16).

In May, 1994, Clinton remarked that with regard to Haiti "we cannot afford to discount the prospect of a military option."[41] Later that month the House debated several amendments to limit his use of military force in Haiti. The amendment that passed, 223 to 201, was another nonbinding measure, declaring it to be the sense of Congress that the United States should not take military action against Haiti "unless the President first certifies to Congress that clear and present danger to citizens of the United States or United States interests requires such action."[42] An alternative amendment, offered by Congressmen Dellums and Hamilton, was rejected, but it too opposed military action unless Clinton justified it.

The amendment that passed in May, anemic as it was, did not last for long. Two weeks later the House rejected it on a separate vote.[43] Why this flipflop? The Republican vote on the two amendments stayed fairly constant: 169 to 3 on the first amendment, and 171 to 3 on the second. The amendment failed the second time because of shifts among the Democrats: 54 Democrats supported the first amendment and only 24 supported the second. A swing of 30 votes was enough to change the results from 223 to 201 in favor to 226 to 195 in opposition.[44] Congressman Porter Goss (R-Fla.), sponsor of the first amendment, offered this explanation: "I think what a reasonable observer might conclude is that it is because the President of the United States wants to invade Haiti, if not with Congress' blessing, then with Congress' silence."[45]

Clinton intensified the pressure on Haiti, combining economic sanctions with threats of military force.[46] On June 29, the Senate considered nonbinding language to oppose military operations in Haiti unless certain conditions were met. The author of this sense-of-Congress amendment, Judd Gregg (R-N.H.), spoke of using the power of the purse to restrict the president, and yet accepted the president as the prime mover in military operations. His amendment stated that no funds should be obligated or expended for any U.S. military operation in Haiti unless such operations were authorized in advance by Congress. Of course this was offered as "sense of the Congress." Gregg next recognized some exceptions to his amendment. Troops could be deployed to Haiti to protect or evacuate U.S. citizens, and whenever "vital to the national security interests of the United States." The person to make the latter determination was the president.[47] Congress was out of the picture.

Even though Gregg discussed his amendment in terms of the Constitution and the War Powers Resolution, he did not believe that Congress should have to authorize military actions in advance. Rather, Clinton should simply explain to Congress what he had decided: "So this sense of the Senate makes it clear that we as a body expect the President . . . to come to us in advance and explain whether or not and why . . . he wishes to pursue military operations in Haiti."[48] If officials in the administration felt "they must use a military response in order to put Mr. Aristide back in power, then that is the right of the President of the United States to make that decision."[49]

Gregg later removed the sense-of-Congress language and expressed his amendment as a binding rule of law. Yet the construction of the amendment remained the same. No funds could be used to deploy U.S. forces to Haiti unless: (1) such operations were authorized in advance by the Congress, (2) force was necessary to protect U.S. citizens, or (3) the president decided that force was necessary to protect vital national security interests. To avoid the funding restriction, Gregg explained that Clinton need only "first contact and advise us in advance before he uses military force in an invasion of Haiti."[50]

Both supporters and opponents of the Gregg amendment read the president's

BOX 16

Nonbinding Language on Haiti

(b) LIMITATION.—It is the sense of Congress that funds appropriated by this Act should not be obligated or expended for United States military operations in Haiti unless—

(1) authorized in advance by the Congress; or

(2) the temporary deployment of United States Armed Forces into Haiti is necessary in order to protect or evacuate United States citizens from a situation of imminent danger and the President reports as soon as practicable to Congress after the initiation of the temporary deployment, but in no case later than forty-eight hours after the initiation of the temporary deployment; or

(3) the deployment of United States Armed Forces into Haiti is vital to the national security interests of the United States, including but not limited to the protection of American citizens in Haiti, there is not sufficient time to seek and receive Congressional authorization, and the President reports as soon as practicable to Congress after the initiation of the deployment, but in no case later than forty-eight hours after the initiation of the deployment; or

(4) the President transmits to the Congress a written report pursuant to subsection (c).

(c) REPORT.—It is the sense of Congress that the limitation in subsection (b) should not apply if the President reports in advance to Congress that the intended deployment of United States Armed Forces into Haiti—

(1) is justified by United States national security interests;

(2) will be undertaken only after necessary steps have been taken to ensure the safety and security of United States Armed Forces, including steps to ensure that United States Armed Forces will not become targets due to the nature of their rules of engagement;

(3) will be undertaken only after an assessment that—

(A) the proposed mission and objectives are most appropriate for the United States Armed Forces rather than civilian personnel or armed forces from other nations, and

> (B) that the United States Armed Forces proposed for deployment are necessary and sufficient to accomplish the objectives of the proposed mission;
>
> (4) will be undertaken only after clear objectives for the deployment are established;
>
> (5) will be undertaken only after an exit strategy for ending the deployment has been identified; and
>
> (6) will be undertaken only after the financial costs of the deployment are estimated.
>
> Source: 107 Stat. 1474, sec. 8147 (1993).

war powers expansively. Senator Jesse Helms (R-N.C.), a supporter, stated: "The President, of course, has constitutional authority to order such an invasion. Nobody questions that."[51] Senator John McCain (R-Ariz.), an opponent, said that "for us to prospectively tell the President of the United States that he cannot enter into military action anyplace in the world, in my view is a clear violation of his powers as Commander in Chief under the Constitution of the United States."[52]

Senators cited precedents to justify unilateral presidential action. Senator McCain discussed actions during the Jefferson administration in dealing with the Barbary pirates. "That was done without a declaration of war. That set a precedent for operations like Grenada, Panama, et cetera." Senator Christopher Dodd (D-Conn.) agreed that the reference to the Barbary pirates "is a good historical example."[53] However, President Jefferson took only *defensive* actions against the Barbary pirates. When Congress returned, he sought authority for offensive actions. Congress passed at least ten statutes authorizing Presidents Jefferson and Madison to take military action against the Barbary pirates.[54] The war against the Barbary pirates was not declared, but it was authorized.

Gregg's amendment lost, 34 to 65. At that point the Senate voted 93 to 4 in favor of another sense-of-Congress amendment, this one identical to language adopted by the Senate on October 21, 1993 (when it was accepted 98 to 2). The basic thrust was to lodge power with the president. Congress should authorize military actions in Haiti unless U.S. citizens were in danger or the president decided that force was vital to U.S. interests.[55]

On July 31, 1994, the Security Council adopted a resolution "inviting" all states—particularly those in the region of Haiti—to use "all necessary means" to remove the military leadership on that island.[56] The Senate responded with a nonbinding resolution that stated that the Security Council resolution "does not constitute authorization for the deployment of United States Armed Forces in Haiti under the Constitution of the United States or pursuant to the War Powers Resolution (Public Law 93-148)." The Senate language passed by a vote of 100 to 0.[57] A number of lawmakers were offended by the concept of the administration seeking "authority" from the Security Council but not from Congress. Senator Helms remarked: ". . . the administration has gone, hat in hand, to the United Nations to ask the permission of the U.N. Security Council to invade Haiti. But the President, as has been emphasized here, has not bothered to ask the approval of the United States Congress to go to war—and that is what it amounts to—against Haiti. For the past 3 weeks, the President's advisers have been running around the United Nations in New York City lobbying the Russians and lobbying the French for permission to invade Haiti, but the permission of Congress, which is required by the United States Constitution, has not been sought."[58]

At a news conference on August 3, Clinton once again denied that he needed support or authority from Congress to invade Haiti: "Like my predecessors of both parties, I have not agreed that I was constitutionally mandated to get it."[59] In a nationwide televised address on September 15, he told the American public that he was prepared to use military force to invade Haiti, referring to the Security Council resolution of July 31 and his willingness to lead a multinational force "to carry out the will of the United Nations."[60] No word from Clinton about carrying out the will of Congress or the American public.

The public and a substantial majority of legislators assailed the planned invasion. Criticized in the past for currying public favor and failing to lead, Clinton now seemed to glory in the idea of acting against the grain. He was determined to proceed with the invasion: "But regardless [of this opposition], this is what I believe is the right thing to do. I realize it is unpopular. I know it is unpopular. I know the timing is unpopular. I know the whole thing is unpopular. But I believe it is the right thing."[61] There seemed to be no attention to doing the legal thing, the authorized thing, the constitutional thing.

Clinton emphasized the need to keep commitments: "I'd like to mention just one other thing that is equally important, and that is the reliability of the United States and the United Nations once we say we're going to do something."[62] Who was "we"? It was not Congress or the American public. It was a commitment made unilaterally by the president acting in concert with a Security Council resolution he helped pass.

The planned invasion was never carried out. Negotiations by former President Jimmy Carter (with Senator Sam Nunn and Colin Powell) convinced the military leaders to step down and permit Aristide's return. Nearly 20,000 U.S. troops were sent to Haiti to provide stability.[63] House and Senate debates were strongly critical of Clinton's insistence that he could act militarily against Haiti without legislative authority. A resolution, introduced to provide retroactive authorization for the use of U.S. armed forces in Haiti, was rejected in favor of substitute language stating that "the President should have sought and welcomed Congressional approval before deploying United States Forces to Haiti.[64] A remark by Senator Max Baucus (D-Mont.) reflected the mood of many legislators: "The President did not seek my approval for occupying Haiti. And he will not get my approval now."[65] This legislative response was generally critical of Clinton's actions, but he reinforced the precedent of acting under the "authority" of the United Nations rather than Congress. It was a precedent he would build on.

Commitment to Bosnia

In concert with the United Nations and NATO, the Clinton administration participated in humanitarian airlifts in Sarajevo and helped enforce a "no-fly zone" (a ban on unauthorized flights over Bosnia-Herzegovina). In his first year in office, Clinton indicated that he would need authorization from Congress before ordering air strikes in Bosnia. At a news conference on May 7, 1993, he stated: "If I decide to ask the American people and the United States Congress to support an approach that would include the use of air power, I would have a very specific, clearly defined strategy. . . ." At that same news conference, he switched from the word "support" to *authority:* "I assure you today that if I decide to ask for the authority to use air power from the Congress and from the American people. . . ."[66]

In another exchange with reporters, on September 8, he said he would support U.S. participation along with other NATO nations in Bosnia but added: "Of course in the United States, as all of you know, anything we do has to have the support of the Congress. I would seek the support of the Congress to do that. . . . if we can get the Congress to support it, then I think we should participate. . . . [Military action in Bosnia] has to be able to be enforced or, if you will, be guaranteed by a peacekeeping force from NATO, not the United Nations but NATO. And of course, for me to do it, the Congress would have to agree."[67]

He later wrote to the party leaders in the Senate—George Mitchell (D-Maine) and Bob Dole (R-Kans.)—encouraging them to vote for "authorization of any military involvement in Bosnia."[68] Other statements by Clinton in 1993 seemed to degrade Congress to a mere consultative body. He told reporters on September 27 that "it is clear to everyone that the United States could not fulfill a peacekeeping role in Bosnia unless the Congress supported it. And I will be consulting with all the appropriate congressional leadership in both parties. . . ."[69] The language of authorization had changed to mere "support," in whatever form that would take. Actual legal authority from Congress, in advance, was no longer mentioned.

In September, 1993, Senator Dole said that he had intended to offer an amendment to restrict Clinton's military options in Bosnia. Dole was about to require advance approval from Congress before Clinton could deploy any additional U.S. forces to Bosnia-Herzegovina. Exceptions were allowed for conducting humanitarian relief operations and enforcing the no-fly zone. However, Dole then announced that he would not offer the amendment. His amendment was limited to the deployment of ground forces. It said nothing about requiring congressional approval for air strikes.[70]

Clinton opposed efforts by Congress to restrict his military options. He objected to any legislative language that "unduly restricted the ability of the President to make foreign policy."[71] He did not think "we should have an amendment which would tie the President's hands and make us unable to fulfill our NATO commitments."[72] As with Haiti and the United Nations, "our" commitments would be decided solely by the president, not by Congress. When asked whether he would veto legislation that required him to ask and get the consent of Congress before using troops in Haiti and Bosnia, his answer rambled but implied that Congress existed to provide advice, not authority, and that the crucial decision for using force had to be left to the president: "All I can tell you is that I think I have a big responsibility to try to appropriately consult with Members of Congress in both parties—whenever we are in the process of making a decision that might lead to the use of force. I believe that. But I think that, clearly, the Constitution leaves the President, for good and sufficient reasons, the ultimate decisionmaking authority. . . . [T]he President must make the ultimate decision, and I think it's a mistake to cut those decisions off in advance."[73]

Throughout 1993, Clinton continued to oppose any legislative language that "would make it unreasonably difficult for me or any President to operate militarily with other nations when it is in our interest to do so—and as we have done effectively for half a century through NATO."[74] Yet over that entire half-century, NATO had never once used military force. On the basis of nonexistent precedents, Clinton wanted discretion to do what no president had ever done.

On October 20, the Senate settled for sense-of-Congress language. It attracted a vote of 99 to 1 for these words: "It is the sense of Congress that none of the funds appropriated or otherwise made available by this Act should be available for the purposes of deploying United States Armed Forces to participate in the implementation of a peace settlement in Bosnia-Herzegovina, unless previously authorized by Congress."[75] In explaining that the amendment did not impose any legally binding restriction on the president, Senator George Mitchell supported the provision "because it does not purport to impose prior restraints upon a President performing the duties assigned him under the Constitution." Mitchell did "not favor prior restraints. I believe they plainly violate the Constitution."[76] By opposing prior restraint, Mitchell left the decision of military force solely to the president, a position that contradicted what Mitchell called a central principle of the Constitution, which "intended to prevent the accumulation of power in any one branch of Government, in any institution, or individual."[77]

The Senate language in the above paragraph was enacted into law: mere sense-of-Congress language with no legally binding effect.[78] With regard to the commitment of U.S. military forces to Bosnia, Congress left the door to unilateral presidential action open wide.

AIR STRIKES AGAINST THE SERBS

In 1994, Clinton began threatening air strikes against Serbian militias in Bosnia. There were no further statements about seeking authority from Congress. Decisions to use air power would be taken in response to UN Security Council resolutions, operating through NATO's military command. Clinton explained: "the authority under which air strikes can proceed, NATO acting out of area pursuant to U.N. authority, requires the common agreement of our NATO allies."[79] In other words, Clinton would have to obtain approval from England, France, Italy, and other NATO allies, but not from Congress.

Air strikes began in February, 1994. U.S. jets shot down four Serbian bombers over Bosnia, the first time in the history of NATO that its forces had been engaged in combat. Clinton reported to Congress that the actions were "conducted under the authority of U.N. Security Council resolutions and in full compliance with NATO procedures."[80] To Clinton, compliance with the Constitution did not have the same priority or urgency. He saw no need to obtain authority from Congress. Authority from international and regional institutions would do just as well, if not better. On April 11, Clinton told reporters that the air strikes "were conducted in strict accordance of existing U.N. policy." The Security Council resolution "gives NATO the authority to act. We are acting solely under the existing U.N. resolution which has been approved by the Security Council."[81] Air strikes continued in April, August, and November.

In May, 1994, the administration released its proposals for reforming multilateral peace operations. The subordinate status of Congress was clear. Of six major guidelines, one promised "better forms of cooperation between the Executive, the Congress and the American public on peace operations." The "flow of information and consultation between the executive branch and Congress" would be increased and regularized, and the president would seek bipartisan support—but not authorization—from Congress and the American people.[82] The president would need authority from the United Nations and NATO; talking with some members of Congress would suffice.

Congress did not challenge Clinton's authority to conduct air strikes in Bosnia. Instead, lawmakers debated lifting the arms embargo to give Bosnian Muslims greater capacity to protect themselves against the Serbs. A Senate amendment to require Clinton to terminate the U.S. arms embargo lost on a vote of 50 to 50. The amendment was particularly controversial because termination would have been unilateral on the part of the United States, putting it at odds with Security Council policy.[83] The House voted to end the arms embargo but no such requirement was enacted into law.[84]

NATO conducted limited air strikes during the first half of 1995. When Bosnian Serb forces overran the UN-designated "safe area" of Sbrebrenica, NATO carried out the war's biggest air raid at the end of August, 1995.[85] On September 1, Clinton explained to congressional leaders the procedures followed for ordering air strikes on Bosnia. The United Nations and NATO participated in the decision; Congress did not. The North Atlantic Council (NAC) "approved" a number of measures and "agreed" that any direct attacks against remaining safe areas would justify air operations as determined "by the common judgment of NATO and U.N. military commanders."[86] Clinton said he authorized the actions "in conjunction with our NATO allies to implement the relevant U.N. Security Council resolutions and NATO decisions."[87] Nothing about acting in conjunction with Congress or statutory authority. On September 12, he regarded the bombing attacks as "authorized by the United Nations."[88]

GROUND TROOPS TO BOSNIA

The next escalation of U.S. military action was Clinton's decision to introduce ground forces into Bosnia in 1995. The issue had been debated for three years, but it picked up steam again in May, 1995, and continued to be widely discussed in subsequent months. The number of American soldiers to be sent to Bosnia was put at about 25,000. On a separate issue, Congress finally got the votes to lift the arms embargo, but Clinton vetoed the bill on August 11.

On September 29, the Senate debated an amendment regarding troops to Bosnia. Once again, however, Senators chose legally nonbinding language. It would be the "sense of the Senate" that no funds should be used to deploy combat-equipped U.S. forces for any ground operations in Bosnia and Herzegovina unless "Congress approves in advance the deployment of such forces." Exceptions were made to allow the president to deploy U.S. ground forces if needed to evacuate U.S. peacekeeping forces from a "situation of imminent danger, to undertake emergency air rescue operations, or to provide for the airborne delivery of humanitarian supplies."[89]

Debate on this amendment illustrates how much legislators deferred to the president on the deployment of troops. The author of the amendment, Senator Gregg, argued that "it is appropriate that we as a Congress act to either approve that action or disapprove that action." He suggested this allocation of power: "Clearly, the power to undertake actions which put American soldiers' lives in harm's way lies primarily and first with the President, but obviously we as a Congress also play a major role, not only on the appropriating side but, more importantly, on the side of being concerned for our soldiers, many of whom will obviously be our constituents."[90]

Gregg felt "strongly that prior to the President taking this action, he should come to the Congress and ask for our approval." However, nothing in the amendment required congressional approval. Senator Sam Nunn (D-Ga.) supported the amendment only because it did not have the effect of law: "If it did tie the President's hands at this critical juncture while the peace negotiations are underway, I would oppose it and vote against it."[91] Senator John Kerry (D-Mass.) agreed that if the amendment's language had been legally binding, many senators would have opposed it.[92]

Senator Paul Simon (D-Ill.) announced that he would vote against the amendment, even though it was a "sense of the Senate," because foreign policy cannot be effective "if Congress micromanages it." Senator Bill Cohen (R-Maine) disputed that point, noting that Clinton was about to deploy 25,000 troops "to one of the most hostile regions in the world" and "without having any sort of defined plan presented to us."[93] The Gregg amendment passed the Senate, 94 to 2.[94]

As Congress continued to consider different restrictions on troops to Bosnia, Secretary of State Warren Christopher warned that Clinton would not be "bound" by any congressional ban on funding. The administration said it was prepared to go ahead regardless of what Congress legislated.[95] At a news conference on October 19, Clinton engaged in this conversation with reporters:

> Q. Would you go ahead, then, and send the troops, even if Congress does not approve?
>
> *The President.* I am not going to lay down any of my constitutional prerogatives here today. I have said before and I will say again, I would welcome and I hope I get an expression of congressional support. I think it's important for the United States to be united in doing this. . . . I believe in the end, the Congress will support this operation.[96]

The House debated, repeatedly, the president's authority to commit ground troops to Bosnia. On October 30, by a vote of 315 to 103, the House passed a nonbinding resolution that U.S. troops should not be deployed without congressional approval.[97] The resolution included language about the peace negotiations in Bosnia (see box 17). Ninety-three Democrats—nearly half of those in the House—joined 222 Republicans to support the resolution. Although House Minority Leader Dick Gephardt voted against the resolution, he said that "none of us wants to see American troops in Bosnia without the prior approval of this body."[98] He supported the second part of the resolution requiring congressional authorization for the deployment, but not the first part about the negotiation process. He thought that part of the resolution was too disruptive of ongoing negotiations. Other Democrats, like Lee Hamilton and James Moran, voted against the resolution but agreed that Congress should have to approve the sending of U.S. ground troops to Bosnia.[99]

The House majority of 315 to 103 for a nonbinding resolution slipped a bit on November 17, when the House voted on legislation that would have legal effect. This bill prohibited the use of funds to deploy U.S. ground troops in Bosnia unless Congress specifically appropriated money for that purpose. The margin declined to 242 to 171.[100] Instead of the 93 Democrats supporting the measure on October 30, only 28 Democrats backed a legally binding requirement.

Hamilton's position expressed in the past—that the president needed prior authorization from Congress for military deployments—had changed. He opposed the bill because it "ties the hands of the President. It tells the commander in chief that he cannot deploy troops to Bosnia, period. When you are the commander in chief, you have the power to deploy troops. That is fundamental, and this bill takes away that power."[101] If the president, as commander in chief, has the fundamental power to deploy troops, why should there ever be

---

BOX 17

More Nonbinding Language

Resolved, That it is the sense of the House of Representatives that—

(1) in the negotiation of any peace agreement between the parties to the conflict in the Republic of Bosnia and Herzegovina, there should not be a presumption, and it should not be considered to be a prerequisite to the successful conclusion of such a negotiation, that enforcement of such an agreement will involve deployment of United States Armed Forces on the ground in the territory of the Republic of Bosnia and Herzegovina; and

(2) no United States Armed Forces should be deployed on the ground in the territory of the Republic of Bosnia and Herzegovina to enforce a peace agreement until the Congress has approved such a deployment.

Source: 141 *Cong. Rec.* H11398 (daily ed. Oct. 30, 1995) (H. Res. 247)

---

prior authorization? Also, the bill did not say that Clinton "cannot deploy troops to Bosnia, period." He could deploy them, but only after Congress had appropriated funds specifically for that objective. As Benjamin Gilman, chairman of the House Committee on International Relations later noted: "This resolution does not rule out the deployment of United States forces to Bosnia, but it does make certain that the President come to the Congress first."[102]

Some Democrats who had supported the October 30 measure, because it was nonbinding, backed away from the November 17 version. John Spratt of South Carolina remarked: "We have to and can send the President strong signals, as we did when we passed McHale-Buyer, 315-to-103. But this bill is more than a warning signal; it flat-out prohibits the President from sending any U.S. ground troops to Bosnia as part of any peacekeeping operation unless funds are specifically appropriated."[103]

Twelve Republicans voted against the November 17 version. James B. Longley, Jr., of Maine, said he was "not a supporter of putting American troops on the ground in Bosnia. I think it would be a terrible mistake." Nevertheless, he deferred to the president: "I have to respect the authority of the Commander in Chief to conduct foreign policy. . . . I think there is no greater threat to American lives than a Congress that attempts to micromanage foreign policy. I have told the President that I would respect his authority as Commander in Chief."[104] How is it "micromanagement" to debate sending ground troops to Bosnia? Why are American lives threatened when Congress opposes military intervention? Clearly, American lives are threatened more when the president puts them in harm's way. And why did Longley's respect for the president exceed his respect for the Constitution?

The administration expressed interest in obtaining legislative support—but not legislative authority. In a letter to Senator Robert C. Byrd on October 19, Clinton invited "an expression of support by Congress."[105] He told reporters on October 31 that if a peace agreement were reached it would request "an expression of support" in Congress for committing United States troops to a NATO implementation force.[106] In a letter to Speaker Newt Gingrich on November 13, Clinton continued to avoid any suggestion that he needed authorization from Congress before sending U.S. ground forces to Bosnia.[107]

Addressing the nation on November 27, Clinton justified the deployment as a way of stopping "the killing of innocent civilians, especially children, and at the same time, to bring stability to Central Europe, a region of the world that is vital to our national interests. It is the right thing to do."[108] That language parallels Clinton's justification for invading Haiti: it was the right thing, even if not the legal thing. On December 6, having approved the NATO operation plan for sending ground troops to Bosnia, he said he would be requesting "an expression of support from the Congress."[109] The support never came.

The response in Congress depended greatly on what Bob Dole, the Senate majority leader, would do. On November 27, he made it clear that legislative prerogatives were subordinate to presidential interests. It was Dole's view that Clinton had "the authority and the power under the Constitution to do what he feels should be done regardless of what Congress does."[110] There would be no checks and balance system, no tussling for power. Once the president had announced his policy, legislators would dutifully fall in line. Congress, as an independent branch, did not exist. It was not remotely coequal.

Dole spoke as the Republican front-runner for president in 1996. Instead of demonstrating leadership and protecting institutional and constitutional interests, he deferred to the president and the polls: "We need to find some way to be able to support the President and I think we need to wait and see what the American reaction is."[111] Other Republican candidates were similarly guarded. Steve Forbes opposed the deployment but said that Clinton had the authority to send troops to Bosnia, and, if that happened, "We have to support the troops while they're there." Lamar Alexander remarked about Clinton: "I intend to continue to listen to him and do my best to support him, but I believe he's wrong." Why support a president when you think he is wrong? Pat Buchanan was the only Republican candidate to say flatly that Clinton lacked constitutional authority to send troops to Bosnia without approval from Congress.[112]

Other Senators developed the idea that presidential commitments abroad, even if misguided, were sacrosanct. Slade Gorton (R-Wash.) believed that Clinton's commitment to Bosnia "was both unwise and improvident. Nonetheless, it was made by the President."[113] A few senators rejected that theory. Jon Kyl (R-Ariz.) insisted that Congress "has to make it clear to the President that he cannot simply go around making premature commitments without the advice and consent of the Congress."[114] Senator Byrd also spoke out in defense of congressional war prerogatives,[115] as did Senators Kay Bailey Hutchison (R-Tex.),[116] Russ Feingold (D-Wis.),[117] and James Inhofe (R-Okla.).[118]

On December 13 and 14, the Senate considered several measures regarding U.S. troops to Bosnia. One approach was a nonbinding resolution with two parts: expressing congressional opposition to sending the troops, while also "strongly" supporting the troops.[119] Senators tried to walk a fine line, not wanting their opposition to the deployment to be interpreted as a lack of support for U.S. soldiers. This resolution fell, 47 to 52. The Senate also rejected a House bill prohibiting the use of defense funds for the deployment of ground troops to Bosnia unless the funds were specifically appropriated by law. That bill failed on a vote of 22 to 77.[120] The Senate then passed, 69 to 30, a multipart bill providing support for American troops but expressing "reservations" about sending them to Bosnia (see box 18).[121]

Senator Dole explained some of the purposes behind the bill that passed. One was to shift responsibility from Congress to the president. Dole said that Clinton "made this decision and he takes responsibility. It was his decision to send troops and his decision alone."[122] Translation: if anything went wrong, it would be Clinton's fault, not Congress's. Second, the Senate was expressing doubts about the merits of sending troops to Bosnia. Dole remarked: "This resolution does not endorse the President's decision. It does not endorse the agreement reached in Dayton."[123] Dole elaborated: "We can posture and complain about the President's decision. I do not like it. He knows I do not like it. I told him I do not like it."[124] The bill was a way for senators to oppose the president's policy but praise the soldiers being sent to carry it out. It made no sense.

On the same day as these Senate votes, the House acted on a series of measures related to Bosnia. By 210 to 218, the House failed to pass a bill prohibiting funds from being used to deploy troops to Bosnia. It next voted 287 to 141 to pass a nonbinding House resolution regarding enforcement of the peace agree-

BOX 18

Touching All the Bases

S.J. Res. 44

Whereas beginning on February 24, 1993, President Clinton committed the United States to participate in implementing a peace agreement in Bosnia and Herzegovina without prior consultation with Congress; . . .

Whereas on December 3, 1995, President Clinton approved Operation Joint Endeavor and deployment of United States Armed Forces to Bosnia and Herzegovina began immediately thereafter: Now therefore be it

Resolved by the Senate and the House of Representatives of the United States of America in Congress assembled,

SECTION I. SUPPORT FOR UNITED STATES ARMED FORCES.

The Congress unequivocally supports the men and women of our Armed Forces who are carrying out their missions in support of peace in Bosnia and Herzegovina with professional excellence, dedicated patriotism and exemplary bravery, and believes they must be given all necessary resources and support to carry out their mission and ensure their security.

SECTION 2. DEPLOYMENT OF UNITED STATES ARMED FORCES.

(a) Notwithstanding reservations expressed about President Clinton's decision to deploy United States Armed Forces to Bosnia and Herzegovina and recognizing that:

(1) the President has decided to deploy United States Armed Forces. . . .

(2) the deployment of United States Armed Forces has begun; and

(3) preserving United States credibility is a strategic interest, the President may only fulfill his commitment to deploy United States Armed Forces in Bosnia and Herzegovina for approximately one year . . . subject to the conditions in subsection (b) [which required the president to make available to Congress his determinations on several matters].

Source: 141 *Cong. Rec.* S18552 (daily ed. Dec. 13, 1995).

ment. The resolution expressed "serious concerns and opposition to the President's policy" but declared that the House was confident that U.S. troops "will perform their responsibilities with professional excellence, dedicated patriotism, and exemplary courage." Like the Senate, the House wanted it both ways. Another House resolution, "unequivocally" supporting American troops but omitting direct criticism of the president's policy, lost 190 to 237.[125]

In the end, President Clinton was able to deploy 20,000 American ground troops to Bosnia without first seeking or obtaining authority from Congress.

FUNDING THE BOSNIA COMMITMENT

On December 21, Clinton said he expected that the military mission to Bosnia "can be accomplished in about a year."[126] No one following the issue could have believed that. A year later, on December 17, 1996, he extended the troop deployment for another "18 months."[127] He approved NATO's operation plan for the Stabilization Force (SFOR) as the successor to his 1995 initiative and welcomed NATO's decision to approve the plan and the "Activation Order that will *authorize* the start of SFOR's mission."[128] Authority would come from allies, not Congress.

The eighteen-month extension came and went, with the Clinton administration no longer attempting to set an endpoint to the commitment in Bosnia. On March 3, 1998, President Clinton told Congress that he did not propose "a fixed end-date" for U.S. troops in Bosnia.[129] Efforts by Congress to force withdrawal of troops by a date certain or to require authorization for continued deployment failed.[130] By December, 1999, U.S. troops were still in Bosnia.

The Clinton administration initially estimated the cost of the Bosnia intervention at $1 billion or more.[131] A month and a half later Clinton put the cost at $1.5 billion.[132] By 1999, the cost had climbed beyond $10 billion. The administration was able to fund the commitment initially without coming to Congress for an appropriation specifying funds for Bosnia.

One source of funds was the defense appropriations bill. Because the bill contained $7 billion more than Clinton had requested, a veto seemed likely, yet he let the bill become law after realizing that some of the surplus funds would come in handy for Bosnia. He accepted the defense bill "because my Administration has reached agreement with Congressional leaders to provide funding, out of the funds contained in this bill, for the troop deployment and other efforts to secure peace in Bosnia."[133] Although he had not asked for funds for Bosnia, he would use them for that purpose.

Notice the language. He had reached agreement not with Congress but with "congressional leaders." Whatever the original purpose of funds in the defense bill, Clinton and a handful of legislators would siphon funds from appropriations without congressional deliberation or votes. Some Republican leaders had agreed to rechannel at least $1.5 billion of the defense funds for the Bosnia deployment.[134]

On January 22, 1996, the administration asked Congress to reprogram $991 million from various Pentagon programs to finance part of the Bosnia commitment. The reprogramming request, which required approval only from certain congressional committees rather than from Congress as a whole, reflected savings from lower-than-expected inflation. In other words, by revising economic assumptions and projections, the administration liberated about a billion dollars for Bosnia.[135]

What a process! Congress sends a defense appropriations bill to committees, hearings are held, the bill is reported in each chamber, amendments are debated, and a compromise package finally emerges from conference committee ready for the president's signature. At no point along the line does Congress approve funds for U.S. ground troops to Bosnia. Clinton then allows the bill to become law after working out an agreement with some Republican leaders or committees that money in the bill can be used for the Bosnia deployment. This process circumvents full congressional debate and control, as well as public control.

A second source of funds magically appeared. The administration discovered a billion dollars that no one seemingly had known about in the National Reconnaissance Office, which is part of the intelligence community. That untapped fund quickly grew to more than $2 billion. Of that amount, $820 million was diverted to the mission in Bosnia.[136] The lesson? When the need is great, money will be found.

War against Yugoslavia

In October, 1998, the Clinton administration was once again threatening the Serbs with air strikes, this time because of Serb attacks on the ethnic Albanian majority in Kosovo. At a news conference on October 8, Clinton stated: "Yesterday I decided that the United States would vote to give NATO the authority to carry out military strikes against Serbia if President Milosevic continues to defy the international community."[137] An interesting sentence: "*I* decided that the United States. . . ." Whatever Clinton decided would be America's policy. The decision to go to war against another country was in the hands of one person, exactly what the framers hoped to avoid. Clinton supported giving *NATO* authority instead of Congress voting to give the *president* authority.

Clinton's chief foreign policy advisers went to Capitol Hill to consult with legislators but not to obtain their approval.[138] Although Congress was to be given no formal role in the use of force against the Serbs, legislatures in other NATO countries took votes to authorize military action in Yugoslavia. The Italian Parliament had to vote approval for the NATO strikes.[139] The German Supreme Court ruled that the Bundestag, which had been dissolved with the election that ousted Chancellor Kohl, had to be recalled to approve deployment of German aircraft and troops to Kosovo.[140] The U.S. Congress, supposedly the strongest legislature in the world, was content to watch from the back seat.

On March 11, 1999, with Clinton close to unleashing air strikes against Serbia, the House voted on a resolution to support U.S. armed forces as part of a NATO *peacekeeping* operation. The resolution—purporting to "authorize" Clinton to deploy U.S. forces to implement a peace agreement—passed 219 to 191.[141] However, legislators were voting on a concurrent resolution (H. Con. Res. 42); Congress cannot authorize anything in a concurrent resolution because it is not legally binding. Authorization requires a bill or joint resolution, both of which are presented to the president for his signature or veto. A concurrent resolution passes both chambers but is not presented. Lawmakers voted on something that started out as a joint resolution but changed at some point to a concurrent resolution, with no one alert enough or willing enough to change the word "authorize" to something more appropriate, like "support."

A second point: members of the House clearly anticipated a peace agreement between Serbs and Kosovars. The House was not supporting military action. The Kosovars eventually accepted the plan, but the Serbs did not. Therefore, the House vote cannot be taken as support for the bombing operation that would begin within two weeks.

By the time the Senate voted on March 23, negotiations had collapsed and air strikes were imminent. The Senate voted 58 to 41 in support of military air operations and missile strikes against the Federal Republic of Yugoslavia (Serbia and Montenegro).[142] Like the House, the Senate made the mistake of using the word "authorize" in a concurrent resolution (S. Con. Res. 21). The war against Yugoslavia began on March 24.

Following these votes in the House and the Senate and the outbreak of war, Congressman Jim Leach (R-Ohio) wrote an op-ed piece that correctly said that the War Powers Resolution "stands as a declaration that war is too profound a business to be left to a single individual." That value was indeed uppermost in the minds of the framers. And yet Leach claimed that Clinton was "on solid legal ground for the military steps he has taken."[143] Neither the House nor the Senate vote provided legal support for Clinton. He operated against the

Constitution and without any statutory support. There was no legal or constitutional ground for his actions.

On April 28, after the first month of bombing, the House took a series of
votes on war in Yugoslavia. It voted 249 to 180 to prohibit the use of appropriated funds for the deployment of U.S. ground forces unless first authorized by
Congress. A motion to direct the removal of U.S. armed forces from Yugoslavia failed, 139 to 290. A resolution to declare a state of war between the United
States and Yugoslavia fell, 2 to 427. A fourth vote, to authorize the air operations and missile strikes, lost on a tie vote, 213 to 213.

Newspaper editorials and commentators derided the House for these multiple and supposedly conflicting votes, but the House articulated some basic
values. It insisted that Congress authorize the introduction of ground troops,
and it refused to grant authority for the air strikes. Lawmakers pointed to the
irony of President Clinton seeking the approval of eighteen NATO nations but
not the approval of Congress. Congressman Ernest Istook (R-Okla.) remarked:
"President Clinton asked many nations to agree to attack Yugoslavia, but he
failed to get permission from one crucial country, America."[144]

The House debate prompted Clinton to write to Senate Majority Leader
Trent Lott, emphasizing again that air power would prevail. However, if he
were to change his policy and support the introduction of ground troops, "I
can assure you that I would fully consult with the Congress. Indeed, without
regard to our differing constitutional views on the use of force, I would ask for
Congressional support before introducing U.S. ground forces into Kosovo into
a non-permissive environment."[145] This letter was widely interpreted to mean
that Clinton would seek congressional authority before introducing ground
troops, but the letter only promised consultation and a request for legislative
"support." If Congress were to deny that support, nothing in the letter would
have stopped Clinton from introducing ground troops on what he considered
to be his own independent constitutional authority.

In contrast to the House, the Senate decided to duck the issue. Senator John
McCain offered a joint resolution to authorize President Clinton to use "all
necessary force and other means, in concert with United States allies, to ac-
complish United States and North Atlantic Treaty Organization objectives in
the Federal Republic of Yugoslavia (Serbia and Montenegro)." The clear intent
was to give congressional support to continued air strikes as well as anything
else the president decided to do, including the introduction of ground troops.
Supporters of the resolution claimed that it gave Congress an opportunity to
take responsibility, but Senator Kay Bailey Hutchison offered a more convincing interpretation (see box 19).

BOX 19
Hutchison Objects to Serbia Resolution

The resolution is wrong for other reasons. Those who offer this resolution believe it is necessary because Congress has a responsibility to act. I don't think this resolution is an exercise of responsibility. I think it is an abdication of responsibility. It tells the President, in so many words, don't bother us anymore with this war. Congress doesn't want to know what your plan is. We don't want to know what it is going to cost. We don't want to know from you what the exit strategy is. Congress doesn't want to authorize the use of ground forces. In short, we are saying, President Clinton, go fix it and don't bother us, send us the bill.

Source: 145 *Cong. Rec.* S4533–34 (daily ed. May 3, 1999).

Rather than consider the resolution on its merits, with possible amendments, the Senate resorted to procedure and tabled it, 78 to 22.[146] Had the resolution passed, the legal purpose was unclear. McCain at times described his amendment as unnecessary because the president already had, McCain said, sufficient authority under the Constitution to do whatever he liked militarily: "the Presidency already has its authority. . . . If the Senate does nothing, . . . the President has the power to commit all armies to the conflict in Yugoslavia tomorrow."[147] Then why enact the legislation? To push Clinton to do what he could do anyway? In that case, the McCain resolution would have operated more like a nonbinding, sense-of-Congress measure.

A few weeks later the Senate tabled another amendment, this one by Senator Arlen Specter (R-Pa.) to direct the president to seek approval from Congress before introducing ground troops into Yugoslavia. Failure to obtain approval would deny the president funds to conduct the operation.[148] Specter said: "it is high time that Congress stood up on its hind legs and said we are not going to be involved in wars unless Congress authorizes them."[149] Later he argued: "We don't have the authority to delegate our constitutional authority."[150] His amendment was tabled, 52 to 48. An amendment by Senator Bob Smith (R-N.H.), to prohibit funding for military operations in Yugoslavia unless Congress enacted specific authorization, was tabled 77 to 21.[151]

Through these successive tabling motions, the Senate might as well have considered one final motion: "Do we want to exercise our constitutional powers and participate in matters of war?" Tabled, 63 to 37.

During the bombing of Serbia and Kosovo, Congressman Tom Campbell (R-Calif.) went to court with twenty-five other House colleagues to seek a declaration that President Clinton had violated the Constitution and the War Powers Resolution by conducting the air offensive without congressional authorization. On June 8, a district judge held that Campbell did not have standing to raise his claims. Although each House had taken a number of votes, sometimes supporting Clinton and sometimes not, Congress had never as an entire institution ordered Clinton to cease military operations. In that sense, there was no "constitutional impasse" or "actual confrontation" for the court to resolve. Instead, the court was faced with a typical lawsuit where a small group of members of Congress objected to presidential conduct. As the court noted: "If Congress had directed the President to remove forces from their positions and he had refused to do so or if Congress had refused to appropriate or authorize the use of funds for the air strikes in Yugoslavia and the President had decided to spend that money (or money earmarked for other purposes) anyway, that likely would have constituted an actual confrontation sufficient to confer standing on legislative plaintiffs."[152]

Afghanistan and the Sudan

Other American military actions occurred during 1998, again without congressional authorization. In August, President Clinton ordered cruise missiles into Afghanistan to attack paramilitary camps and into Sudan to destroy a pharmaceutical factory. He justified this use of military force as a retaliation for bombings earlier in the month against U.S. embassies in Africa. The administration claimed that Osama bin Laden was behind the embassy attacks, that he used the training complex in Afghanistan, and that he was somehow related to the pharmaceutical plant.

Clinton explained that he selected the two targets because "of the imminent threat they presented to our national security."[153] It was never clear why the pharmaceutical factory in Sudan represented an "imminent threat." Although Clinton claimed that the plant was "involved in the production of materials for chemical weapons,"[154] questions were raised as to whether the plant was producing a precursor chemical for a nerve gas or an agricultural insecticide.[155] The Pentagon later conceded that it was unaware that the plant produced "a large share of the medicine used in the Sudan."[156]

In February, 1999, a Saudi businessman who owned the pharmaceutical plant went to court to demand that the Clinton administration compensate him for the facility and release millions of dollars in assets frozen by U.S. officials on the ground that he was linked to bin Laden. He denied that he had any relationship to bin Laden and also denied that his plant produced chemicals for a nerve gas.[157] In May, the administration released $24 million of his assets but refused to clear his name. A senior White House official said that the administration continued to have "concerns" about him, but that the concerns were based on sensitive intelligence sources and methods the administration did not want to disclose. His attorney responded: "We deal in a world of facts and evidence; the government appears to be hiding behind suggestion and innuendo."[158] More than a year after the attack on Sudan, news reports still questioned the legitimacy of bombing the plant.[159]

Continued Action against Iraq

Clinton's launching of missiles against Baghdad in June, 1993, would be followed by further military actions. In September, 1996, he ordered the launching of more cruise missiles against Iraq in response to an attack by Iraqi forces against the Kurdish-controlled city of Irbil in northern Iraq. Cruise missiles also struck air defense systems in southern Iraq. Clinton explained that the missiles "sent the following message to Saddam Hussein: When you abuse your own people or threaten your neighbors, you must pay a price."[160]

There was no claim here of self-defense or the need to protect the lives of Americans. The principle—if that word can be used—was different: Whenever foreign leaders abuse their people and threaten their neighbors, an American president can take military action to punish them. With that standard, how many nations could a president attack? Quite a long list. Start with Russia and China and then turn to smaller but still substantial countries in Asia, Africa, and other continents. Clinton's argument here is even less credible than his cruise missile attack against Baghdad. Clinton's decision to launch cruise missiles in 1996 coincided with his reelection race and preparations to deliver an acceptance speech at the Democratic convention.

Toward the end of January, 1998, Clinton threatened once again to bomb Iraq, this time because Saddam Hussein had refused to give UN inspectors full access to examine Iraqi sites for possible nuclear, chemical, and biological programs. The bombing was postponed when UN Secretary General Kofi Annan visited Baghdad in February and negotiated a settlement with Iraq. The Clinton administration accepted the settlement, with reservations, but made clear that military force remained an option if Iraq failed to comply with the new agreement.

Congressional leaders had drafted a resolution (S. Con. Res. 71) that condemned Iraq and urged Clinton to take "all necessary and appropriate actions to respond." The language had an eerie resemblance to the Tonkin Gulf Resolution of 1964, which authorized President Johnson to use all necessary force in Vietnam. Senator Max Cleland, Democrat from Georgia, led a handful of Democrats in opposing the resolution. It was never adopted.[161]

The closest anyone ever came to a legal justification for the bombing relies on the following argument. When Congress passed the authorization bill in January, 1991, empowering President Bush to take military action against Iraq, it somehow gave advance blessing to whatever the UN Security Council might do in the future in issuing resolutions on Iraq. On its face, such a claim—delegating war in perpetuity—would seem preposterous. Congress could no more surrender to an international body its prerogatives over foreign policy than it could its power of the purse.

Here are the specifics of the argument. On January 14, 1991, Congress enacted P.L. 102-1 to authorize U.S. armed force against Iraq. President Bush could use military force pursuant to UN Security Council Resolution 678 "in order to achieve implementation of Security Council Resolutions 660, 661, 662, 664, 665, 666, 667, 669, 670, 674, and 677."[162] This statute is usually interpreted as congressional authority to drive Iraq out of Kuwait, which was the purpose of Resolution 678, adopted on November 29, 1990. All the earlier resolutions, from 660 to 677, prepared the way for 678. Resolution 660, passed on August 2, 1990, condemned Iraq's invasion of Kuwait and demanded immediate withdrawal. Resolution 661 imposed economic sanctions. Resolutions 662 to 677 reinforced the earlier resolutions and added other restrictions.

How could it be argued that Congress on January 14, 1991, had transferred its constitutional power to the UN Security Council? Here is the reasoning. Resolution 678 authorized member states to use all necessary means "to uphold and implement resolution 660 (1990) and all subsequent relevant resolutions and to restore international peace and security in the area."[163] Supporters of presidential power argued that the phrase "all subsequent relevant resolutions" meant that whatever the Security Council promulgated after January 14, 1991, would be automatically sanctioned by P.L. 102-1.

The language in Resolution 678 is somewhat ambiguous. What does "subsequent" refer to? Any resolution issued after 678? Or any resolution issued after 660 but before 678? It could be read either way. The natural reading is the latter one, because the objective was to oust Iraq from Kuwait. President Bush never had authority to send ground troops north to Baghdad. That would have exceeded his statutory authority and violated the understanding of other nations that were part of the multilateral alliance.

The most unnatural reading would be to conclude that Congress, in passing P.L. 102-1, had transferred its constitutional powers to the Security Council and that henceforth the magnitude of the American military commitment would be decided by UN resolutions, not congressional statutes. Under this far-fetched theory, whatever the Security Council decided would compel Congress to vote the necessary appropriations. Congressional debate on P.L. 102-1 provides zero support for that theory.

On February 19, 1998, during a visit to Tennessee State University, Secretary of State Madeleine Albright was asked how Clinton could order military action against Iraq after opposing American policy in Vietnam. Her response: "We are talking about using military force, but we are not talking about a war. That is an important distinction."[164]

What a fine line! How many people in the country, or in the administration, understood such distinctions? Were the Iraqi people supposed to feel relief that President Clinton planned military force rather than a war? Does the president's need to obtain prior congressional authority arise only in time of war but not with military force? Albright's reasoning would eviscerate the congressional war power and the constitutional system of checks and balances.

In December, 1998, President Clinton ordered four days of bombing in Iraq. He justified the military action as an effort to attack Iraq's nuclear, chemical, and biological weapons programs and because Iraq had failed to cooperate completely with UN weapons inspectors.[165] He also explained that U.S. credibility would suffer if it did not fulfill its earlier threat to use military action if Iraq interfered with UN inspectors: "if Saddam can cripple the weapons inspection system and get away with it, he would conclude that the international community, led by the United States, has simply lost its will. . . . If we turn our backs on his defiance, the credibility of U.S. power as a check against Saddam will be destroyed."[166] Yet the Pentagon later disclosed that American and British forces were "taking care to avoid hitting Iraqi factories suspected of producing chemical and biological weapons" for fear of unleashing plumes of poisons on civilians.[167]

In a letter to Congress, Clinton argued that the military operation in Iraq was "consistent with and has been taken in support of numerous U.N. Security Council resolutions, including Resolutions 678 and 687." In this same message, he claimed that he acted under the authorization of P.L. 102-1, enacted in January, 1991.[168] There is no support for that legal argument. In the midst of the four-day bombing, the House passed a nonbinding resolution supporting the armed forces and reaffirming the policy of removing Saddam Hussein. Congressman David Skaggs, Democrat of Colorado, faulted both Clinton and Congress for violating the war power provisions of the Constitution (see box 20).

As a result of the December bombing, there were now *no* UN inspectors to monitor chemical, biological, and nuclear capability in Iraq. Moreover, the administration apparently jettisoned its legal reliance on UN Security Council resolutions. Secretary of State Albright and Secretary of Defense William S. Cohen warned that the United States and Britain would continue to act militarily against Iraq, with or without the approval of other allies or the UN Security Council.[169] Over the next eight months, the United States and Britain conducted repeated air strikes against Iraq, firing more than 1,100 missiles against 359 targets, or triple the number of targets attacked during the four-day operation in December, 1998.[170]

BOX 20

Skaggs on Constitutional Duties

Mr. Speaker, of course we want to support American troops as they carry out this dangerous and important mission. But let us not lose sight of the sad fact that President Clinton has acted in violation of the Constitution in ordering these attacks without authority of Congress. And let us not forget as well that the decision to go to war is vested in Congress and not in the Commander in Chief and that we too share blame for this violation of the Constitution because we have time and again defaulted in our responsibility and obligation to insist on our proper constitutional role.

. . . this administration engages in a contrived bit of legal sophistry to conjure up a pretext of legality where none exists.

Shame on him. And shame on us for letting other Presidents and this one take away one of the most important powers vested in Congress, which the American people have a right to expect us, here, to exercise in their behalf.

Source: 144 *Cong. Rec.* H11727 (daily ed. Dec. 17, 1998).

Legislative Leaders

Instead of challenging the military initiatives of Presidents Bush and Clinton and reclaiming legislative power, members of Congress generally came to the defense of presidential prerogatives. That pattern prevailed regardless of whether the president was from the legislator's party or not. Legislators seemed more interested in protecting the executive branch than their own.

Consider the position of Senator George Mitchell (D-Maine). In 1991, as Senate majority leader, Mitchell vigorously challenged Bush's claim that he could use military force against Iraq without congressional authorization. Mitchell argued that the framers knew that "the decision to commit the Nation to war should not be left in the hands of one man . . . if [President Bush] now decides to use those forces in what would plainly be war he is legally obligated to seek the prior approval of the Congress."[171] Two years later Mitchell opposed legislative language that would have required President Clinton to obtain advance approval from Congress before sending U.S. forces to Bosnia-Herzegovina. Instead, Mitchell supported a nonbinding, sense-of-Congress resolution urging the president to seek congressional authorization. His proposal, he explained, "does not purport to impose prior restraints upon a President performing the duties assigned him under the Constitution."[172] He did not "favor prior restraints. I believe they plainly violate the Constitution."[173] On this fundamental constitutional principle, Mitchell adopted one position for Bush and the opposite position for Clinton.

Under Mitchell's second theory, the decision to commit the country to war could be "left in the hands of one man." The requirement for prior approval had been replaced by a prohibition on prior approval. His conflicting positions might be explained by having to serve two roles as Senate majority leader: protecting the Senate as an institution and facilitating President Clinton's legislative agenda. No doubt these two roles make it difficult to singlemindedly safeguard legislative prerogatives, but if a constitutional principle is worth fighting for under one president, it is worth fighting for under the next. Otherwise, a lawmaker's position is dictated merely by short-term partisan calculations.

Even more disturbing, in terms of the ability of Congress to protect itself as an institution, are statements by Republican leaders in the Senate and the House who spoke openly and forcefully in defense of President Clinton's broad and unreviewable powers as commander in chief. Objecting to any legislative constraints on Clinton's decision to use military force in Bosnia in 1995, Senate Majority Leader Dole said that Clinton had the constitutional authority "to do what he feels should be done regardless of what Congress does" (see box 21). In an interview with CBS News, Dole remarked: "No doubt about it, whether Congress agrees or not, troops will go to Bosnia."[174]

Following this philosophy of government, Congress had no authority to check the president or insist on prior approval for offensive actions against other nations. If the president decided on a course of action, Congress was powerless to resist. Its only duty was to appropriate the funds needed for the military commitment and perhaps later decide whether to terminate funding for an operation that had gone sour. But it had no business blocking what a president wanted to do.

In January, 1999, former President George Bush spoke to members of the Senate. He said that he had relied heavily on Dole "and not only did he not let me down. He was the model Party leader in the Senate—never putting his agenda ahead of the President's."[175] Under this theory, the decision to deploy troops is in the hands of one man (the president) and the duty of the Senate majority leader is to serve the president, not the Senate.

Senator McCain, Republican from Arizona, made similar comments during the debate on military intervention in Bosnia. According to McCain, Congress had no constitutional grounds for challenging Clinton's policy: "The President will be sending 20,000 Americans to Bosnia for 1 year, whether we approve or disapprove. . . . The President has the authority under the Constitution to do so, and he intends to exercise that authority with or without our approval."[176] Not only was Clinton defending what he claimed to be his executive prerogatives, he had help from leading members of the opposition party in Congress.

Is it true that Clinton could have ignored statutory language that restricted the movement of troops? In 1976, Congress prohibited all assistance for conducting military or paramilitary operations on Angola.[177] In 1986, Congress used language in an appropriation bill to prohibit U.S. forces from operating within twenty miles of the Nicaraguan border while providing assistance to the Contras.[178] No one in the executive branch objected that these statutory restrictions were unconstitutional. Congress can use the power of the purse to limit the president both before he acts and after he acts.

A statement by Speaker Newt Gingrich in 1995 is remarkable. The House was debating an amendment to repeal the War Powers Resolution, except for the reporting and consultation provisions. Gingrich was the last person to speak on the amendment. In supporting the repeal, he argued that a major motivation was to augment presidential power. He appealed to the House "to, at least on paper, increase the power of President Clinton."[179] Gingrich said he wanted to "strengthen the current Democratic president because he is the President of

---

BOX 21

Dole on Presidential Power

Now, in my view the President has the authority and the power under the Constitution to do what he feels should be done regardless of what Congress does. But we also have a responsibility to our constituents and, I think, to the President of the United States to give him our best advice. . . .

. . . It is time for a reality check in the Congress. The fact is that President Clinton has decided to send United States Forces to Bosnia. The fact is that these troops will be sent—and indeed some are already there. The fact is by next week, there will be a couple thousand American soldiers on the ground in Bosnia.

The President has the constitutional power as Commander in Chief to send these forces. The Congress cannot stop this troop deployment from happening. The President and senior advisers have repeatedly said they will proceed with the deployment, whatever the Congress does. If we would try to cut off funds we would harm the men and women in the military who have already begun to arrive in Bosnia.

. . . We have one President at a time. He is the Commander in Chief. He has made this decision. I do not agree with it. I think it is a mistake.

Source: 141 *Cong. Rec.* S17529, S17862 (daily ed. Nov. 27 and 30, 1995).

---

the United States. And the President of the United States on a bipartisan basis deserves to be strengthened in foreign affairs and strengthened in national security."[180] Presidential war power expands because it is promoted not only by executive initiatives but by legislative leaders.

In December, 1998, after President Clinton had ordered bombing strikes in Iraq, Gingrich supported the action with this reasoning: "I believe, as a practical matter, both under our Constitution and in the nature of how human beings function, the daily leadership has to be an executive function, and the President of the United States has to provide that leadership every day, 365 days a year."[181] Although Gingrich identified a second value—"We are a Nation under law"[182]—he saw no need for Congress to authorize military actions. It was enough that he was "briefed on [the air strikes] in advance."[183] A number of other House members insisted that it was necessary for President Clinton to come to Congress to seek advance authorization.[184]

In the Senate, Majority Leader Trent Lott initially opposed the planned military strike against Iraq, stating that "Both the timing and the policy are subject to question."[185] However, his statement was qualified in this respect: "If, however, military action is taken, all Americans will fully support our troops in battle."[186] He followed through on that the next day, announcing: "Once the decision is made and the action is underway, you support it."[187] Under this reasoning, once a president decides to use military force, congressional debate and analysis are not allowed and the system of constitutional checks and balances is suspended.

The Media

Journalists have encouraged the public to believe that the president has the constitutional authority to initiate war. In several articles in 1995, a reporter for *The New York Times* stated that President Clinton "does not need the approval of Congress to send troops to the Balkans."[188] I wrote to the reporter: "Instead of saying, flatly, that Clinton doesn't need the support of Congress, I wish you would say that according to him, and according to some people like Dole, he doesn't need it. There are a number of people, including myself, who believe that he cannot act constitutionally unless he has not only the support but the authority of Congress. The legal and constitutional picture is more complex than you paint it."[189]

My letter had some effect, because five days later the reporter wrote in an article: "The President says he does not need Congressional authorization for the mission."[190] Yet the earlier comments in *The New York Times* had already influenced other publications. One newspaper, *The Hill,* initially wrote: "Clinton says he'd welcome congressional support, but doesn't think he needs it. . . . But the Constitution is clear. Only Congress has the ability to declare war."[191] A month later this newspaper reversed course, stating: "Although President Clinton has the constitutional authority to send U.S. troops to lead a NATO peacekeeping force, and could do so even if Congress votes otherwise, he could be taking an enormous political risk. . . ."[192] I called the editor to ask why the newspaper had changed its legal position and what basis it had for recognizing such constitutional power for the president. The editor told me that the staff believed the president had unilateral power because *The New York Times* said so. Without any basis other than careless wording in a leading newspaper—

wording that would later be corrected—*The Hill* wrote an editorial that reached a large audience and helped misinform citizens. An editorial by the *Washington Post* nonchalantly remarked: "It is true that President Clinton is asking Congress to approve a Bosnia deployment that he has the formal power to order without asking."[193]

Newspaper response to Senator Dole's position on troops to Bosnia is revealing. He said, "I obviously want to support the president. . . . We need to find some way to be able to support the president and I think we need to wait and see what the American reaction is."[194] As Senate majority leader, why was he so inclined to support the president instead of his institution (or the Constitution)? As leader of his chamber, why was he waiting for public reaction?

When Dole finally took a position, it was curiously supportive of the president but critical of the president's policy in sending troops. He said: "We have one president at a time. He is the commander in chief. He's made this decision. I don't agree with it. I think it's a mistake. We had a better option, many better options."[195] Even though Dole concluded that it was a mistake to send American troops to Bosnia, he backed the president.

Reporters praised his position. A columnist for the *Washington Post* wrote that Dole's "old values" emerged on Bosnia. His position gave the world "a glimpse of what many colleagues regard as the essential Dole: the wounded, decorated World War II veteran who never forgot how to salute his commander in chief."[196] Saluting the president in World War II as an enlisted man is one thing; there is no comparable duty for a Senate majority leader to salute the president.

Although Dole was willing to argue with presidents on foreign policy, the columnist noted that he "does not challenge their decisions when troops are headed into harm's way."[197] Why not? If troops are headed into harm's way needlessly, and better options are available, why defer to the president? One of Dole's colleagues, John McCain of Arizona, remarked: "I think what you saw in Bob Dole was an instinctive respect for the office of president and the Constitution."[198] It is not respectful of the Constitution for a senator to surrender legislative authority to the president, especially when he thinks that the president's authority is misguided.

An op-ed piece by David Broder of the *Washington Post* called Dole "Clear and Consistent on Bosnia."[199] But Broder admitted that Dole "never has wanted U.S. troops on the ground" in Bosnia—the very policy that Clinton was pursuing. What was the basis for this reporter's applause?

Mary McGrory of the *Washington Post* credited Dole with an act of patriotism: "Dole, a decorated World War II veteran, executed an immaculate salute to the president."[200] Dole, as an enlisted man in World War II, did indeed salute the leadership and decisions of President Franklin D. Roosevelt, as did every other member of the military. In 1995, as Senate majority leader, there was no such obligation to salute whatever President Clinton decided. Instead, Dole had an obligation to support and defend the Constitution, including the prerogatives assigned to Congress.

On June 26, 1993, President Clinton ordered air strikes against Iraq in response to a failed assassination attempt of former President Bush during a visit to Kuwait. In September, 1996, Clinton ordered the launching of cruise missiles against Iraq, both in the north and the south. These operations coincided with Clinton's reelection race and preparations to deliver his acceptance speech at the Democratic convention. The press chose to interpret the attack as evidence of a strong leader. According to one journalist, Clinton's use of force more than a dozen times in his first term "has served to lay to rest many of the early popular doubts about his fitness to serve as commander in chief."[201]

What a strange interpretation. In his eight years in office, President Eisenhower rarely threatened military force, but there was never a doubt about his fitness as commander in chief. Repeated use of force should call into doubt a president's judgment. While bestowing this praise on Clinton, the journalist offered another observation without recognizing how much the story clashed. White House aides acknowledged that "there was a domestic political component in Clinton's decision to punish Iraqi leader Saddam Hussein for his move against Kurdish-inhabited areas in northern Iraq two months before a U.S. presidential election."[202] To use force against another country for domestic reasons is evidence of unfitness.

Military commitments by President Bush expanded the scope of executive power, especially his claim that he could mount an offensive war against Iraq without coming to Congress for authority. Recognizing that unilateral action by the United States would reinforce the "cowboy" image of American foreign policy, he sought a resolution from the UN Security Council and forged a large alliance of participating nations. But he never sought authority from Congress. President Clinton expanded executive power even further, sidestepping Congress by seeking "authority" from the Security Council and NATO.[203] Congress never found an effective way to protect its institutional interests. Large majorities would coalesce around nonbinding resolutions, but as soon as the resolution veered toward legally binding language, or as the deadline for action came clearly into view, Congress backed off. By 1999, there appeared to be no limit on what a president could do in committing the nation to war.

5

Spending Powers after World War II

A year after the War Powers Resolution, Congress passed the Congressional Budget and Impoundment Control Act of 1974, also widely touted as an effort to reassert legislative power. This statute has had a complex and mixed history, but there is good reason to conclude that it helped President Reagan in 1981 pass a budget plan that led to a five-fold increase in the national debt. By 1981, the total national debt (accumulated since 1789) had reached a trillion dollars. Largely because of the budget changes in 1981, the debt soared to *five* trillion by 1999. The explosion of deficits produced the Gramm-Rudman-Hollings Act of 1985, a statute that abdicated legislative power not so much to the president as to automatic formulas and triggers. With Reagan's encouragement, the drumbeat for transferring greater spending power to the president prompted Congress to consider another abdication, the Line Item Veto Act of 1996.

Impoundment Battles

The decision of presidents not to spend funds appropriated by Congress has had a long and tortured history. Impoundment precedents can be found in every administration, starting with George Washington. By and large, presidents withheld funds whenever they thought they could get away with it and retreated hastily whenever lawmakers screamed with sufficient intensity.[1]

The picture changed dramatically with Richard Nixon's election in 1968. The White House began to develop a legal theory that justified impoundment as an inherent constitutional power of the president. If such impoundment actions were constitutional in origin, lawmakers could do nothing by statute— much less by issuing complaints—to check the president.

Alarmed by this development, a subcommittee of the Senate Judiciary Committee set aside three days for hearings in March, 1971. Subcommittee chairman Sam J. Ervin, Jr. (D-N.C.), recognized that impoundments could be a useful and proper tool for effecting savings and for avoiding deficiencies in appropriations accounts. Impoundment would be appropriate when Congress passed appropriations "as nothing more than a ceiling on expenditures, leaving it to the discretion of the executive branch to expend the funds."[2] But when impoundment was exercised as an exclusive power of the president, without regard to statutory limits or directives, it threatened the constitutional power of Congress to decide budget priorities. It was the president's duty under Article II of the Constitution to "take Care that the Laws be faithfully executed," and that obligation applied not only to laws he liked but laws he may not have entirely supported or even asked for. Ervin pointed out that the framers "intended that [the president] execute all laws passed by the Congress, irrespective of any personal, political, or philosophic views he might have. He has no authority under the Constitution to decide which laws will be executed or to what extent they will be enforced. Yet, by using the impounding technique, the president is able to do just that. He is able to effect policy by determining which of the laws passed by Congress he will enforce and to what extent."[3]

As Ervin noted, impoundment enabled the president "to effect an item or line veto" in violation of the Constitution, "which only empowers him to veto entire bills." By impounding appropriated funds, the president was able to "modify, reshape, or nullify completely" laws passed by Congress, thus exercising an essential part of the legislative power. He charged that this "illegal exercise" of presidential power "flies directly in the face of clear constitutional provisions to the contrary."[4]

Executive Claims

The legal position of the Nixon administration was articulated by Caspar W. Weinberger, deputy director of the Office of Management and Budget (OMB). He testified that while it is the responsibility of Congress to decide what to appropriate, it "does not follow from this, however, that the expenditure of government funds involves an exclusively legislative function; in fact, the [Constitution] seems to assume that the expenditure of funds—as distinguished from the granting of authority to withdraw them from the Treasury—is an executive function." Weinberger also said that "a law appropriating funds is permissive and not mandatory in nature."[5]

From those two principles, it would appear that impoundment was fully sanctioned by the Constitution and subject to no constraints from Congress. Weinberger reinforced his point by arguing that the president, under the Constitution, has a "general management power" that requires discretionary decisions and judgment.[6] Moreover, he admonished Congress in these terms: "the whole nature of the appropriation process is such that Congress is, in one way or another, virtually prevented from taking an overall look at the effect of their total actions."[7]

During the 1972 election campaign, the impoundment battle heated up. President Nixon charged that Congress, as an institution, acted irresponsibly on federal spending. He attributed this behavior to the procedures that Congress used to consider the budget, asserting that Congress "not only does not consider the total financial picture when it votes on a particular spending bill, it does not even contain a mechanism to do so if it wished."[8] Budget problems resulted from the "hoary and traditional procedure of the Congress, which now permits action on the various spending programs as if they were unrelated and independent actions."[9] White House aides joined the attack on Congress. John Ehrlichman, the president's domestic adviser, blasted the "credit-card Congress" for adding billions to the budget. He likened the lawmakers to a spendthrift brother-in-law "who has gotten hold of the family credit card and is running up big bills" with no thought of paying them.[10]

This was a bold move, calculated to put Congress on the defensive. Did Congress defend itself? Hardly. Many members even outdid the president in decrying the irresponsibility of Congress. They told their constituents that fiscal sanity could not be restored until Congress altered its procedures and organization. The facts did not support such a simplistic picture, but legislators seemed to enjoy downgrading their own institution. While traveling around the country with ten members of the House of Representatives, Richard Fenno listened to them flail away at Congress. They consistently criticized Congress and portrayed themselves "as a fighter against its manifest evils. Members run for Congress by running against Congress."[11] The mathematics here were peculiar. Each member of Congress was responsible; collectively they were a disaster.

Easily available budget data demonstrated that Nixon's picture of Congress was a caricature, for Congress had little net effect on total budget spending during his years in office. Congress reduced Nixon's appropriations requests for fiscal years 1969 through 1973 by a total of $30.9 billion. That reduction was offset by a $30.5 billion increase in spending authorized by backdoor devices (such as contract authority on the clean-water program) and mandatory entitlements.[12] In short, pretty much of a wash. The budget deficits during the

Nixon years were caused mainly by the loss of tax revenues due to the recession of 1970, not to runaway federal spending.[13]

During hearings in the fall of 1972, the Nixon administration actually defended the president's reliance on budget deficits to stimulate the economy. Secretary of the Treasury George Shultz said that it was a "good thing and a courageous thing." Senator Abraham Ribicoff (D-Conn.) wondered about that: "I am still puzzled. If it is courageous for the president to build in a deficit in his budget, why is it less than courageous for Congress to build in a deficit in its budget? Why is it right for the president and wrong for Congress?"[14] The question went unanswered.

Nixon proposed a spending ceiling of $250 billion for fiscal 1973. If outlays threatened to exceed that level, he wanted complete discretion to decide which programs to curtail or eliminate. Both Houses supported the ceiling but could not agree on a formula to limit presidential discretion. When Congress failed to pass legislation to support Nixon's proposal, he announced that he would withhold appropriated funds from a number of domestic programs. Phoenix-like, the spending ceiling emerged from the ashes, this time in the form of an administratively imposed ceiling. Secretary Shultz announced that the president had reviewed the budget and "now feels sure that he can hold the outlays in the fiscal 1973 budget to $250 billion, and he is determined to do so."[15]

During December, 1972, and January, 1973, the Nixon administration announced major cancellations and cutbacks. Although presidents had impounded funds in the past, the Nixon impoundments were unprecedented in scope, severity, and truculence. Never before had congressional priorities and prerogatives been so altered and jeopardized.[16]

The White House stepped up the public relations campaign by preparing a 145-page kit of materials to be used against Congress. Government officials, when meeting with citizens groups, were directed to spice up their talks with lampoons and "horror stories" about the "spendthrift" Democratic-controlled Congress. Typical quips were drafted to be included in speeches (see box 22).

This White House gambit backfired. Senators Edmund Muskie (D-Maine) and Hubert Humphrey (D-Minn.) asked the General Accounting Office to determine whether the administration's effort violated a law called "Lobbying with Appropriated Moneys Act."[17] Comptroller General Elmer B. Staats concluded that the kit violated language in an appropriations act that restricted funds for publicity or propaganda purposes designed to support or defeat pending legislation.[18] After a Ralph Nader litigation unit (Public Citizen, Inc.) went to court, claiming that the White House had violated public law, a White House official in an affidavit stated that all copies of the kit had been returned for destruction. The suit was subsequently dismissed on the ground that it was moot.[19]

Congress Retaliates

The arbitrary and heavy-handed impoundments by the Nixon administration provoked Congress to draft legislation to curb presidential power. During hearings in 1973, Senator Ervin responded to unchecked and unregulated executive impoundments by raising the question "whether the Congress of the United States will remain a viable institution or whether the current trend toward the executive use of legislative power is to continue unabated until we have arrived at a presidential form of government."[20] Executive initiatives had brought the dispute to a head, but Ervin looked also to deficiencies within Congress: "the executive branch has been able to seize power so brazenly only because the Congress has lacked the courage and foresight to maintain its constitutional position. The Congress has failed as an institution to equip itself physically to carry out its legislative duties independent of the executive branch, much less to perform its important function of overseeing the activities of the executive branch in administering the programs it has enacted. Moreover, as individuals, many of us have found it more comfortable to have somebody else— the President—make the hard decisions and relieve us of responsibility."[21]

Senator Ervin proposed legislation that would require the president to notify Congress whenever he impounded funds. The impoundment would cease unless Congress approved the impoundment within sixty calendar days of continuous session. He hoped that the legislation would help Congress "restore itself to its intended role under our Constitution."[22] Some Republicans offered their support. Senator Jacob K. Javits, Republican of New York, said that "we are deprived of the power of the Congress when the line item veto is employed under the guise of impoundment, and that is exactly what is happening."[23] Senator Edward J. Gurney, Republican of Florida, regarded Nixon's impoundments as "a necessary, short-term evil" but also believed that the scope and degree of the impoundments "have resulted in a very undesirable exercise of Executive power. It is a use of power which the words of our Constitution do not contemplate."[24]

Administration officials did not back off. At the 1973 hearings they defended impoundment as an essential weapon in the fight against inflation, deficit spending, and waste.[25] Roy L. Ash, OMB director-designate, testified that "the present difficulty results from the lack of a congressional mechanism to review and act upon the overall government fiscal situation in advance of taking appropria-

---

BOX 22

White House Quips on Congress

"This may look like a Santa Claus Congress—but it's got a bagful of bad news for the taxpayer."

"Just because the Congress passes the buck doesn't mean the President has to spend it."

"When Congress can't add, Senator [Hugh] Scott (the Republican leader) has said the President must subtract. Otherwise the budget will keep on multiplying and the taxpayer's dollar will keep on dividing."

"When one man helps himself to another man's bank account, that's called embezzlement. But when a big-spending congressman helps himself to the taxpayer's income with higher prices and taxes, then it's called 'compassion.'"

Source: Mike Causey, "Administration Supplies One-Liners," *Washington Post,* Apr. 6, 1973, p. D17.

---

tion and other legislative actions."[26] But the problem, Ash said, ran deeper than that. Even if Congress succeeded in establishing a mechanism to relate specific items of spending to total spending, total revenues, and total borrowing, Congress "still cannot perform the job of spending money." The administration of detailed projects is "undeniably within the executive authority."[27]

The representative from the Justice Department, Deputy Attorney General Joseph T. Sneed, called the Senate bill "wholly impractical, profoundly unwise, and of very doubtful constitutionality."[28] He claimed that the bill "seeks to reverse 170 years of Presidential practice."[29] Sneed denied that the presidential exercise of impoundment was "usurpation; rather it is in the great tradition of checks and balances upon which our Constitution is based."[30] He questioned whether Congress had the power to convert the chief executive into a "Chief Clerk."[31]

Impoundment Control Act

The Senate took the initiative in passing anti-impoundment legislation. At first the House avoided such legislation because many members feared that voters would interpret congressional pressure to release impounded funds as pro-spending. But the House soon realized that impoundment control was an essential element of budget reform because, in its absence, congressional decisions on budget priorities could easily be frustrated by the administration. Senate proponents of impoundment legislation offered both political and policy reasons for combining it with budget reform. Nixon had often castigated Congress for its lack of effective budget control mechanisms. Thus he would find it difficult to veto impoundment control if it were part of a larger budget reform package. Once both Houses of Congress came to recognize the desirability of joining impoundment control with budget reform, they passed the Impoundment Control Act as Title X of the budget reform act of 1974.

The Nixon administration had seized upon some language in the Antideficiency Act, which had been enacted in 1905 to ensure that executive agencies would not overspend their appropriations. As a means of achieving that objective, the president could establish budgetary reserves by apportioning an appropriation "to provide for contingencies, or to effect savings whenever savings are made possible by and through changes in requirements, greater efficiency of operations, or *other developments* subsequent to the date on which such appropriation was made available." The congressional objective in enacting this statute was to save money that was not needed to achieve the purposes of the appropriation.

President Nixon used the "other developments" language to justify refusals to spend appropriated funds on independent policy grounds, such as disagreements with Congress over the wisdom of particular programs and a desire to reduce overall federal spending in order to fight inflation. The Impoundment Control Act narrowed the president's authority to accumulate budgetary reserves by removing "other developments" from the Antideficiency Act.

The Impoundment Control Act established a comprehensive scheme for congressional review of impoundment actions in order to ensure that the president did not abuse his authority. The act recognized two types of impoundment: rescissions and deferrals. If the president wanted to rescind (cancel) budget authority, he would have to transmit a special message to Congress and obtain the support of both Houses within forty-five days of continuous session. If Congress denied its support, the president would have to make the budget authority available to the appropriate agencies for obligation and expenditure.

Both Houses explained the constitutional basis for the rescission procedure. Congressman Richard Bolling, who managed the Budget Act in the House, argued that rescission needed the explicit support of Congress because it represented a change to a previous law. He noted: "Inasmuch as a rescission represents the undoing of what Congress previously enacted, it is entirely appropriate that no rescission be authorized except by affirmative vote of both Houses."[32]

Forcing Congress to act again and again through the legislative process, sometimes by extraordinary majority (to override presidential vetoes), was considered institutionally demeaning. Senator Ervin first thought it was appropriate for the president to rescind funds unless "affirmatively vetoed by the Congress within 60 days."[33] He soon abandoned that position and insisted that rescissions had to be affirmatively ratified by Congress (see box 23).

For deferrals, the Impoundment Control Act required the president to submit a special message to Congress whenever he proposed to defer spending of appropriated funds. He would have to make the budget authority available for obligation if either House of Congress passed an "impoundment resolution" that disapproved the proposed deferral. The Supreme Court's decision in *INS v. Chadha* (1983) invalidated all types of legislative vetoes, including the one-House veto for deferrals.

Did this mean that the president could defer funds without a legislative check? Were the two branches to be at war again? Hearings by the House Committee on Rules in 1986 reviewed what had happened after the *Chadha* decision. Chairman Claude Pepper correctly noted that from 1983 to 1985, "both branches treated the deferral process gingerly. The number of deferrals proposed by the President and the number disapproved by Congress were modest in those years. The President, to his credit, did not try to expand his power."[34]

The truce collapsed in 1986, when President Reagan sent Congress a large number of deferrals. Now that Congress lacked a one-House veto, Reagan had in effect item-veto power. When OMB Director James C. Miller III appeared at the House hearings, he rubbed it in. Congressman Joe Moakley (D-Mass.) asked: "Do you think for one minute that the Congress would have given the President the right to defer if we thought we would not have the one-House veto?" Miller replied: "You took a risk. You took a risk in utilizing the one-House veto. . . . you rolled the dice and the President won in that regard."[35]

The dispute reached federal court, where it was determined that the one-House legislative veto was tied inextricably to the deferral authority. Because they were inseverable, the deferral authority therefore vanished with the legislative veto. Congress promptly converted the judicial decision into statutory law.[36]

The Budget Act of 1974

Although the budget deficits during the Nixon years could be tied more closely to economic performance than to legislative deficiencies, a congressional study

---

BOX 23

Ervin on Impoundment Procedure

Mr. President, I would like to state to the Senate very briefly why I changed the provision of the bill from a veto by the Congress to the requirement that there by an affirmative ratification of the impoundment by the Congress. We have an expression down in North Carolina that the people ought not to make monkeys of themselves. And I think that this amendment [requiring Congress to disapprove by concurrent resolution], if adopted, would mean that the Senate more or less would be making monkeys of themselves.

In the first place, . . . Congress has the undoubted power of the purse under the Constitution. It is conceivable that Congress might have to vote four times before it could make it obligatory upon the executive branch of the Government to spend a single penny of the appropriated funds in a given instance. [Ervin explained that Congress might have to pass an authorization bill, override a veto of that bill, pass an appropriation bill, and override a veto of that bill.]

If the amendment . . . were to be adopted, Congress would have to vote a fifth time [leading to a sixth vote by Congress to override the expected presidential veto.]

Source: 119 *Cong. Rec.* 15237–38 (1973).

---

committee quickly blamed Congress and its procedures. In a report released in 1973, the Joint Study Committee on Budget Control (JSC) linked the increasing size of budget deficits to procedural inadequacies within Congress: "The constant continuation of deficits plus their increasing size illustrates the need for Congress to obtain better control over the budget." The committee concluded that "the failure to arrive at congressional budget decisions on an overall basis has been a contributory factor" in the continuation of deficits. No committee was responsible for deciding "whether or not total outlays are appropriate in view of the current situation. . . . As a result, each spending bill tends to be considered by Congress as a separate entity, and any assessment of relative priorities among spending programs for the most part is made solely within the context of the bill before Congress."[37]

This description was overdrawn and incorrect. Such stereotypes were used to exaggerate the need for reorganization and reform. In fact, the "old system" was not nearly so fragmented, incoherent, and irresponsible. The Joint Committee on Reduction of Federal Expenditures prepared "scorekeeping reports" and circulated them on a regular basis. Those reports were printed in the *Congressional Record*. Legislators therefore knew, from month to month, how congressional action compared to the president's budget. Through informal techniques, Congress managed to coordinate its actions and change the shape of the president's budget without exceeding its size. The results reveal a systematic and responsible pattern, not chaos. Congressional totals remained within the ballpark of the president's budget. Legislative spending did not spin wildly out of control.

Nevertheless, congressional reformers in 1974 assumed that lawmakers would behave more responsibly if they voted explicitly on budget aggregates and faced up to totals, rather than decide spending actions in "piecemeal" fashion on separate appropriations and legislative bills. In 1974, as now, it was difficult to defend fragmentation, splintering, and decentralization when reformers pressed eagerly for "coordination," "coherence," and a "unified budget process."

To many, the model of the executive budget looked appealing. The Budget and Accounting Act of 1921 had assumed that presidential control and responsibility would be improved by centralizing the budget process in the executive branch. There has been no retreat from that principle for the president, but advantages for the chief executive do not necessarily apply to Congress. The risks are high when Congress, possessing very different institutional qualities, tries to emulate the executive branch.

The Budget Act of 1974 anticipated a contest between two budgets: presidential and congressional. The analogy is weak because the president is head of the executive branch, which is fortified by a central budget office. There is no head in Congress, and there could be no comparable powers for a congressional budget office. Congress is inherently decentralized between two chambers, two parties, and various appropriation, authorization, and tax committees. No amount of procedural tinkering can hide that reality.

These considerations had no effect on the drive for budget reform. Comprehensiveness was the order of the day. The 1974 statute created Budget Committees in each House and made them responsible for reporting budget resolutions with five aggregates: total budget authority, total outlays, total revenues, the surplus or deficit, and public debt. Outlays and budget authority would be organized in terms of major "functional categories" (such as national defense, transportation, and agriculture) to permit legislative debate on budget priorities. Adoption of a budget resolution would guide the individual efforts of authorization, appropriation, and tax committees. The Budget Act established the Congressional Budget Office (CBO) to give legislators technical support, but it could never have the same institutional power as OMB. The executive branch is largely hierarchical. No such quality applies to Congress, which is essentially collegial in its operations.

The Downside of Acting Comprehensively

The new procedures and organization mandated by the 1974 legislation looked impressive on the surface, but there was no guarantee that comprehensive action by Congress would yield more responsibility or heightened accountability. Increasing the size of a legislative vehicle—from an appropriations bill to a budget resolution—could introduce new, unanticipated problems. It is difficult enough to pass individual appropriations, tax, and entitlement bills. Compromises and delicate tradeoffs must be fashioned to build majority support.

Why would it be any easier to pass a comprehensive budget resolution, where all parties would seek to have their interests included? Such a step magnifies the scope of legislative conflict and encourages additional concessions to members and interest groups. As the cost of doing business in Congress increases, so does the need for obfuscation and deception. That has been one of the major lessons since 1974. When legislative conflict exceeds a certain point, the result is escapist budgeting. Members become less, not more, responsible.

By centralizing the legislative process, the Budget Act of 1974 made it more difficult to pass a budget and increased the likelihood of political deadlock.[38] The larger the legislative vehicle, the harder it is to attract a majority. As noted by John Gilmour, the "genius of the old [pre-1974] practice of considering the budget only in pieces, never as a whole, was that it minimized the possibility of stalemate."[39]

Conflicts in executive budget-making force concessions from agencies that compete for a relatively fixed aggregate. These agencies are subordinate to the central control of the president assisted by OMB. Agency appetites can be controlled. Conditions in Congress are entirely different. There is no central control and therefore no reason to expect that greater conflict will produce budgetary restraint. Spending pressures in Congress can be relieved by voting more money or by adopting fanciful economic projections. Congress has done them all.

Rudolph Penner, former CBO director, made some interesting comments about the capacity of Congress to function better under a decentralized, informal system than under a system that appears to be more coherent and responsible (see box 24). He called attention to a crucial fact: the president and Congress

---

BOX 24

Virtues of Informality

[Former CBO Director Rudolph Penner]: I have always been struck by the fact in looking at the history of the [budget] process that it appeared chaotic in the late 19th century and early 20th century, but the results were very good in terms of budget discipline, yielding balanced budgets or surpluses most of the time, unless there was really a good reason to run a deficit.

Now we have a process that looks very elegant on paper, but it is leading to very dishonest and disorderly results. It is my strong feeling that, while Gramm-Rudman may have done some good in reducing the deficit as we measure it, it has also done an enormous amount of harm in spawning a large number of gimmicks that make it very difficult to analyze the budget anymore. These gimmicks make investors and other outsiders lose confidence in the Government. Gramm-Rudman has also shortened the time horizon of decisionmaking so that policies are judged mainly according to their effects on this year's cash flow deficit as opposed to their longer run effects on economic efficiency and equity.

And frankly, I would get rid of Gramm-Rudman. I am one of those public policy analysts who thought the 1974 process was a good idea when it was first invented. I have to confess to a lot of disappointment and frustration as to how it actually worked out. I think the criticisms of that process, that it was too complex and too time consuming, are right on the mark. . . .

Source: "Budget Process Reform," hearing before the House Committee on the Budget, 101st Cong., 2d sess., pp. 20–21 (1990).

---

can decide budget issues reasonably well through the normal, fragmented political process, disorderly as it is. The two branches performed less well under the statutory disincentives of the Budget Act of 1974. The Budget Committees, created to improve legislative responsibility, became another access point for members who had been rebuffed by the authorization and appropriations committees. If lawmakers set total spending at a generous level in a budget resolution, as they did in the initial years, the result was increased pressure for higher spending.

The appropriations committees found it difficult to argue against amendments for more spending when their bills fell below the amount allowed in a budget resolution. That fact created a new incentive or rationale for additional spending. Instead of reporting bills with less money than the president had requested (the previous pattern), the choice was now to spend "up to" the figure inserted in the budget resolution. A chief clerk of an appropriations subcommittee complained that the spending limits in a budget resolution had been set too high: "We were faced with pressure to spend up to the full budget allocation. It's almost as if the Budget Committee bent over backwards to give Appropriations all that it wanted and then some."[40] Because of these calculations, the Budget Act legitimized spending that would not have occurred under the previous system.[41]

Instead of keeping within the president's aggregates, legislators could vote on generous ceilings in a budget resolution and then announce proudly to their constituents that they have "stayed within the budget." Congressman Tom Steed (D-Okla.), managing the Treasury–Postal Service appropriations bill for fiscal 1977, stated in a floor message: "Although we are over the President's budget, we are under the legislative budget. . . . This particular bill will be well within the limit set by the Committee on the Budget of the Congress."[42] In time, the public would no longer know whether a bill "below budget" was below the allocation in the budget resolution or the president's budget.

In 1978, Congressman Delbert Latta (R-Ohio) declared that the Budget Act had been converted into "big spenders' biggest ally."[43] The Budget Committees encouraged "more spending by putting [their] blessing on many social welfare proposals so inflationary that the House, left to its own devices, would probably not approve many of them."[44] Congressman Barber Conable (R-N.Y.) objected to the new budget process because it sanctioned higher numbers for programs, giving them "an aura of responsibility they would not otherwise have had."[45] In 1979, the chairman of the House Budget Committee, Bob Giaimo (D-Conn.), conceded that budget resolutions had included sizable funding increases for program after program, "almost regardless of its effectiveness."[46]

Reagan's 1981 Initiative

Budget resolutions were praised because they represented a vehicle for centralized, systematic, and coherent legislative action—all intended to strengthen Congress. Under some conditions, however, the process of passing a budget resolution could strengthen *the president*. Those conditions materialized in 1981 when President Ronald Reagan attracted the necessary votes from Republicans and conservative Democrats to gain control over the budget resolution in both Houses. The budget resolution became the blueprint for enforcing his priorities for a tax cut, defense buildup, and retrenchment of domestic programs. The budget resolution therefore advanced presidential, not congressional, goals. Once the White House had seized control of the budget resolution, subsequent action on the tax bill, appropriations bills, and the reconciliation bill became the necessary steps to implement presidential policy. When Reagan's theory of supply-side economics failed to generate predicted revenues, the nation faced budget deficits of $150 billion to $200 billion a year. At the time President Reagan entered office, the national debt (accumulated from 1789 to 1981) stood at approximately $1 trillion. In his first four years that number doubled and by the time he left office it had climbed to $3 trillion.

Would the actions in 1981 have happened without a budget resolution? Possibly, but Reagan would have faced almost insurmountable hurdles in trying to enact his radical program with the pre-1974 budgetary process. Most likely his program would have been chopped to bits by successive committee and subcommittee action. The budget resolution gave him the centralizing vehicle he needed.

Budget analysts generally agree with this assessment. Penner asked: "Would the dramatic actions of 1981 have been possible without the process? It is a question that no one will ever be able to answer with certainty. I believe, however, that it would have been difficult to achieve these results using the old, muddled way of formulating budgets."[47] Penner concluded that Reagan's objectives would have been much harder to achieve had he been forced to negotiate with the decentralized power structure that existed in Congress before 1974. Allen Schick made a similar point (see box 25).

Reagan's high-risk strategy sparked an explosion of budget deficits. It is highly unlikely that an error of that magnitude would have occurred with the decentralized process that existed before 1974. The incrementalism of that process functioned as an effective brake on radical proposals.

The Budget Act of 1974 strengthened Reagan's hand by forcing Congress to vote on an overall budget plan. David Stockman, Reagan's OMB director from 1981 to 1985, explained how the centralized congressional process became a convenient instrument for implementing White House goals. The constitutional prerogatives of Congress "would have to be, in effect, suspended. Enacting the Reagan Administration's economic program meant rubber stamp approval, nothing less. The world's so-called greatest deliberative body would have to be reduced to the status of a ministerial arm of the White House."[48] For the budget plan to work, Congress had to "forfeit its independence."[49]

BOX 25

Virtues of Fragmentation

Historically, the president has been at a disadvantage vis-à-vis Congress in their periodic budget conflicts. Congress excels as an institution that fragments issues and avoids decisions on overall objectives. Before installation of the congressional budget process, this fragmented behavior characterized legislative consideration of the president's budget. Appropriations were splintered into more than a dozen bills, tax legislation was walled off from spending decisions, and Congress did not have to vote on the totals. Members were able to profess support for the president's objectives while "nickel and diming" the budget in their action on appropriations and other spending measures.

Source: Allen Schick, "How the Budget Was Won and Lost," in *President and Congress: Assessing Reagan's First Year,* ed. by Norman J. Ornstein, p. 25.

The danger of permitting a president, or the executive branch, this much control over Congress is reflected in Stockman's own assessment of the expertise available in the White House and OMB. After leaving office he admitted: "a plan for radical and abrupt change required deep comprehension—and we had none of it."[50] He conceded that he had "built an edifice of doctrine, but not a theory of governance."[51]

For those who associate the executive branch with expertise and objectivity, take a look at a key decision on the 1981 budget. It was well known within the White House that the initial allocation of a nine percent annual growth rate for the Defense Department was unacceptably high, especially with the large tax cut. In order to prevent large deficits, it was necessary to pare back the increase to five or seven percent. On September 9, 1981, Stockman met at a "shootout" with President Reagan and Secretary of Defense Caspar Weinberger. After some discussion, Weinberger unveiled a large chart showing three cartoon characters representing different defense budgets: the Carter budget (a tiny soldier without a rifle), the Stockman budget (a bespectacled little soldier holding a small wooden rifle), and the Weinberger budget (a big, square-jawed, fully armed GI Joe). Weinberger got his nine percent.[52] Imagine the ridicule directed at a congressional committee that analyzed a national security issue in this fashion.

The record of 1981 exposed serious weaknesses within Congress. Instead of depending on its supposedly superior analytical capability gained from the 1974 statute, including CBO and the Budget Committees, Congress embraced the administration's flawed and false premises. What explains the continued support for the 1974 statute? Congressman Trent Lott (R-Miss.) put it this way in 1985: "The primary reason is that it is worthwhile politically. Members of Congress use the budget process to give the appearance that they are doing something about the deficits or dealing with the budget. In my judgment, they are using it as political cover so that they can continue to be fiscally irresponsible."[53]

Gramm-Rudman-Hollings

The astonishing growth of budget deficits after 1981, combined with Reagan's refusal to offer constructive solutions, paved the way for the Gramm-Rudman-Hollings (GRH) Act of 1985. This statute symbolized many things: an admission that the congressional budget process created in 1974 was helpless in dealing with deficits in the range of $200 billion a year; a conclusion that the political stalemate between Reagan and Congress required a statutory framework to force action; and an unwillingness in Congress to delegate any additional authorities or powers to the executive branch. Instead of helping matters, GRH led to continued increases in budget deficits and a further loss of accountability. Budgeting escapism reached new heights of ingenuity. By 1990, both branches agreed to abandon GRH.

Gramm-Rudman created a statutory schedule to eliminate deficits by fiscal 1991. Beginning with a deficit of $171.9 billion for fiscal 1986, the statute directed a decrease in that level by about $36 billion each year over a five-year period. The president's budget and the congressional budget resolution were supposed to adhere to those targets. If in any fiscal year the projected deficit exceeded the statutory allowance by more than $10 billion, a "sequestration" process would be triggered to make across-the-board cuts to meet the statutory target. Half of those cuts were to come from defense; a number of social programs were exempted.

Gramm-Rudman suffered from many deficiencies. By focusing primarily on a deficit number for a particular year, it encouraged both branches to play games by making short-run calculations that aggravated long-run problems. Various accounting tricks were devised, such as shifting costs from a current year to a previous one (or to the next), or raising revenue for a current year at the cost of losing much larger revenues for future years.[54] Other gimmicks: selling federal assets, accelerating the payments of loans, moving items off-budget, and estimating higher revenue on the theory that tax laws would be enforced more vigorously.[55] Allen Schick offered this judgment: "GRH started out as a process for reducing the deficit and has become a means of hiding the deficit and running away from responsibility."[56]

The GRH deficit targets also discouraged timely action on appropriations bills. Instead of cutting some programs that might have to be cut again through sequestration, appropriations bills were delayed and greater reliance placed on continuing resolutions. Congressman David Obey (D-Wis.) said that as long as Gramm-Rudman existed, there was an incentive for the Appropriations Committees to delay coming to the floor, "because even if they cut their own bill and meet the spending limitations required under a budget resolution, that does not guarantee that every other committee will perform, and so they can wind up having their bill cut twice."[57] Eventually, crucial decisions were shifted to "budget summits" held at the White House or other locations, excluding most legislators and preventing "the normal give and take of congressional deliberations."[58]

The crutch of Gramm-Rudman made it easier for the two branches to avoid painful decisions. The task was relatively simple: offer budget projections that met the Gramm-Rudman deficit targets. If actual deficits soared beyond those optimistic predictions, the statutory mission was nonetheless fully satisfied. Because the public was under the illusion that the deficit crisis was being addressed, Congress and the president were under less political pressure to do something real. Senator Jim Sasser (D-Tenn.), chairman of the Senate Budget Committee, summed up the issue in 1989 (see box 26).

Representative Marty Russo (D-Ill.), member of the House Budget Committee, made a similar point in 1990. He explained how the two branches routinely practiced deceit with budget deficits: "The President submits a budget that relies on very optimistic economic and technical assumptions and questionable savings proposals to meet the Gramm-Rudman deficit target. Congress attacks the assumptions and proposals as phony, but uses them in the budget resolution anyway."[59] Congress accepted the president's phony figures because honest numbers (which were available) would have increased the projected deficit and made Congress look like the "big spender." Once the president ducked responsibility by submitting a disingenuous budget, politics required Congress to embrace the same mistaken assumptions.

Gramm-Rudman never met any of its deficit targets. The target for fiscal 1986 was $171.9. The actual deficit: $221.2 billion. The target for the next year was $144 billion; the actual deficit came close ($149.8 billion). The deficit for fiscal 1988 was supposed to be $108 billion; it reached $155.2 billion.[60] When it

---

BOX 26

Benefits of Obfuscation

[Senator Jim Sasser (D-Tenn.), chairman of the Senate Budget Committee]: Now, the record simply, unhappily, does not support the notion that Gramm-Rudman has worked as a deficit reducer. Instead, the Gramm-Rudman game and the gaming of the system has actually replaced deficit reduction in many ways.

As I said the other day, we have ended up with two sets of books. This Government keeps two sets of books. First, we keep a set for the Gramm-Rudman game—and this is a useful fiction manipulated to give the illusion of progress—and second, we keep a set of books that are the real books. This is the real deficit. And we neglect getting around to doing something about the real deficit because of the Gramm-Rudman set of books we keep.

Now, it should be no surprise that an artificial construction is giving us artificial results, and that is exactly what Gramm-Rudman is, an artificial construction. But perhaps the ingenuity of some at the art of gaming this artificial construction is surprising. We have all decried the gimmickry, even as we have used them ourselves, to reach the Gramm-Rudman targets, but the simple fact is that Gramm-Rudman encourages these practices.

Source: "Budget Reform Proposals," joint hearings before the Senate Committees on Governmental Affairs and the Budget, 101st Cong., 1st sess., pp. 2–3 (1989).

---

became obvious that the deficit targets of Gramm-Rudman could not be reached, the two branches enacted a law in 1987 known as Gramm-Rudman II. The new statute pushed the fantasy forward by two years, anticipating a deficit of zero by fiscal 1993. The deficit for that year reached $255 billion.[61]

Punting to the Courts (I)

Various drafts of the Gramm-Rudman bill depended on congressional agencies (either the Congressional Budget Office or the General Accounting Office) to carry out what seemed to be clearly executive duties. In one of the bills, the OMB director and the CBO director were tasked with jointly estimating the levels of total revenues and budget outlays, determining whether the deficit for a particular fiscal year would exceed the maximum deficit amount assigned for that year, and specifying the percentages by which certain expenditures should be reduced to eliminate the excesses.[62] Upon receipt of this OMB-CBO report, the president would issue an order eliminating the amount of the deficit excess.

The Senate conducted no hearings on the constitutionality of Gramm-Rudman. The House Committee on Government Operations held a hearing on October 17, 1985, inviting four people to testify. I joined Comptroller General Charles Bowsher, OMB Director Jim Miller, and CBO Director Rudolph Penner. I was the only one to address the constitutional issue. In addition to making some general points about the bill's effect of subordinating Congress to presidential power, I stated that CBO, because it was part of the legislative branch, could not be given "substantive enforcement responsibilities, as would be the case under Gramm-Rudman."[63] I concluded that *Buckley v. Valeo* (1976) prohibited Congress from imposing substantive and enforcement responsibilities on legislative officers. I urged that constitutional questions—especially those involving the balance between executive and legislative power—should be handled by Congress, not the courts: "The courts in the past, I think, have made clear that you cannot expect other branches of government to protect your own powers. You have to do that for yourselves."[64]

The fact that I was the only one to testify on constitutional issues prompted Congressman Mike Synar (D-Okla.) to remark to me: "you sit there as the only person whom I can find in this city or anywhere in this country who has done the type of constitutional scrutiny and analysis which is necessary to give any of us assurances that we are not going down a path that may be dangerous."[65]

During floor consideration, Senator Bennett Johnston (D-La.) objected that "we have here an abdication of power and an abdication of responsibility by Congress."[66] He offered an amendment to give Congress a greater role in deciding what to cut, but his proposal was never taken up.[67] Although both chambers passed the legislation, constitutional challenges continued. Laurence Tribe of the Harvard Law School noted that a "legislative officer" (the CBO director) played an "important part in making the unavoidably discretionary decisions that suspend operation of the entire law during recessions, and that trigger presidential action to slash entitlements and impound funds so as to comply with the deficit ceilings. Giving such executive duties to a legislative officer is almost certainly unconstitutional."[68]

By the time the bill emerged from conference committee, it was decided to authorize the comptroller general, at the General Accounting Office, to certify the results submitted by CBO and OMB. Senator Bob Packwood (R-Ore.)

argued that the addition of GAO, "which indeed is an executive agency . . . cures the allegation of unconstitutionality."[69] One would be hard-pressed to call GAO an executive agency. If the statute was defective on that point, a section was added to give any member of Congress an opportunity to challenge, through a process of expedited review, the constitutionality of this provision. The matter would be first decided by a three-judge court and go from there immediately to the Supreme Court.[70]

Several legislators vigorously protested the transfer of legislative power to CBO, OMB, and GAO. Congressman Henry Waxman (D-Calif.) detailed his objections (see box 27). Congressman James Scheuer (D-N.Y.) agreed that Congress "should not place the ultimate authority for budgetary matters in the hands of unelected bureaucrats at OMB, GAO, and CBO who don't directly represent the will of the people."[71] To Congressman Henry Hyde (R-Ill.), "the vice of Gramm-Rudman is it confines to a mindless, unfeeling, unthinking, bloodless formula the judgments—the sensitive, hard judgments—that we were elected to make. When we go to voters and say, 'Trust us. We'll exercise our judgment based on our conscience and our experience,' and then we lateral over to a computer the judgments on defense and on so many important issues, that is cowardice, and I cannot buy it."[72] Congressman Peter Rodino (D-N.J.) believed the legislation to be unconstitutional because it would "deprive the Congress, the peoples' most directly elected Representatives, of substantial governing authority—establishing a radical precedent that will invite further erosion of Congress' constitutionally delegated powers."[73] In the Senate, Robert C. Byrd remarked that "this process represents the most significant abdication of the responsibility of Congress to determine the fiscal priorities of the Nation that I have seen in my 33 years on Capitol Hill."[74] Nevertheless, the conference report was agreed to by the House, 271 to 154, and by the Senate, 61 to 31.[75]

The three-judge court held that the delegation of certain executive powers to the comptroller general, who is appointed by the president with the advice and consent of the Senate but removable by a joint resolution of Congress, was unconstitutional.[76] That ruling was affirmed by the Supreme Court.[77] Fundamentally, Congress could not give executive powers to an agent of Congress.

Spending Caps

In 1990, both branches agreed to abandon fixed deficit targets. They now turned toward caps on spending, with the hope that deficits would decline over the years. The agreement by President Bush to raise taxes as part of the 1990 pack-

---

BOX 27

Abdicating Spending Decisions

[Congressman Henry Waxman (D-Calif.)]: There is only one reason why a proposition so irresponsible has come so far: Because all of us are scared to death of being labelled as having voted against a balanced budget.

All of Gramm-Rudman comes down to this one political fear, the fear of the big lie against us in our next campaign. Majorities of each House are afraid that opponents might use this vote to confuse the issues so badly that we might not be able to explain that the Gramm-Rudman sham is itself unbalanced.

I am sad that the Congress thinks so little of itself. It is our job to look at each Government effort—each tax incentive, each subsidy, each grant—to evaluate its success, and to choose to continue it, revise it, or end it. It's politically painful work, especially in a time of limited public resources, but it should be done.

But rather than facing up to this responsibility, we are today adopting Government by automatic pilot. We are establishing a financial doomsday machine that will make our choices for us and that will be beyond our control. . . .

This is a shameful bill. It is unworthy of this House. It is unworthy of the trust that the American people have placed in us. We are betraying this trust by handing our jobs over to bureaucrats, triggers, and automatic decisions. . . .

We cannot delegate our authority to make laws to CBO or OMB or GAO or even to the president. The drafters of the Constitution most fundamentally wanted the voters to have a say in who makes laws and wanted the voters to be able to get to these elected representatives.

Source: 131 *Cong. Rec.* 36075 (1985).

---

age became a key factor in his defeat in 1992. The following year, President Clinton proposed a package of spending cuts and revenue increases to control deficits, and federal deficits finally started to decline. In 1997, Clinton and Congress agreed to another budget deal, providing for a modest tax cut (the first since 1981) and extending the spending caps on discretionary spending. As part of the agreement, Clinton received an additional $33 billion in new domestic spending. With these successive actions and a healthy economy, fiscal 1998 actually closed with a small surplus.

Spending caps signal many things. They are meant to demonstrate discipline and constraint, but they also reveal that lawmakers have no faith in the regular legislative process or the budget statute of 1974. Arbitrary ceilings are set well in advance of congressional action on appropriations bills and entitlement legislation. If members remain under the caps, they can claim that they lived within established boundaries. But if caps are set at generous levels (as they have been), they invite spending that might not have occurred. Caps encourage legislators to spend up to the limit. If the Appropriations Committees were to report bills below the caps, pressure would build for floor amendments to spend whatever the caps allow. To avoid these floor fights, the Appropriations Committee have an incentive to report bills that touch but do not exceed the caps.

Caps can be broken if Congress feels a need to. Exceptions are allowed for "emergency spending," and just what constitutes an emergency depends on how much political support there is for a program. In 1998, in the rush to complete the budget, both Congress and President Clinton agreed to about $21 billion in emergency spending beyond the levels set by caps. The same practice continued in 1999. "Emergency spending" was allowed for such programs as emergency farm disaster, the war in Yugoslavia, and natural disasters. Ironically, "emergency spending" was also assigned to funding for the 2000 census, although ever since the Constitution of 1787 we have required a census every ten years. In 1999 the spending cap was exceeded by $37 billion.

The spending ceilings of 1990, 1993, and 1997 have some parallels to Gramm-Rudman. All of these statutes attempted to create specific targets years in advance, creating both expectations and disappointments. Although the failures of the spending caps have not been as serious as with Gramm-Rudman, there are some similarities: (1) trying to predict several years in advance what will happen, instead of dealing with budget issues year by year, and (2) having to play statistical games to satisfy preordained numbers. The result is greater cynicism about the budget process and less confidence that the regular legislative and political system can be relied on. For both Gramm-Rudman and the spending ceilings, there was an apparent lack of faith that a future Congress would have the political judgment and courage to make the right choices. Yet what makes the lawmakers of one Congress (the Congress setting the limits) so much smarter and responsible than the lawmakers subject to those limits?

Spending ceilings and deficit limits depend on technical computations called "baselines," which are projections of budget outcomes. Definitions of baselines have changed over the years, moving from "current services" to "current law" to "current policy," but they can be manipulated to make a spending increase look like a "cut" and to project deficit "reductions" when the deficit actually increases. Technical adjustments to baselines easily confuse the press and the public and make elected officials look responsible and accountable when they are not.[78]

Momentum Builds for an Item Veto

Because of the phenomenal increase in deficits in the 1980s, members of Congress began to debate measures to increase the president's power to rescind (cancel) appropriated funds. What a strange development. Because the president had submitted an irresponsible budget proposal in 1981 that led to intolerable annual deficits, Congress decided to reward the president with additional powers.

In this push to augment executive power, constitutional requirements and legislative prerogatives were of marginal interest. In 1984, Senator Mack Mattingly (R-Ga.) offered an amendment to give the president item-veto authority over appropriations bills. He proposed an override vote of a majority of each chamber rather than the two-thirds required by the Constitution.[79] After Senator Lawton Chiles (D-Fla.) voiced concern about "rewriting the Constitution" by statute, Senator Alan Dixon (R-Ill.) admitted that "as a lawyer, I have some difficulty about the constitutional viability of this approach."[80] Dixon nevertheless wanted to dispose of the constitutional issue this way: "it is for the courts, not the Senate. Nobody knows, because the courts have never ruled. . . . It comes down, then, to the question of whether this is a good idea." Bottom line: let judges wrestle with the constitutional issue.

Senator Pete Domenici (R-N.M.) disagreed that "something as patently unconstitutional as this ought to be passed" and tossed to the courts for resolution. Senator John Stennis (D-Miss.) noted that the Mattingly amendment failed to touch the "top, side, or bottom of the real Constitution that we have and live under." Senate Majority Leader Howard Baker (R-Tenn.) remarked that "we are attempting to deal with a constitutional issue in a statutory form."[81]

At that point, Chiles raised a point of order "that the bill is legislation which changes the Constitution of the United States."[82] Following Senate precedents, the Chair submitted the question to the Senate. Before the question could be debated, however, Mattingly moved to table the point of order. That tactic failed by the remarkably narrow margin of 45 to 46. During debate on the point of order, Baker said that just as the Supreme Court could review and pass on the enactments of Congress, "it is equally true, and the precedent is just as old, that the Senate of the United States must first exercise its own judgment as to whether a matter before it conforms with or violates the Constitution."[83] With regard to claims that courts had not yet ruled on the statutory grant of item-veto power to the president, Chiles remarked that the question "is so clear that no court, from a justice of the peace on, has ever had to rule on it."[84] Dixon responded that the law is "unsettled" and that the "only question is whether we have the courage to let the Supreme Court of the United States decide. This Senate is not the place where 100 separate Senators make that kind of judicial decision . . . ." How did it take courage to duck an issue and shove it to courts?

Senator Slade Gorton (R-Wash.) found the arguments in favor of the amendment "profoundly disturbing" because none of the proponents seemed to believe that the proposal was constitutional.[85] He chided Dixon and Mattingly for failing to do the necessary legal analysis (see box 28). Senator Paul Sarbanes (D-Md.), siding with Gorton and Chiles, agreed that there had been no prior litigation on the proposal because it was "patently unconstitutional." He offered this analogy:

> Suppose someone submitted a legislative proposal to change the term of the President to 2 years, or the Senate to four, or the House to three. Suppose I put in that legislative proposal; then say, well, the Supreme Court has never ruled on this question. . . .
>
> What happens to our own responsibility to make a judgment to uphold the Constitution, and make a judgment with respect to whether a proposition before us has any slim claim to constitutional validity? . . .

Senator Dale Bumpers (D-Ark.) supported Sarbanes by commenting: "Each one of us held up our hand, took the oath of office, and said we will uphold the Constitution of the United States. There was no caveat. You did not say, 'I will uphold the Constitution of the United States only on those cases where precedent is well-established.' You did not say, 'I will uphold the Constitution unless something is presented to the Senate that the Court has never ruled on, in which case I will vote for it so the Supreme Court can rule.'" The Senate rejected the Mattingly amendment, voting 56 to 34 in favor of Chiles's point of order.[86]

President Reagan pressed repeatedly for an item veto.[87] In his State of the Union message in 1988, he objected to the large "mega bills" that Congress had sent him: a continuing resolution and a reconciliation bill. He told legislators

---

BOX 28

Gorton on the Constitutional Oath

[Y]ou swore an oath, as I did, when you became Members of this body to uphold the Constitution of the United States. You cannot hide behind the fact that the Supreme Court of the United States has final authority on constitutional questions. You cannot hide behind that proposition to ignore your own duty properly to interpret the Constitution, which you have inherited after 200 years of history. It is your duty to make a judgment as to whether or not this amendment is constitutional.

If you can in good faith say you believe that it is, you can vote in the way which the Senator from Illinois has made a claim. But to duck your responsibility on the ground that sometime, at some future date, the Supreme Court will have final authority over the question is to ignore your oath which you swore when you became a Member of this body.

Source: 130 *Cong. Rec.* 10862 (1984).

---

that if he had an item veto he would have deleted funds for cranberry research, blueberry research, the study of crawfish, and the commercialization of wildflowers.[88] Watching this address at home, I knew that projects of that size would not be in bills presented to the president and that Reagan could not have "item vetoed" them. At work the next day, I checked the conference report and found $92,000 for blueberry research, $260,000 for cranberry research, $50,000 for the wildflowers, but looked in vain for the study of crawfish. The report did mention $660,000 for aquaculture, with $200,000 set aside for "research in Louisiana." I called the House appropriations subcommittee and asked whether those words referred to a crawfish study. The staffer confirmed that they did. At a time when federal deficits were running about $200 billion a year, President Reagan identified four projects with a grand total of $602,000.

More important than this nickel-and-dime scenario, Reagan misled the nation about what he could do. Had he possessed the kind of item veto that governors had (and that he had asked for), he could not have canceled the four programs. They were not in the bills presented to him. A president cannot veto what is not in front of him. The four programs were listed elsewhere in the conference report and legislative history. A governor's item veto would not have reached them.

I called a friend at OMB and asked how they could have allowed Reagan to appear so misinformed and confused in a nationally televised address. I was told that the White House had farmed out that section of the speech to a public relations firm, which gleefully discovered the blueberries and other items, believing them to be eye-catchers for the public. The public relations firm lacked the knowledge about the budgetary process to know the difference between what could be item vetoed and what could not. Here is an abdication by the White House to a private agency.

Inherent Item Veto

Some members of Congress encouraged Presidents Reagan and Bush to exercise an "inherent item veto." Under this curious theory, the Constitution—ever since 1789—has included an item veto, although no one noticed it until the 1980s. The idea was first publicized by Stephen Glazier, who wrote an op-ed piece in the *Wall Street Journal* in 1987, entitled "Reagan Already Has Line-Item Veto." Glazier insisted that a line-item veto was justified because Congress had resorted to passing "omnibus" bills that eroded the president's original veto power. Faced with the "bunching up" of disparate provisions, the president could act in self-defense to veto individual items. He could "unbunch" bills by vetoing line items and riders. Glazier argued that because no president had ever asserted this power, "the courts have never had an opportunity to bless the action."[89]

There is actually nothing new about "omnibus" appropriations bills and nothing new about riders. The first appropriations bill, enacted on September 29, 1789, included $216,000 for the civil list, $137,000 for the Department of War, $190,000 to discharge warrants issued by the previous Board of Treasury, and $96,000 to pay the pensions for invalids.[90] That was it. Four lump-sum dollar amounts for the whole of government, covering only thirteen lines in the U.S. Statutes. President Washington received the bill in that form: take it or leave it. A similar omnibus appropriation bill was enacted on March 26, 1790.[91]

Lawmakers in the First Congress, many of them having served as delegates to the Philadelphia Convention, obviously saw no constitutional problems in "bunching up" a number of subjects and combining them to form a single bill. President Washington never protested that his general veto power was eviscerated by these omnibus bills. Writing to Edmund Randolph on September 23, 1793, Washington stated his understanding of the veto power: "From the nature of the Constitution, I must approve all the parts of a Bill, or reject it in toto."[92]

Omnibus appropriations bills continued. In 1794, Congress split appropriations into two bills: one for the general government and the other for the military.[93] After the establishment of a separate Department of Navy in 1798, Congress acted on three appropriations bills: one for the general government and separate ones for the army and the navy.[94] The contemporary practice of passing thirteen appropriations bills is relatively "un-omnibus" compared to these precedents.

Nor was there anything new about appropriations riders. On August 13, 1787, the delegates to the constitutional convention debated the procedure for passing tax bills in the House and allowing amendments in the Senate. George Mason expressed concern that the Senate might introduce "the practice of tacking foreign matter to money bills."[95] Thomas Jefferson's *Manual of Parliamentary Practice,* prepared during the years of his vice presidency from 1797 to 1801, also referred to the custom of adding nongermane amendments to bills: "Amendments may be made so as totally to alter the nature of the proposition; and it is a way of getting rid of a proposition by making it bear a sense different from what it was intended by the movers, so that they vote against it themselves."[96]

Some lawmakers, responding to Glazier's thesis, thought it would be a good idea to embrace the inherent item veto and see what happened. Senator Bob Dole (R-Kans.), running for president in 1988, said that although no president had used the power, "it might be worth a try." If it meant provoking a constitutional test when he received a bill "larded with fat, I will do it. Then we'll let the courts decide."[97] Dole's presidential bid failed, but other legislators also found the idea appealing. Senator William V. Roth (R-Del.) and Congressman Chalmers P. Wylie (R-Ohio) urged President Reagan to use the inherent item veto.[98] Instead of protecting their own power, these legislators were willing to give it away unless the courts decided to return it.

In 1988, an all-day conference was held to examine the merits of an inherent item veto. I was among the majority of the speakers who threw cold water on the notion of an inherent item veto. Charles J. Cooper, who had headed the Office of Legal Counsel in the Department of Justice, could find nothing in the constitutional text, structure, or history to support this idea. Members of the audience stirred uneasily, wondering how a conference sponsored by two conservative groups could backfire in this manner. The last speaker was Robert Bork. Surely he would come to the rescue, but Bork also found the idea without merit. He said it was a strange argument that a constitutional power would sit around, unnoticed, for two hundred years.[99] Cooper authored a lengthy Justice Department memo, finding no support for an inherent item veto.[100]

By 1991, the idea of an inherent item veto had attracted the support of four senators and forty-eight House members. They urged President Bush to try the item veto and provoke a test case in court.[101] However, in 1992, Bush announced that his constitutional advisers had convinced him that there was no legal support for an inherent item veto: "our able Attorney General [William Barr], in whom I have full confidence, and my trusted White House Counsel [C. Boyden Gray], backed up by legal opinions from most of the legal scholars, feel that I do not have that line-item veto authority. And this opinion was shared by the Attorney General in the previous administration."[102]

The controversy continued into the Clinton administration. In 1994, the Senate Judiciary Committee held hearings on a bill expressing the sense of the Senate that the president "currently has authority under the Constitution to veto individual items of appropriation and that the President should exercise that authority without awaiting the enactment of additional authorization."[103] The sponsor of this legislation, Senator Arlen Specter (R-Pa.), argued that the notion of an inherent item veto was one "on which reasonable minds could differ," and, that being the case, why not submit it to the Supreme Court and have the dispute settled there?[104]

Basic message: members of Congress should transfer legislative power to the president and see whether courts will return the power to Congress (see box 29). However, each branch is supposed to protect its own prerogatives. The framers did not expect Congress to surrender legislative power to the president and wait for a judicial ruling to decide the matter.[105]

GAO's Study

In January, 1992, the General Accounting Office released a report that claimed that if President Reagan possessed an item veto, he could have saved up to $70 billion over a six-year period.[106] Senator Robert C. Byrd, chairman of the Appropriations Committee, was furious at GAO for initiating and releasing the report. He wondered why GAO, as a legislative agency, "would allow itself to be used to stick a knife in the back of the Congress."[107] Reflecting on all his years in Congress, Byrd concluded: "that is the weakest report that I have seen from the General Accounting Office—shabby. It is fatally flawed."[108]

Senator Byrd asked me to evaluate the GAO study. Drawing on the same set of data used by GAO, I concluded that a more realistic and more useful estimate of savings over the six-year period would be $2–3 billion and probably less. I also cautioned that a president, armed with an item veto, could use that leverage to force a quid pro quo that would retain a legislator's project in return for an expensive White House priority, pushing spending up.[109]

BOX 29
Specter Invites a Test Case

. . . after extensive legal research and analysis, I now urge the
President to exercise the line-item veto without further legislative action. I do so because I believe, after a careful review of the historical
record, that the President already has the authority under the Constitution to veto individual items of appropriation in an appropriations bill
and that neither an amendment to the Constitution nor legislation
granting enhanced rescission authority is necessary.

. . . the President's use of the line-item veto will almost certainly
engender a court challenge if the veto is not overridden. The courts will
then decide whether the Constitution authorizes the line-item veto. If
they find it does, then the matter will be settled. If they find it does
not, then Congress may revisit the issue and decide whether to amend
the Constitution or grant statutory enhanced rescission authority to
the President.

Source: 140 *Cong. Rec.* 6429, 6431 (1994).

After my analysis, Comptroller General Bowsher wrote to Senator Byrd,
acknowledging that actual savings over the six years would have been much
less than the theoretically maximum potential savings GAO had projected. In
fact, such savings could have been "close to zero." Bowsher admitted that one
could conceive of situations in which the "net effect of item veto power would
be to increase spending," because presidents intent on building legislative support for their own spending programs could back programs or projects favored
by senators and representatives. He regretted highlighting the $70 billion fig-
ure and contributing to a "misleading impression."[110] Although GAO backed
away from its report, it would be cited by Congress four years later as support
for giving the president an item veto.

Rescission Reforms

From 1985 to 1995, Congress held a series of hearings to explore different ways
of granting the president some form of expanded impoundment power. During that period I testified nine times on every variety of item-veto authority:

separate enrollment, constitutional amendments, the inherent item veto, expedited rescission, and enhanced rescission. With this array of options, it wasn't unusual for lawmakers to confuse one term with another (particularly expedited and enhanced rescission).

In 1992, 1993, and 1994, the House of Representatives passed legislation to make it easier for the president to rescind funds. Instead of allowing Congress to ignore the president's rescission proposals, "expedited rescission" would require at least one House to vote on the president's recommendations.[111] In debating these measures, lawmakers indulged in institutional self-flagellation. On the issue of transferring the item veto to the president, House Minority Leader Bob Michel (R-Ill.) said he would be asked: "Bob, why would you give up your legislative authority to an all-powerful chief executive?" His response: "Because we have loused it up here in the Congress. That is why."[112]

Expedited rescission attracted support partly because some legislators recognized that it would shift less power to the president than a full-fledged item veto. Even so, the debate on expedited rescission gave lawmakers another opportunity to pummel their own institution. Congressman Harris Fawell (R-Ill.) told opponents of the bill that Congress "is like an alcoholic being denied his power to drink himself to death. Congress feels it has got to continue to imbibe in overspending. One of these days I expect somebody over there will snap and say, 'Stop me before I spend again.'"[113]

Some legislators spoke more realistically about the interest that both branches have in spending federal funds. Presidents have their own lists of favored programs. Congressman Jim Slattery, Democrat of Kansas, supported expedited rescission but cautioned that item-veto authority would shift power to the president and make it easier for presidents to fund programs they wanted (see box 30). Congressman David Price, Democrat of North Carolina, noted that presidents "almost always ask for more money than Congress is willing to appropriate." During the previous twelve years, Presidents Reagan and Bush had requested nearly $60 billion more than Congress was willing to appropriate.[114]

The Senate took no action on the expedited rescission bills passed by the House. Instead, they voted on a separate reform, called "enhanced rescission." Under this procedure, the president's rescission proposal would become law unless Congress disapproved. The president could veto the disapproval resolution, forcing Congress to muster a two-thirds majority in each House to override the president.[115] Senator McCain (R-Ariz.), one of the proponents of enhanced rescission, pointed to the discredited GAO study as partial justification for delegating greater power to the president.[116] He added: "given Congress' predilection for pork barrel spending, omnibus spending bills and

BOX 30

Slatterly on Presidential Pork

Any suggestion that this legislation is not going to change the way this body does business is dead wrong. This gives the President an important new power. And I must confess that I have a deep concern about preserving the balance of power between the executive and legislative branches of Government. I believe that every Member of this body that has taken an oath of office to defend the Constitution should be concerned about our balance of powers. . . .

I have spent hundreds of hours trying to kill the B-2 bomber and hundreds of hours trying to kill the super collider. Both projects wanted by President Bush and President Reagan. They wanted to spend the money. I wanted to stop spending the money.

Now, had those presidents had line-item veto power, they could have come to me and said, "Congressman, back off of your effort to kill those spending projects or I am going to line item everything in an appropriation bill that has something to do with Kansas."

Source: 139 *Cong. Rec.* 8525 (1993).

continuing resolutions, it would seem only prudent and constitutional to provide the President with functional veto power. . . . It should be self-evident to all Senators that controlling spending is something that the Congress is completely unable to do."[117]

Senator Byrd, a steadfast opponent of transferring any form of item-veto power to the president, offered a lengthy address in which he set forth the governing constitutional principles.[118] Under the procedure followed in the Senate, the McCain amendment required 60 votes to waive a provision of the Budget Act. The vote on the amendment was 44 to 54.[119] A year later McCain's amendment attracted a vote of 45 to 52.[120]

A rescission battle in 1992 between President Bush and Congress illustrates how both branches participate in "pork-barrel" spending. Running for reelection, Bush hoped to put Congress on the defensive by proposing the rescission of funds for seemingly frivolous programs, including asparagus research, celery research, prickly pear research, Vidalia onion storage, and manure disposal.[121] He thought the names of these federally funded programs would be so laughable and indefensible that legislators would be forced to support him. A series of proposals from Bush brought the total rescission request to $7.9 billion.

If Bush wanted to play fun and games, Congress was ready. Senator Byrd put the White House on notice that there "is plenty of 'pork' . . . at the other end of Pennsylvania Avenue."[122] Congress began to search for silly-sounding programs promoted by the executive branch, ranging from a study of the significance of holism in German-speaking society to a $94,000 study of why people fear going to the dentist. "Any child who has to go to the dentist will tell you why he fears the dentist," Byrd said. "It hurts."[123]

Congress accepted some of the Bush proposals but substituted other cuts in programs favored by the administration. Just as Bush felt that some legislative programs were wasteful and "pork," Congress reached similar judgments about executive-approved projects, including National Science Foundation research grants for "monogamy and aggression in fish in Nicaragua; the well-being of middle-class lawyers; status attainment in Chinese urban areas; sexual mimicry of swallowtail butterflies; and song production in freely behaving birds."[124] Congress came up with a list of $8.2 billion in rescissions, which were enacted into law. After this political blood-letting, Bush abandoned his rescission strategy.

Line Item Veto Act

With the Republican victories in the 1994 elections and the drafting of the "Contract with America" by House Republicans, Congress had the votes and the legislative platform to pass even stronger item-veto powers for the president. Instead of "expedited rescission," House Republicans supported the version of item-veto authority that would transfer greater power to the president: "enhanced rescission." After a bill became law, the president would recommend rescissions and those proposals would become law within twenty days unless Congress disapproved by bill or joint resolution. The president could veto the disapproval bill, forcing Congress to muster a two-thirds majority in each House to override the veto.[125]

Enhanced rescission reversed the power relationship between Congress and the president. The 1974 statute put the burden on the president, within a specified number of days, to convince Congress to rescind funds. Under the new Republican version, presidential rescissions would take effect unless Congress disapproved the president and overrode a veto.

On January 12, 1995, the House Committee on Government Reform and Oversight and the Senate Committee on Governmental Affairs held joint hearings to consider enhanced rescission. Senator Dan Coats (R-Ind.), a strong proponent of the item veto, singled Congress out for rebuke. He argued that presidential power had to be increased to compensate for legislative irresponsibility. Congress "cannot discipline itself. . . . [It] is selfish and greedy and out of touch with the American people [and] cannot put the national interest ahead of parochial interests or special interests."[126]

Later in the hearings, Congressman John Spratt (D-S.C.) asked OMB Director Alice Rivlin how much she thought was "wasteful and unwarranted" in bills submitted to the president, and how much he "could realistically glean out of a bill, how much can we reduce the deficit if the President has this scalpel, this instrument in his control?" She replied: "I would think that it would be a relatively small proportion of discretionary spending that would be a candidate for a line-item veto."[127] She told another member of Congress: "I don't believe that this would be a large dollar figure. It is likely to be a relatively small percentage of total spending."[128]

CBO Director Robert Reischauer agreed that the item veto would not produce much in savings. The impact would be quite different: giving presidential spending a preference over congressional spending. Evidence at the state level "suggests that the item veto has not been used primarily to hold down overall State spending, but rather it has been used by Governors to substitute their priorities for those of the legislatures." Experience at the national level convinced Reischauer that presidents would like item-veto authority to direct greater resources to their own spending agenda.[129]

Floor Debate

The enhanced rescission bill passed the House in February, 1995.[130] One Republican claimed that the legislation had the backing of 70 percent of the American public, who "are fed up with pork-barrel spending by this Congress."[131] Another Republican charged that Congress "has proved incapable of making the tough decisions."[132] The bill picked up support from both sides of the aisle. A Democrat remarked that Congress "has not responsibly exercised the power of the purse for years. We have been downright irresponsible with this power."[133]

The Senate wrestled with two strategies: enhanced rescission, as advocated by Senator McCain, and expedited rescission, supported by Senator Dominici. The committees of jurisdiction—Senate Budget and Senate Governmental Affairs—couldn't decide which version to recommend, so they reported both versions.[134] It looked like the bills would go to the floor and be fought over until one prevailed.

Just as that was about to happen, the Senate defeated the balanced budget amendment. It fell short by a single vote because of Senator Mark Hatfield's opposition. Comparisons were drawn between Speaker Newt Gingrich's ability to move the item-veto bill through the House quickly and the difficulty that Senate Majority Leader Bob Dole had in controlling events in his chamber. About to announce for the presidency, Dole did not want another bloody conflict among Republicans. As Senator McCain said, "The spectacle of Republicans fighting Republicans is not what we had in mind November 8th" when the Republicans took both Houses of Congress.[135]

The McCain and Domenici bills were yanked in favor of a substitute that had been considered and rejected a decade back: "separate enrollment." This procedure would convert the present thirteen appropriations bills into about ten thousand bills. A committee report from Senate Governmental Affairs patiently and painstakingly explained that the itemization of bills at the state level ($2,000 for this, $2,500 for that) made no sense at the federal level.[136] Congress passes lump-sum appropriations to give agencies greater latitude to move money around in the middle of a fiscal year to respond to changing circumstances.

With separate enrollment, a clerk would take an appropriations bill after it had passed both Houses and break it into separate paragraphs, sections, and numbers, with each part made into a bill and presented to the president. This procedure would yield thousands and thousands of bills, restricting agencies to comparatively small amounts and preventing them from shifting funds over the course of a fiscal year. No committee hearings had been held to analyze this proposal and no committee report explained its reach. The Senate, anxious to pass something, embraced separate enrollment.[137]

When a bill passes both Houses in different forms, conferees are appointed quickly to work out a compromise. Republicans were slow to go to conference on the item-veto bills because they were reluctant to give President Clinton, in the middle of a presidential election year, authority he could exploit for political and partisan reasons (which is what he, or any other president, would do). However, by not acting, Republicans were vulnerable to the charge that if they were so eager to grant the president an item veto, why weren't they going to conference?

The logjam broke in 1996. Dole, now a declared candidate for president, wanted to display his leadership abilities by getting a bill through Congress.[138] Under these pressures, the bill popped out of conference. Interestingly, one of the arguments in the conference report was the defective GAO report that claimed that a presidential item veto could save $70 billion over a six-year period.[139] During floor debate, Senator McCain also cited the $70 billion figure, as did Congressman John Duncan (R-Tenn.).[140] Evidently, whenever a study is released to the public it remains in the intellectual stream forever, even when the authors repudiate their own product. Killed by its creator, the GAO study had a life of its own.

The conferees agreed basically on the House version: enhanced rescission. The new law put the burden on Congress to disapprove presidential rescission proposals within a thirty-day period. Along with rescission of discretionary appropriations, the president could cancel any new item of direct spending (entitlements) and certain limited tax benefits. Even supporters of the item veto bill recognized the breadth of power being transferred from Congress to the president. Senator Ted Stevens (R-Ala.), chairman of the Appropriations Committee, called the bill "the most significant delegation of authority by the Congress to the President since the Constitution was ratified in 1789."[141] Clinton received the bill and signed into law the Line Item Veto Act of 1996.[142]

Clinton's Item Vetoes

The Line Item Veto Act, enacted on April 9, 1996, did not take effect until January 1, 1997. To ease its passage, the conferees decided that Clinton should not have access to this authority during the 1996 presidential election. When Clinton was reelected and exercised the item veto, it had a relatively small effect on the federal budget. The total savings, over a five-year period, came to less than $600 million. His cancellations for fiscal year 1998 were about $355 million out of a total budget of $1.7 billion.[143] The totals would have been somewhat higher had Clinton's original recommendations become law. Congress disapproved one of the cancellation packages and the administration reversed itself on another package after conceding that it lacked authority to do what it did.

On October 6, 1997, Clinton used his item-veto authority to cancel thirty-eight projects in the military construction appropriations bill. Estimating that the cancellations would save nearly $290 million over a five-year period, he identified three criteria that supposedly guided the selections: (1) the Defense Department concluded that the projects were not a priority at this time, (2) they did not make an immediate contribution to the housing, education, recreation, child care, health, or religious life of the military service, and (3) they would not have been built in fiscal year 1998 in any event.[144]

The selections came under heavy fire. The Senate Appropriations Committee held hearings and took testimony from the Air Force, Navy, and Army. The military witnesses testified that the canceled projects were mission-essential and could be commenced in 1998.[145] On October 30, the Senate voted 69 to 30 to disapprove the cancellations. The bipartisan opposition to Clinton's action was strong, Republicans voting 42 to 12 and Democrats 27 to 18 for the disapproval resolution. On November 8, the House voted 352 to 64 for the disapproval resolution. The party split: 193 to 23 for Republicans and 158 to 41 for Democrats. A House Independent also voted for the resolution. Clinton vetoed the disapproval resolution but was easily overridden, the House voting 347 to 69 and the Senate 78 to 20.

Also reversed, by the administration itself, was a Clinton cancellation that involved the federal retirement system, affecting employees who elected to switch from the Civil Service Retirement System (CSRS) to the Federal Employees Retirement System (FERS). Clinton claimed that the action would save $854 million over five years. The proposal never made much sense, legally. It was reported as a cancellation of discretionary budget authority. Every other cancellation of this type showed estimated savings in budget *outlays*. The FERS proposal, instead, showed "receipt changes." If there had been a cancellation of budget authority, there should have been outlay savings.

Clinton's action was immediately challenged by Congress. Senator Stevens, chairman of the Appropriations Committee, and Senator Domenici, chairman of the Budget Committee, both agreed that the change in the FERS policy did not constitute "budget authority."[146] Clinton later recanted on the issue. Administration officials admitted that he did not have the authority to use item-veto authority against the retirement program.[147]

Clinton offered some interesting explanations for his relatively modest use of cancellation authority. With regard to items of new direct spending (entitlements), out of many eligible candidates he canceled only one. The record is similar with "limited tax benefits" that assist one hundred or fewer taxpayers. Out of seventy-nine opportunities to veto those items, he canceled two. Clinton explained that thirty of the tax items had been recommended by the Treasury Department to fix flaws in current law, and another dozen or more were put in by Congress by agreement with Treasury to fix other procedural problems.[148] Reporters were puzzled by this limited use of item-veto authority. Why did Clinton not eliminate more of what—in the words of one reporter—"sounds like the very definition of a special interest goodie"? Clinton explained: "Well, it's certainly the definition of a special interest group, but not all special interests are always in conflict with the general interest. If that were true, our country would not have survived for over 200 years."[149] Put another way, a limited tax benefit is a special interest if a legislator wants it and a matter of general interest if the president wants it.

While it is true that Clinton made modest use of cancellation authority, the political impact of the statute was not modest. Far more damaging to legislative prerogatives was the message that Congress sent in enacting this law: "We are irresponsible and unable to control ourselves. We need to depend on the president to protect the national interest." The abdication of spirit and institutional self-respect was much greater than the transfer of statutory authority.

Punting to the Courts (II)

As though uncertain about the legality of their own handiwork, members of Congress included in the Line Item Veto Act a procedure allowing for expedited review in the courts for challenges that the statute violated the Constitution.[150] Senator Byrd, an opponent of the bill, objected to this procedure as well. Congress, he said, should resolve constitutional issues within its own chambers rather than shifting them to the courts (see box 31).

Other legislators expected the Supreme Court to protect legislative prerogatives. Marge Roukema (R-N.J.) said she was convinced "that the Supreme Court of the United States will save this Congress from itself."[151] Bill Clinger, Republican from Pennsylvania and chairman of the House committee with jurisdiction over the item-veto bill, offered this response to those who objected that the bill was unconstitutional: "It is not really our job to determine what is constitutional or what is not unconstitutional [*sic*]."[152]

In 1997, a district court held that the Line Item Veto Act was unconstitutional because it violated the legislative procedures set forth in Article I.[153] On appeal, the Supreme Court ruled that the plaintiffs (members of Congress) lacked standing to bring the case.[154] The following year, a district judge found standing for private plaintiffs and held the statute unconstitutional; the Supreme Court affirmed.[155] Speaking for the Court, Justice John Paul Stevens held that the Line Item Veto Act violated the Presentment Clause by departing from the "finely wrought" constitutional procedures established for the enactment of law. He said that the cancellation authority represented the repeal of law that could be accomplished only through the regular legislative process, including bicameralism and presentment. As a result of this litigation, legislative and spending prerogatives were returned to Congress, but not because legislators were willing to defend their own institution. It took another branch to do the constitutional analysis that Congress should have performed by itself.

That is not the end of the story. In their dissents, Justices Antonin Scalia and Stephen Breyer pointed to other statutory methods that could give the president some semblance of item-veto authority, without raising any of the

BOX 31

Byrd Objects to Expedited Review

Constitutional problems in the bill? Proponents say not to worry. Section 3 authorizes expedited review of constitutional challenges. Any member of Congress or any individual adversely affected by the item veto bill may bring an action, in the U.S. District Court for the District of Columbia, for declaratory judgment and injunctive relief on the ground that a provision violates the Constitution. . . .

Evidently the authors of this legislation had substantial concern about the constitutionality of their handiwork. A provision for expedited review to resolve constitutional issues is not boilerplate in most bills. You may remember that when we included a provision for expedited review in the Gramm-Rudman-Hollings Act of 1985, the result was a Supreme Court opinion that held that the procedure giving the Comptroller General the power to determine sequestration of funds violated the Constitution.

Why are we trying to pass a bill that raises such serious and substantial constitutional questions? We should be resolving these questions on our own. All of us take an oath of office to support and defend the Constitution. During the process of considering a bill, it is our duty to identify—and correct—constitutional problems. . . . It is irresponsible to simply punt to the courts, hoping that the judiciary will somehow catch our mistakes.

Source: 142 *Cong. Rec.* S2942–43 (daily ed. Mar. 27, 1996).

constitutional issues that were identified by the district court or the Supreme Court. Justice Scalia pointed to earlier statutes, never before challenged, that appropriated to the president sums "not exceeding" specified amounts.[156] Presidents, exercising this discretionary authority, could spend the full amount or less than the full amount. As Scalia noted: "The short of the matter is this: Had the Line Item Veto Act authorized the President to 'decline to spend' any item of spending contained in the Balanced Budget Act of 1997, there is not the slightest doubt that authorization would have been constitutional."[157] Justice Breyer, joined by Justices Sandra Day O'Connor and Scalia, described another permissible approach. Congress can vote funds for a particular activity unless the president determines, and so certifies, that the expenditure would not be in the national interest.[158] There are many such precedents.

If Congress wants to transfer to the president discretionary authority over the level of federal expenditures, there are many constitutional ways of doing that. Enactment of these proposals, however, would come at a cost. They continue to send a not very subtle message that members of Congress are chronically and incurably irresponsible in exercising the spending power and must rely on the finer, nobler instincts of the president to delete wasteful programs and projects. That picture of our political institutions is not supported by what we know about the two branches. It is too demeaning to Congress (and representative government) and too flattering and reverential about the presidency.

In the years following World War II, Congress revealed other uncertainties about its institutional purpose and capability. Functions that had been discharged from 1789 to 1950 now seemed increasingly difficult, prompting legislators to seek relief by novel statutory procedures or by amending the Constitution. Three examples are the chronic problems of raising federal pay and debate over constitutional amendments for a balanced budget and for term limits.

Congressional Pay

The Constitution provides that senators and representatives "shall receive a Compensation for their Services, to be ascertained by Law, and paid out of the Treasury of the United States." In implementing this provision, legislators throughout the nineteenth century and early twentieth century have found it awkward and excruciating to raise their own salaries, but that is what the Constitution requires.

Members of Congress often complained about the "delicate" task of setting their own pay levels. Many found it burdensome and embarrassing to act as judges in their own cause. Often their efforts backfired. For example, in 1816 Congress changed the compensation of legislators from $6 a day to $1,500 a session, making the new salary retroactive to cover the first session of the Fourteenth Congress. The increase came "at the close of a bloody and expensive war" with England.[159] After the elections of 1816, there was such agitation for repeal that Congress dutifully returned to the former per diem standard of $6 a day. One legislator noted that the compensation bill had excited more discontent than the Alien and Sedition Acts, the Quasi-War with France, the internal taxes of 1798, Jefferson's embargo, the War of 1812, the Treaty of Ghent, "or any one measure of the Government, from its existence."[160]

The ultimate in backdating occurred on March 3, 1873, the day before the Forty-second Congress adjourned. On that day the Congress raised the annual salary of a legislator to $7,500 and made the salary increase applicable to the whole of the Forty-second Congress. Each member thus received a $5,000 bonus or windfall for the two-year period. Adding to the controversy, the increase had been added as a rider to an appropriations bill instead of following the traditional (at that time) route of a legislative bill.

Within a year, Congress acted to repeal this pay increase. Members had a field day in denouncing the action of the Forty-second Congress. The Democratic Convention held in New York in October, 1873, adopted a resolution containing this language: "We condemn and denounce the salary grab, and all Congressmen, democratic or republican, who voted for it, or who have not renounced all share in plunder seized for a service already done and paid for."[161] The repeal law stated that all moneys appropriated as compensation for the members of the Forty-second Congress, in excess of the mileage and allowances fixed by law at the start of that Congress, "and which shall not have been drawn by the members of said Congress respectively, or which having been drawn, have been returned in any form to the United States, are hereby covered into the Treasury of the United States, and are declared to be the moneys of the United States absolutely, the same as if they had never been appropriated as aforesaid."[162]

These were gruesome experiences for legislators, but by one means or another they managed to raise their pay periodically from 1789 to the 1960s. Soon, however, they began to look for automatic increases that would not depend on legislative action. In 1967, Congress established a commission to recommend every four years the rates of compensation for members of Congress, justices of the Supreme Court, federal judges, and certain high-ranking government officials. The president, after receiving these recommendations, would submit to Congress his own proposals for salaries. They would take effect within thirty days unless disapproved by either House or replaced by a different salary schedule enacted into law. Legislation in 1970 adopted a similar scheme, allowing for increases in federal salaries unless either House disapproved within thirty days.[163]

Would these mechanisms remove the "politics" of pay adjustments? Not likely. The first report of the pay commission led to a pay increase in 1969. The second quadrennial report, submitted a year late, was defeated by Congress in 1974. Presidents Nixon and Ford, appealing to the country for spending constraints, repeatedly tried to delay salary increases or keep them below the line of comparability established by the pay commission. In 1972, Nixon's refusal to submit an alternative pay plan provoked a rebuke from an appellate court for violating the law.[164] By 1977, top executive officials, judges, and members of Congress had received only one raise.

Congressman Larry Pressler asked the courts to declare unconstitutional the statutory procedure for setting legislative compensation, arguing that the system of allowing salary adjustments without affirmative action by both Houses of Congress violated the Ascertainment Clause (legislators shall receive a compensation "to be ascertained by law"). A district court in 1976 decided that the constitutional meaning of "ascertain" was satisfied by the statutory procedure.[165]

The history of federal pay after 1976 found legislators entangled in painful rollcall votes and deft parliamentary maneuvers, writhing again and again over their compensation and the salaries of executive and judicial officials. The pay issue continued to dog Congress. In 1989, in one of his last official actions, President Reagan recommended a 51 percent salary hike for members of Congress. The huge increase was needed because regular (and more modest) pay increases had been repeatedly blocked by Congress. The increase was scheduled to take effect on February 8 unless both Houses voted to disapprove. Constituents and the media heaped scorn on lawmakers for seeking a salary increase without taking a vote. Having absorbed a public beating for several weeks, Congress created the worst of all worlds by deciding to disapprove the pay increase (not only for themselves but for all of government). Congressman Vic Fazio (D-Calif.), one of the few to vote for the pay raise, expressed regret at the inability of legislators to defend themselves (see box 32). The House and the Senate voted on February 7 to kill the pay raise.[166] So much for clever delegations and automatic procedures. Legislation enacted at the end of 1989 now requires Congress to approve, by recorded vote, pay increases.[167]

Balanced Budget Amendment

Throughout the 1980s and 1990s, members of Congress debated the merits of an amendment to the U.S. Constitution to require a "balanced budget." This proposal was another way to advertise that Congress is irresponsible and cannot be trusted. Instead of confronting and resolving fiscal problems within their own institution, lawmakers hoped to place coercive language in the Constitution to compel Congress to act responsibly. As Congressman Gerald Solomon (R-N.Y.) noted in 1995: "Madame Speaker, Congress has repeatedly shown that it is not prepared to deal responsibly with the problems without some kind of a prod. The enactment of a balanced budget amendment will help to give Congress—and this is the point—it will help to give Congress that prod, that

BOX 32

Fazio on Salary Increases

. . . if we are to have any success when we ultimately come to the floor with solutions to these problems, we are going to need more self-respect for ourselves and respect for the institution.

We are going to need to show some courage individually. We no longer are going to be in a position to hand this problem to some process or some person and assume it will be taken care of for us. We are going to have to venture something of ourselves if we are going to make any progress.

We are not going to be able to allow those among us who are candidates for Governor or Senator to demagog this issue at the expense of all the Members. We are not going to be able to allow the wealthy among us who really have nothing to gain from a pay raise like this to put the rest of us at a disadvantage, to burden us with arguments centered around the charge of greed.

Most of us, frankly, have not had the courage to speak out. We have not taken the opportunity to rebut those charges that have been made so carelessly in the media.

And the media in general did a very poor job. They provided, in some cases, biased coverage. We became cartoon cannon fodder for trash television and for talk radio, but we did not make our own case, even though we had more editorial and public interest support, including Common Cause, than we have ever had before. We fell prey to the deception of the rabble rousers. . . .

We can do it if we have the courage to try. If we fail, it will be our fault, and no one else's.

Source: 135 *Cong. Rec.* 1709 (1989).

spine, that backbone and, for some who need it, the excuse to do what the American people have to do, and that is to live within means."[168]

At first blush the idea of a balanced budget amendment may seem compelling, but closer scrutiny reveals a less attractive picture. The amendment would do little to balance the budget and do much to unbalance political institutions. It would increase presidential power and shift a number of fiscal and budgetary decisions to federal judges. In turn, it would weaken Congress and representative government and further erode public confidence in government. Citizens would discover what we have learned about state constitutional amendments for a balanced budget: They do not eliminate indebtedness.

Advocates of the balanced budget amendment promised a future of fiscal discipline. For example, President Reagan in 1984 claimed that the amendment "would force the Federal Government to do what so many States and municipalities and all average Americans are forced to do—to live within its means and stop mortgaging our children's future."[169] Any truth to that? No.

States and "average Americans" do not live within their means. They borrow. If states spent only what they took in as revenues, there would be no need for the limits on indebtedness that are placed in state constitutions. Nor would we hear of state and municipal bond offerings, or states worrying about their bond ratings. States do not "balance their budgets." They balance their operating (or general) budgets and run debts in their capital budgets. Big debts. Over the years they have devised a number of techniques for creating and concealing debts.

Side-by-side with state balanced budget requirements, the total state-local debt continues to climb. Justice Shirley S. Abrahamson of the Wisconsin Supreme Court captured this paradox nicely: "The history of the Wisconsin constitutional provisions concerning municipal debt manifests both an abhorrence of public debt and a willingness to increase the debt limit, particularly for school purposes."[170] There is no reason to believe that the national government is immune from these political pressures. Requirements for a balanced budget make room for indebtedness, one way or another. We should not deceive the public into thinking that a balanced budget at the federal level will end federal borrowing. It would not.

Most of the borrowing by state and local governments goes for capital expenditures for roads, education, sewerage, housing, and urban renewal. States impose limitations on the authority of state legislatures and local governments to borrow, but these limits are circumvented by the creation of special districts and authorities that have borrowing authority.[171] These circumventions fragment state government and weaken accountability to citizens.

Because the state limits on borrowing usually apply only to "full faith and credit debt" (secured by the general revenues of the government), the temptation is to turn increasingly to *nonguaranteed* bonds to sidestep debt limitations. Full faith and credit debt, which used to account for almost all of state and local long-term debt, has now declined to about thirty percent or less of the total.

What of the institutional impact on the federal government? First, the requirement of a balanced budget is likely to increase presidential powers over the budget. At the state level, governors use balanced-budget requirements to justify greater power over spending by invoking item-veto authority, impounding funds, or shifting expenditures into the next fiscal year. With a balanced budget requirement for the national government, pressure would mount to extend those same powers to the president, exercised either as inherent authorities or as delegated by statute to the president. The one job that Congress does well—deciding budget priorities—would shift increasingly to the president and the executive agencies.

Second, a balanced budget amendment would transfer a number of sensitive fiscal decisions to federal judges. The courts would have to monitor a variety of spending, taxing, and indebtedness actions to see that they conform to the amendment. That is the lesson learned from the states. Judges are not shy about deciding budgetary and fiscal questions, but they are not very good about it either.[172]

Third, the power and prestige of Congress would suffer when citizens discovered that Congress could promise a balanced budget but could not deliver. All the tricks for escaping the deficit targets embodied in the Gramm-Rudman-Hollings Act would be dwarfed by new heights of accounting ingenuity. If citizens want government benefits without being taxed for them, Congress will find ways to disguise the deficit. Instead of dealing with a deficit of known size, honestly displayed, the incentive would be to paper it over, push it underground, and shove it to the future.

Passing a constitutional amendment marks a serious commitment, a solemn promise. By passing a balanced budget amendment, members of Congress would signal to their constituents a determination to grapple with deficits. If in fact the level of the national debt continued to climb through the use of bookkeeping contrivances and new borrowing agencies, the reputation of Congress would further plummet. Having failed to comply with the statutory mandates in Gramm-Rudman and other laws, Congress would advertise that it has no greater respect for constitutional commands. This result would only deepen public cynicism and disrespect for the national legislature. Large deficits in the annual budgets threaten the nation. So do deficits of trust in our governmental institutions.

Term Limits

Arguments for an item veto and a balanced budget amendment rest on the belief that Congress is irresponsible and unworthy of trust. Similarly, term limits are designed to get rid of lawmakers supposedly corrupted by lengthy service. The clear message: "Members of Congress are not honest. The longer they serve, the worse they get." The Contract with America proposed two types of term limits: one to limit the terms of representatives to six years and senators to twelve. An alternative imposed limits of twelve years for both chambers. The punitive spirit behind the proposal is reflected in the title of a book published in 1994 by John Armor: *Why Term Limits? Because They Have It Coming!*

If the goal is a legislature of citizens who are not professional politicians, why not a limit on lifetime service? Otherwise, members of Congress could serve six or twelve years in the House, step aside for two years, and return for another six or twelve years. Or members could serve six or twelve years in the House, twelve years in the Senate, and presumably return to the House for an additional stint. Members of Congress, facing the end of their congressional career, could run for mayor, governor, and other public offices. Term limits would not guarantee public service by nonprofessional citizen legislatures. When the House in 1995 debated amendments to restrict lifetime service of representatives to six years and senators to twelve, those restrictions were defeated 114 to 316. Another lifetime amendment (twelve years in both chambers) was rejected, 164 to 265.

Another issue: Should term limits be merely prospective or also retroactive? If service in Congress has a corrupting effect, why not apply term limits to prior service? If the principle of term limits is to be consistent, current members who have already served twelve years should not be allowed to run again. But advocates of the term limits amendment argued that it was unfair to change the rules in the middle of the game for current lawmakers. An amendment to make term limits retroactive was defeated, 135 to 297. The constitutional amendment only attracted a vote of 227 to 204, far short of the two-thirds majority needed.

Public support for term limits seemed to ignore its impact on the constitutional balance between the executive and legislative branches. Turning members of Congress into citizen-legislators would give them little stake in protecting legislative interests, and it would weaken their power to protect those interests even if they wanted to. Power would flow from Congress to the White House, political appointees, and members of the career bureaucracy. Congressman Henry Hyde (R-Ill.), chairman of the House Judiciary Committee, broke with his party on this issue, refusing to participate in a "dumbing down of democracy" (see box 33).

With Congress weakened in relation to the executive branch, lawmakers would become more, not less, dependent on the expertise eagerly offered by

BOX 33

Hyde on Term Limits

I want to tell you how unpleasant it is to take the well in militant opposition to something that is so near and dear to the hearts of so many of my colleagues and Members whom I revere, but I just cannot be an accessory to the dumbing down of democracy. . . .

When that dentist bends over with the drill whirring, do you not hope he has done that work for a few years?

And when the neurosurgeon has shaved your head and they have made the pencil mark on your skull where they are going to have the incision and he approaches with the electric saw, ask him one question, are you a careerist?

. . . To do your job [as a member of Congress], to have a smattering of ignorance, in Oscar Levant's phrase, you have to know something about the environment, health care, banking and finance and tax policy, farm problems, weapons systems, Bosnia and Herzegovina and North Korea, not to mention Nagorno-Karabakh, foreign policy, the administration of justice, crime and punishment, education and welfare, budgeting in the trillions of dollars and immigration. And I have not scratched the surface.

We need our best people to deal with these issues. We in Congress deal with ultimate issues: life and death, war and peace, drawing the line between liberty and order. . . .

Source: 141 *Cong. Rec.* H3905 (daily ed. Mar. 29, 1995).

interest groups and lobbyists. Far from eliminating or reducing corruption, term limits are more likely to exacerbate the problem. Unable to look forward to a career in Congress, some lawmakers might view lobbyists not merely as sources of information but as potential employers. Congressman Tony Beilenson, Democrat from California, said that because of the six-year term limit in his state, "legislators come into office looking for ways to use their short stint to make their next career move."[173] He said many left after three or four years to take jobs in the industries they had been overseeing as legislators.

The constitutional amendment for term limits did even less well in 1997, attracting a vote of only 217 to 211 in the House. Congressman Hyde reflected on the reason behind the drive for term limits: "The popularity of term limits is a measure of the low esteem our citizens have for politics and politicians. Some of my colleagues may think that is fine. I think it is dangerous." He said that because of the way members of Congress "attack each other and the way we demean this institution in every campaign, it is no wonder we are held in contempt."[174]

When the Nixon administration began to impound funds in heavy-handed fashion, Congress at first reacted by defending its prerogatives. However, after placing restraints on impoundment in the Budget Act of 1974, lawmakers began to wonder if they had limited the president too much and might be vulnerable to the charge of encouraging wasteful spending. At the same time, to give the public the impression of better legislative control over spending, they enacted a complicated process that centralized congressional procedures. It was this change, more than anything else, that allowed President Reagan to gain control of the congressional budget process and enact a plan loaded with fiscal dangers.

The huge deficits that flowed from his policy led, in time, to renewed calls for greater presidential power through some form of an item veto. This result is curious not only in terms of what Congress tried (supposedly) to check in 1974, but in rewarding the presidency for a misguided and irresponsible budget proposal. Throughout the twenty-five years of experience with the Budget Act of 1974, members have made the budget process increasingly technical and generally incomprehensible to the public and to most of the lawmakers. Instead of allowing the political system to operate openly, the process obscures accountability and results.

6

What Might Be Done?

After protecting congressional war and spending prerogatives from 1789 to 1950, why have lawmakers agreed to transfer power to the president in wholesale lots? Congress remains a strong and independent branch in many areas—capable of retaining close control over executive agencies and the president—but in the domains of war and spending it has not acted with confidence, self-respect, or institutional courage. At stake is not just congressional prerogatives but representative government and democratic values.

It could be argued (and has been argued) that the framers' model was appropriate for the eighteenth century but not for contemporary times, when it is supposedly important to concentrate greater power in the president to respond promptly to national emergencies. The framers were fully aware of such arguments and rejected them. Living in a time of crisis and situated on a highly vulnerable eastern seaboard, they decided to vest in Congress the core powers of war and spending. Other than granting the president the power to repel sudden attacks, they relied for their safety on Congress and the deliberative, democratic process. As noted in one study: "Despite glib assertions of the novelty and gravity of the post–Korean war period, the threats confronting the United States during the first quarter century of government under the Constitution imperiled the very independence and survival of the nation. The United States Government fought wars against France and England, the two greatest powers of that period, to protect its existence, preserve the balance of power, and defend its commerce. Notably, both conflicts, the Franco-American War [the Quasi-War of 1798–1800] and the War of 1812, were authorized by statute."[1]

In the years following World War II, there has been more than enough time to seek authorization in advance from Congress before committing the nation to war. If presidents decide that an emergency requires action without first obtaining approval from Congress, it is far better for them to use military force on suspect authority and come later to Congress to explain what they did, why they acted, and ask Congress to provide retroactive authority. The burden would be wholly on the president to make the case. Abuse of executive power would be impeachable. Experiences of recent decades, including Watergate and Iran-Contra, provide impressive support for the framers' fear of executive power. Checks and balances are needed to bring presidential and White House abuses to light.

On any of the disputes dealt with in this book, presidential power could have been blocked had a handful of members, especially committee chairmen, put greater weight on the Constitution and legislative prerogatives. But there are reasons for presidential dominance, and they are unlikely to change unless pressure comes from outside Congress. In crucial respects the framers' plan has failed.

Of course members of Congress do act in a protective manner, but not as Madison and other framers had hoped. Instead of protecting their institution they protect themselves and their reelection chances. Rather than opposing the president on a pending military action, they find it more convenient to acquiesce and avoid possible criticism that they interfered with a necessary mission. Similarly, by authorizing the president to cancel budget items, they protect themselves from the charge that they tolerate wasteful spending.

Why should citizens care if Congress continues to defer to the president? Why not let Congress remain comfortably and passively in the back seat? There would be some justice to that. There can be little respect or affection for an institution that is constantly cringing. However, it is not merely a question of a weak Congress. Public control and democratic values, operating through Congress as the representative branch, are also degraded. For supporters of democratic systems and deliberative procedures, the present course should be one of genuine alarm. There are a number of things that citizens and Congress could do to restore constitutional checks.

Constitutional Law 101

Few members of Congress seem to have much understanding or interest in the constitutional prerogatives they are expected to exercise and defend. After decades of presidents claiming that they can do anything they want as Commander in Chief, and after decades of Congress, the public, and the media pretending that the president is a more trusted guardian of the purse, it is little wonder that lawmakers have become accustomed to a subordinate role.

A few years ago I gave a talk on war powers at a law school. I had hardly begun when a second-year law student cut me off, with palpable irritation in his voice, by asking: "Doesn't the Constitution give the president the power to declare war, subject to the advice and consent of the Senate?" For a moment my supposedly involuntary breathing system failed me. Did he say what I thought he said? Could a second-year law student be that unaware of the text of the Constitution? I moved from those musings to a broader thought. Evidently the student had not manufactured this misconception. He picked it up somewhere from the press, from friends, and other sources. I was not in the midst of a unique and original misreading of the Constitution. Disturbingly, he reflected something deeper.

Early in 1999, on a drive home after work, I listened to a speech that former President George Bush was giving to the Senate. He discussed the difficulty in 1990 of developing a consensus with Congress about the need to take military action against Saddam Hussein. I heard him say there was a difference of opinion about who had the power to declare war. Had I heard him correctly? The Constitution clearly decides that issue, yet how could it still be unsettled in his mind? Had Bush ad-libbed and strayed from the text of his speech? No. I got a copy of his speech the next day and the language was unambiguous: "there was a fundamental difference of opinion between the Senate and the White House over the Senate's role in declaring war—one that dated back to the War Powers Act."[2] Of course the issue dates back much earlier (to the Constitution), and it is not the Senate's but the Congress's role "to declare war." Ignorance by a law student is one thing. To hear a former (and recent) president stumble on such a fundamental point is much more alarming.

I am constantly surprised by arguments put forward by some members of Congress. Increasingly I hear them say that Congress may not use the power of the purse to prevent a president from using military force against another country. They claim that only *after* the president orders troops into combat would it be constitutionally permissible for Congress to deny funds. There is no basis for that position. If there were, legislators would be fighting a rear-guard battle, trying to exercise control after the president had made crucial military and financial commitments. Members may restrict a president's actions prospectively as well as retrospectively. Nothing prohibits Congress from passing legislation to deny funds for something the president is about to do. If such a statutory restriction were challenged in court, there is every reason to believe that courts would uphold it.

The War Power

The system of checks and balances applies as much to military policy (if not more so) as to domestic policy. We cannot expect foreign policy and national security to be formulated well in the hands of an unchecked executive. In a speech in 1998, Congressman Lee Hamilton (D-Ind.) pointed to the value of joint action by Congress and the president: "I believe that a partnership, characterized by creative tension between the president and the Congress, produces a foreign policy that better serves the American national interest—and better reflects the values of the American people—than policy produced by the President alone."[3]

Instead of ducking responsibility on war power issues, legislators could say (as with Bosnia or Yugoslavia) that intervention is necessary, but to be credible—especially for a long-term commitment—there must be joint action between Congress and the president. Unilateral actions by the president are inherently unstable. When the public and interest groups demand that Congress confront the president and behave like a coequal branch, legislators will respond. Public pressure caused Congress in 1973 to cut off funds for the Vietnam War. Even with his vaunted communication skills, President Reagan never convinced the American public that communist or leftist control in Nicaragua justified the deployment of U.S. soldiers to that region. The result was a series of Boland Amendments prohibiting U.S. funds to the Contras in Nicaragua. If there is no outside pressure, Congress will most likely continue to acquiesce and remain passive on presidential war initiatives. Public participation matters.

The contemporary president benefits from some new developments. One is the volunteer army. During the Vietnam War years, citizens protested by burning their draft cards, refusing induction, fleeing to Canada, and participating in mass demonstrations. With the current volunteer army, the passions and outlets for civil disobedience are almost nonexistent. College campuses, once vigorous centers of opposition to the Vietnam War, are largely silent. As Joseph Califano has noted, an all-volunteer army "relieves affluent, vocal, voting Americans of the concern that their children will be at risk of going into combat."[4]

Second, military technology now enables presidents to wage wars with few casualties. During the four days of bombing Iraq in December, 1998, not a single U.S. or British casualty resulted from seventy hours of intensive air strikes involving 650 sorties against nearly one hundred targets.[5] The following year, President Clinton waged war for eleven weeks against Yugoslavia without a single NATO combat casualty.

Third, the growing cost of running for office means that legislators have less time to tend to their institutional duties. As Congressman Hamilton noted in 1998: "Members today must spend a disproportionate amount of time fundraising, which means less time with constituents discussing the issues and less time with colleagues forging legislation and monitoring federal bureaucrats."[6] Less time in Washington, D.C., means less time understanding legislative prerogatives, less time working with colleagues on like-minded issues, and less time forging alliances to retaliate against executive encroachments.

Constitutional Clichés

The president's capacity to conduct war unilaterally expands when legislators, members of the public, and the media routinely accept clichés and superficial maxims about executive power. A coequal and independent Congress requires that tired, trite axioms be dissected and punctured whenever they start to circulate, especially when they parade as received wisdom. Clichés are not merely hackneyed. They discourage thought. They allow public officials to do what they ought not to do.

1. PRESIDENT AS "SOLE ORGAN"

As legal support for broad presidential power, the administration continues to cite language from *Curtiss-Wright* that the president is "sole organ of the nation in its external relations." This phrase comes from a speech by Congressman John Marshall in 1800. As explained in chapter 2, Marshall never argued that the president was the exclusive policymaker in foreign affairs. At no time, either in 1800 or during his long tenure on the Supreme Court, did Marshall ever suggest that the president could act unilaterally to make foreign policy or military policy in the face of statutory restrictions, nor did he ever imply that presidents could conduct offensive wars on their own authority. The president was "sole organ" in *announcing* and *implementing* policy, not in *making* it. National security policy is formulated through the collective effort of the executive and legislative branches, either by treaty or by statute.

2. THE 200 PRECEDENTS

Unilateral presidential actions in committing military troops is often defended by referring to the two hundred or so instances in which presidents have used force without congressional authority.[7] No doubt one can put together a long list of such precedents, but they do not change the constitutional authority of Congress to take the nation from a state of peace to a state of war. Take a close look at the precedents: President James Monroe's use of U.S. forces to expel a group of smugglers in Florida, the landing of a naval party in Argentina in 1890 to protect the U.S. consulate and legation, the chasing of bandits into Mexico, etc. Those actions cannot possibly justify Truman's war against Korea, Bush's operation against Iraq, or Clinton's bombing of Serbia and Kosovo. Moreover, many of the initiatives in the list of two hundred were taken not by presidents but by military commanders.

3. STOPPING POLITICS AT THE WATER'S EDGE

When President Clinton bombed Iraq in December, 1998, the *New York Times* ran an article with this subtitle: "Politics Stop No More At the Water's Edge."[8] Because some legislators questioned Clinton's motives in ordering the attacks the day before the House was scheduled to take up the Articles of Impeachment against Clinton, the reporter claimed that the legislators violated "Washington's long-standing political code. You don't criticize the President, that code says, when American forces stand in harm's way." There is no such code. As the article itself acknowledged, many presidents have run into trouble on Capitol Hill over foreign policy in the half-century since World War II ended. Lyndon Johnson was driven from office for his Vietnam policy. As the reporter notes, Ronald Reagan was accused by some members of Congress and editorial writers of "staging the invasion of Grenada to mute criticism of his failure to protect marines who were killed in Lebanon."[9] Stopping politics at the water's edge is not the practice in America. Instead, it is a formula for a second-class Congress and a muzzled public.

4. SPEAKING WITH ONE VOICE

In the midst of bombing Yugoslavia in 1999, President Clinton urged that "America must continue to speak with a single voice."[10] Stop. The president is not America; he is not the nation. There is no need to revive Louis XIV's *L'état c'est moi*. Nothing is treasonous or disloyal about questioning and disagreeing with military actions ordered by the president. In 1919, a unanimous Supreme Court upheld the criminal indictments of individuals who opposed America's entrance into World War I and spoke out against the draft.[11] The "clear and present danger" test announced in this decision was followed by the "bad tendency" test, which argued that the mere tendency to create evil justifies suppression by the government.[12] In a penetrating critique in the *Harvard Law Review* in 1919, Zechariah Chafee, Jr., argued that it was particularly in time of war that public debate must be left free to challenge governmental policy.[13] More recently, James Lindsay remarked that "the duty facing members of Congress is not to make the president's job easier but to make the country's policies better. And they can only do that by challenging the president."[14]

5. "535 SECRETARIES OF STATE"

Anytime Congress challenges a president's foreign policy, someone is bound to protest: "We cannot have 535 Secretaries of State!" The clear advice to legislators: step back and let the president alone. But the president is never alone, and certainly not in matters of military action. Hundreds of top officials in the executive branch contribute to the president's decision. He is likely to go to the UN Security Council, to NATO, and to allies around the world—not only for support but for approval. Given its constitutional responsibilities, there is no reason for Congress to capitulate to presidential initiatives.

The mathematical test is not "535" but a majority of the House and a majority of the Senate to provide the statutory authority that the Constitution requires. It is similar to the requirement that the president come to Congress for authority before withdrawing funds from the Treasury. In such situations no one objects that "We cannot have 535 Secretaries of the Treasury."

6. "IF WE'RE IN IT, WIN IT"

Once Clinton began bombing Yugoslavia, some supporters (and previous opponents) argued that no matter how ill-advised the military operation might have been, once the United States and NATO decided to intervene it was necessary to "win" the war. As a general policy, that makes no sense and has never been national strategy. The United States has been involved in numerous military actions without insisting on victory, whatever the cost. Examples of America disengaging from military operations short of a successful outcome include Korea, Vietnam, Lebanon in 1983, and Somalia in 1993. Sometimes when we're in, it is smart to get out, and quickly. It is not a national disgrace to disengage from wrong-headed and ill-fated ventures.

"If we're in it, win it" was the attitude that kept the United States mired in Vietnam, absorbing huge casualties with no hope of success. Had the United States followed the policy to win a war once engaged, President Kennedy would have found himself in an air and ground war in Cuba after the Bay of Pigs and the Cuban missile crisis. In both cases he chose a more limited, and more successful, strategy. If we're in it, we have to decide whether it is in the national interest to remain there. The slogan "if we're in it, win it," focuses solely on presence, not purpose. To justify a military operation, and the casualties expected on both sides, we need a better reason. A more useful guideline: If we shouldn't be there, stay out.

7. PRESERVING CREDIBILITY

When Clinton made a commitment to send troops to Bosnia in 1995, some legislators who had opposed his policy now switched positions and claimed that continued resistance would undermine the credibility of the United States, the presidency, and NATO. Similar arguments surfaced with the bombing of Yugoslavia in 1999. Through some mysterious process, a presidential initiative becomes a "vital national interest." Supporters argued that any effort to renege on Clinton's decision, however misguided it might have been, would undermine the credibility of the presidency and NATO. No doubt the credibility of the presidency and NATO is important, but so is the credibility of Congress, the Constitution, the system of checks and balances, and popular control. Presidential shortcuts and legislative acquiescence mark the road from representative government to autocracy.

8. "DOING THE RIGHT THING"

Writing after his presidency, Bush said that had Congress failed to authorize the war against Iraq he would have acted anyway, because "it was the right thing to do." Clinton used precisely the same phrase in justifying his planned invasion of Haiti and his interventions in Bosnia and Yugoslavia. Multibillion-dollar commitments should not be entered into simply because the president says it is the "right thing" and is determined to proceed with or without Congress and with or without public support. That is a superficial foundation for national policy, domestic or foreign. More important than doing the right thing is doing things the right way: following constitutional procedures, developing a national consensus and public support, and working with the legislative branch instead of circumventing it.

9. PROTECTING THE TROOPS

A standard argument in defense of presidential wars is that regardless of how deficient the policy might be it is necessary to offer support because American troops deserve protection. That was the position of the Senate in 1995 when it passed legislation to support American troops in Bosnia but expressed "reservations" about sending them there. Some legislators even suggested that a cutoff of funds would leave American soldiers stranded and without ammunition, food, and clothing. Clearly, that would not be the result. A cutoff of funds means that troops are withdrawn, out of harm's way. Military commitments need to be examined on their merits. If the policy cannot be defended, it makes no sense to fund it or send American soldiers. In such circumstances the best protection for troops is not to have them there.

10. "we'll consult with congress"

Presidents regularly promise to brief legislators and consult with them about military commitments. Cabinet officials, like the secretary of defense, speak earnestly about the need for an open and frank dialogue between the president and Congress. Many legislators seem mollified by these offers. Consultation, however, is not enough. Congress is a legislative body and discharges its constitutional responsibilities by passing statutes that authorize and define national policy. Congress exists to legislate and legitimate, not to have presidents and executive officials simply touch bases with it.

Word Games

For the past half century, presidents and their assistants have resorted to word games to justify military adventures, but semantics are a poor substitute for constitutional principle and effective policy. Truman denied he was "at war" in Korea. It was, instead, a "police action under the United Nations." Even federal courts, operating at some distance from military actions, found that position singularly unpersuasive. As noted before, Secretary of State Albright was asked in 1998 how President Clinton could order military action against Iraq after opposing American policy in Vietnam. Her response: "We are talking about using military force, but we are not talking about a war. That is an important distinction."[15] Supposedly clever distinctions between war and military force do much to undermine democratic and constitutional values. They eviscerate the congressional war power and public control.

The War Powers Resolution

The War Powers Resolution of 1973 is generally considered the high-water mark of congressional reassertion in national security affairs. In fact, it was ill-conceived and badly compromised from the start, replete with tortured ambiguity and self-contradiction. The statute further subordinates Congress to presidential war initiatives and should be repealed in its entirety.[16]

Other than in genuine emergencies or legitimate measures of defensive action, the president should come to Congress in advance for statutory authority. If he must act in a sudden emergency without such authority, he needs to come as soon as possible to receive retroactive authority. That was the Lincoln model in 1861, and it is the appropriate, constitutional procedure for any genuine emergency. In 1995, a conference report noted that President Clinton's initiatives in Somalia, Rwanda, Haiti, and refugee relief in the Caribbean "all mark significant departures from previous emergency deployments of American forces." The conferees expressed the proper constitutional principle by stating their "strong belief" that military deployments "in support of peacekeeping or humanitarian objectives both merit and require advance approval by the Congress."[17]

In 1998, the House passed language to narrow the scope of presidential war power. An amendment, added to the defense appropriations bill, provided that no funds appropriated in that act "may be used to initiate or conduct offensive military operations" by U.S. armed forces except in accordance with the war powers clause of the Constitution, "which vests in Congress the power to declare and authorize war."[18] That language was tabled in the other chamber because senators were scrambling to get out of town for the August recess.[19] If legislators want to reclaim constitutional powers that have drifted to the president and restore Congress as a coequal branch, revisiting this amendment with hearings and full legislative debate is a good place to begin.

When Secretary Albright appeared before the House Appropriations Committee in 1998, Congressman David Skaggs (D-Colo.) asked her to explain what authority President Clinton possessed to initiate further attacks against Iraq. In a statement later supplied to the committee, as an insert for the record, she claimed that the president's constitutional authority as commander in chief allowed him "to use armed forces to protect our national interests."[20] That is a startling interpretation. Whenever the president determines, on his own, that a matter is in the "national interest," he may unleash military force against another nation without ever seeking authority from Congress. Nothing in the Constitution supports that claim of power.

Behaving like a Coequal Branch

During President Reagan's first year in office, Interior Secretary James Watt withheld documents from a House subcommittee, provoking a committee subpoena for the documents and a recommendation by the Committee on Energy and Commerce that Watt be cited for contempt. Attorney General William French Smith claimed that "all of the documents in issue are either necessary and fundamental to the deliberative process presently ongoing in the Executive Branch or relate to sensitive foreign policy considerations."[21]

In fact, the dispute with Watt concerned the impact of Canadian investment and energy policies on American commerce, an issue squarely within the Article I enumerated power of Congress to "regulate Commerce with foreign Nations." The Justice Department seemed to have difficulty reading, much

less following, the text of the Constitution. As the controversy escalated up-
ward to a contempt citation, the documents were released to the committee.[22]

In 1996, the Justice Department issued a memorandum objecting to two
statutes that concerned the rights of federal employees to provide information
to Congress. Both statutory provisions gave executive employees a right to furnish information to either House of Congress or to a committee. The Justice
memo claimed that a congressional enactment "would be unconstitutional if
it were interpreted to divest the president of his control over national security
information in the Executive Branch by vesting lower-ranking personnel in
that Branch with a 'right' to furnish such information to a Member of Congress without receiving official authorization to do so." In defending this position, the Justice Department cited a number of presidential roles, including
commander in chief, head of the executive branch, and "sole organ" of the nation in its external relations.[23]

In order to evaluate the position of the Justice Department, the Senate Select Committee on Intelligence held two days of hearings in 1998. Professor
Peter Raven-Hansen of the George Washington University law school and I
appeared the first day to rebut the department's position that the president has
ultimate and unimpeded authority over the collection, retention, and dissemi-
nation of national security information. On the second day of hearings, I testified alongside an attorney from the Justice Department.[24]

Based on these hearings and its own independent staff analysis, the committee reported legislation despite claims by the Justice Department that the bill
was an unconstitutional invasion of presidential prerogatives. The committee
acted unanimously, voting 19 to 0 to report the bill.[25] The bipartisan vote for
legislative prerogatives was solid. The Senate report said that the administration's
"intransigence on this issue compelled the Committee to act."[26] The bill passed
the Senate by a vote of 93 to 1.[27]

The House Permanent Select Committee on Intelligence took a different
approach in drafting legislation, but also rejected the administration's claim
that the president exercised exclusive control over national security information. I testified before the House committee as well.[28] Like the Senate, the House
committee dismissed the assertion that the president, as commander in chief,
"has ultimate and unimpeded constitutional authority over national security,
or classified, information. Rather, national security is a constitutional responsibility shared by the executive and legislative branches that proceeds according
to the principles and practices of comity."[29] The two committees reported and
enacted legislation with this language: "national security is a shared responsibility, requiring joint efforts and mutual respect by Congress and the Presi-

dent." The statute further provides that Congress, "as a co-equal branch of Government, is empowered by the Constitution to serve as a check on the executive branch; in that capacity, it has 'a need to know' of allegations of wrongdoing within the executive branch, including allegations of wrongdoing in the Intelligence Community."[30]

Litigating War Power Issues

Dozens of war-power issues have been litigated since World War II. The trend in recent decades is for members of Congress to take these disputes to court, hoping that a judge will agree with their constitutional interpretation. But there is little reason to think that these member cases will be successful. Courts have made it plain that they are loath to decide such cases, because just as one group of members will claim that the president has violated the Constitution, so will another group of lawmakers claim that he has acted properly. Judges don't want to be in the middle of this intramural crossfire. They will not referee a case unless the two branches are in irresolute conflict and the entire Congress has exhausted all the institutional remedies available to it. If members want to protect their institution, they must take the time to forge a majority capable of doing battle against the president.

The Spending Power

Rather than duck accountability on spending issues and heap blame on their institution, legislators can point to the clear record that they generally remain within the budget aggregates proposed by the president. Having established their fiscal bona fides, they are then in a position to participate fully in deciding how the totals are to be spent. Under these conditions, there is no need to delegate cancellation or other spending powers to the president, and no need to construct a complicated budget process for the purpose of convincing the public that Congress can act "comprehensively."

Presidential Largesse

It would put executive-legislative relations in better perspective if we acknowledge the obvious: presidents are just as good as Congress in promoting and originating expensive programs. In fact, they are probably better. Really big programs are likely to come from the president: the supercollider, the strategic defense initiative (Star Wars), and the Clinton health plan of 1993. Presidents are more apt to complain about Congress cutting programs than adding to them.

The media helps foster the notion of an irresponsible Congress. A September 9, 1999, *New York Times* article had this arresting title: "Lawmakers' Spending Plans Could Turn Surplus to Deficit." How many readers will go much beyond the headline? The gist of the story was that the Republicans planned additional spending to wipe out a projected $14 billion surplus for the next year and create in its place an $11 billion deficit.[31] A $25 billion swing is quite a lot, suggesting that an undisciplined Congress is solely responsible for turning a good situation into a bad one.

An industrious reader could locate another story, in exactly the same paper, with the title "Lott Says Veto Is Likely to Kill Tax Cut in '99." Doesn't seem to have anything to do with spending, but of course it does. The Republicans proposed a $792 billion tax cut, but President Clinton promised to veto anything of that size. Instead, he wanted a tax cut of about $300 billion in order to direct more funds to education, a prescription drug program for the elderly, and other domestic programs.[32] His list of new spending initiatives was much longer, and more expensive, than what the Republicans had in mind. The headline could just as well have been: "Clinton's Spending Plans Could Turn Surplus to Deficit." But it didn't say that.

A month later, Clinton threatened to veto a foreign aid bill because it provided $1.9 billion less than he requested. He ended up getting the increase. When Republicans considered an across-the-board spending cut of 2.7 percent, the White House attacked the plan as requiring devastating cuts in education, health, transportation, and other domestic programs.[33] Congress had to settle for an across-the-board cut of 0.38 percent. With Clinton threatening to shut the government down unless he got additional funds, Republicans accommodated his demands by including several billion to hire more teachers and police and to acquire western desert and ranch land as part of Clinton's "Lands Legacy" program.[34]

The State of the Union message has become a major showcase for presidential largesse. Prior to the release of the message, newspaper stories carry leaks from the administration, explaining how the president will first benefit this group and next that group. When President Clinton gave his State of the Union message in January, 1999, it was studded with new spending and tax initiatives. He proposed a new pension initiative to use a little over eleven percent of the surplus to establish Universal Savings Accounts to give all Americans the means to save. Next came a tripling of funding for summer school and after-school programs, $200 million "to help States turn around their own failing schools," a six-fold increase in college scholarships for students who commit to teach in the inner cities and isolated rural areas and in Indian communities, building or modernizing 5,000 schools, and raising the minimum wage by $1 an hour over the next two years. Clinton also proposed changes in the tax code that would reduce federal revenue: tax credits of $1,000 for the aged, ailing, or disabled; tax credits and subsidies for working families and for expanded after-school programs; and a new tax credit for stay-at-home parents. He asked Congress for "a dramatic increase in Federal support for adult literacy" and proposed a 28 percent increase in long-term computing research.

Turning to national security, he asked for an increase in funding by almost two-thirds over the next five years to keep terrorists from disrupting computer networks, to prepare local communities for biological and chemical emergencies, to support research into vaccines and treatments, and to restrain the spread of nuclear weapons. He called for a "sustained increase" over the next six years for readiness, for modernization, and for pay and benefits for U.S. troops and their families.

Clinton said his budget would expand support for drug testing and treatment and contain two new initiatives: a $1 billion Liability Agenda to help communities save open space, ease traffic congestion, and grow in ways "that enhance every citizen's quality of life," and a $1 billion Lands Legacy Initiative to preserve places of natural beauty across America.[35] These and other presidential proposals dwarf the projects that members of Congress attempt to steer toward their communities.

The Price of Centralization

Congress could profitably rethink the merits of the Budget Act of 1974. Even when a process is crippled and dysfunctional, it's not easy or comfortable to kick away crutches. But there is good reason to doubt that budget resolutions are an important discipline for enforcing overall budget decisions. It is probably more true that they obscure accountability, invite greater spending, and open the door to greater presidential leverage, as happened in 1981. Centralized procedures in Congress do not automatically yield benefits or improvements. Congress enacted omnibus tariff bills decade after decade until the results became too embarrassing for legislators, at which point the process stopped. The experiment with an Omnibus Appropriation Bill in 1950, seemingly "rational" and "coherent," ended in failure. These precedents should have cautioned Congress about centralizing the budget process in 1974.

Centralizing the budgeting process in 1974 has led to less participation by members of Congress. Put another way, voters and constituents now have less influence through their representatives. There has been an increasing trend toward "summit meetings" that include a handful of executive and legislative leaders to hammer out the final details of a budget plan. The $500 billion omnibus appropriations bill in 1998 included eight appropriations bills, supplemental appropriations, emergency appropriations, a tax cut, and a number of authorization bills. Toward the end of the process, key negotiations were conducted by White House representatives and four legislators: Speaker Gingrich, Minority Leader Gephardt, Senate Majority Leader Lott, and Senate Minority Leader Daschle.

Republican rank-and-file, and even more senior lawmakers, resented the budget summit in 1995 that included only Republican leaders and White House officials.[36] Similar criticism was directed at Speaker Gingrich in 1997 for making budget decisions without including a sufficient number of other Republican lawmakers.[37] In the fall of 1998, Republicans presented Clinton with a single omnibus appropriations bill instead of the thirteen individual appropriations bills. He was thus ideally positioned to threaten a veto and force another shutdown of government (with the public most likely to blame the Republicans) unless he received funding increases for various domestic programs.[38] Republican leaders once again walked into a trap they helped set. The anger and sense of betrayal from Republicans excluded from this process was one of the factors in Gingrich's decision to step down as Speaker and retire from Congress.[39]

By combining a number of bills to form a single, omnibus measure in 1998, lawmakers left themselves no opportunity to offer floor amendments. The decision was to vote up or down, take it or leave it. No legislator claimed to know the contents of the 4,000-page measure. The very size of the bill invited the inclusion of projects that might not have survived in smaller bills. Congressman Joseph Moakley (D-Mass.) remarked: "the good news for the Democrats is this bill contains a lot more Democratic provisions than we could have gotten under the regular legislative procedure if that legislative procedure had taken place in its orderly fashion."[40]

Reduced Accountability

The framers of the Budget Act of 1974 never fully considered the institutional dynamics of budget reform. They never asked: If Congress strengthened its role in budget-making, would that weaken the leadership required of the president? Prior to 1974, the country had one budget: the president's. Congressional actions were easily measured against that single benchmark. The passage of budget resolutions had the effect of undercutting the significance of the president's budget. During debate on an appropriations bill in 1983, members asked whether the bill was below budget or above budget. House Majority Leader Jim Wright (D-Tex.) admitted that the amounts in the bill exceeded the president's budget requests but then noted: "that, of course, is not the budget. Congress makes the budget; the President does not."[41] When there was only one budget—the president's—it was an easy matter to judge whether a bill was below or above budget. Now it is possible for a bill to be above the president's budget but under the amounts allowed by a budget resolution.

This conceptual confusion has done much to weaken accountability to the public. It is difficult to hold either the president or the Congress publicly accountable for the national budget. The country lacks a clear and definitive reference point for measuring presidential leadership and congressional action. Even presidents find this confusion attractive. In 1985, President Reagan announced that he "would accept appropriations bills, even if above my budget, that were within the limits set by Congress' own budget resolution."[42]

The system of multiple budgets—one by the president and another by Congress—creates substantial costs for the country. If the president ducks responsibility by submitting budgets with unrealistic projections of economic growth, interest rates, and inflation, Congress is penalized if it tells the truth. Passing a budget resolution that assumes slower economic growth, higher interest rates, and higher inflation would produce larger deficits, giving the country the false impression that Congress is less responsible than the president. The clear incentive is for Congress to embrace the same false estimates and thereby deliberately deceive the public. Congressman David Obey (D-Wis.), a member of the House Appropriations Committee, remarked in 1982: "under the existing conditions the only kind of budget resolution you can pass today is one that lies. We did it under Carter, we have done it under Reagan, and we are going to do it under every President for as long as any of us are here, unless we change the system, because you cannot get Members under the existing system to face up to what the real numbers do. You always end up having phony economic assumptions and all kinds of phony numbers on estimating."[43]

The budget process adopted in 1974 is highly complex and has grown more so over the years. The more complex the budget process, the less suitable it is for representative government. Few members of Congress and their staff understand the arcane procedures and rules. The general public cannot follow them. That is a high price in a democratic society, where taxpayers and citizens should be able to monitor spending decisions. Congressman John Dingell (D-Mich.) objected in 1984: "What we have done over the past decade is to create a budget process that is so complex as to be incomprehensible to almost every-one. Most of the Members do not understand it beyond a superficial level. The press does not understand it. The business community does not understand it. The financial community does not understand it. And most important of all, the public does not understand it."[44]

The budget process of 1999 is even more complex. During hearings before the House Rules Committee on July 21, 1999, Congressman Obey reflected on his congressional experience that began in 1969 and culminated in being chair-man and ranking member of the House Appropriations Committee. He testified that "there are not 10 percent of the Members of the Congress who really have a detailed understanding" of the budget process, adding that there were even parts he didn't understand. The process has become "so confoundly compli-cated that it takes eight Philadelphia lawyers a week of Sundays to figure out what in god's name some of the provisions mean, and this makes it simply more difficult, and to the extent it's become more difficult for us, you can imagine people trying to penetrate this gibberish to figure out [how] they can affect it from the outside. Almost impossible."[45]

Members of Congress make repeated appeals for "simplification" of the bud-get process, but progress in that direction is impossible as long as lawmakers lack confidence in their ability to function in the regular legislative process, which includes taking responsibility for budget outcomes each year. It is the distrust of regular politics that feeds the mounting complexity of the budget process, leading to budget resolutions, Gramm-Rudman, spending caps, and item-veto authority. Complexity creates a world where politicians can hide and obfuscate.

Proposals to eliminate budget resolutions encounter several objections. Would a more decentralized process lead to runaway spending? The process in place since 1974 may appear to be more coherent and responsible, but it regularly produces irresponsible results. Without a budget resolution, Congress would not be stripped of an enforcement mechanism. Congress is fully capable of using informal, "non-elegant" processes to control the budget. Instead of hid-ing behind budget resolutions, party leaders and committee chairmen can keep aggregates within bounds. If they fail, the president always has the veto power to strike down appropriations bills that are excessive or tax bills that threaten to add to the deficit. Instead of statutes dictating the actions of elected officials (as with Gramm-Rudman), elected officials should tell statutes what to do.

The Budget Committees, no longer responsible for reporting budget reso-lutions, could serve a number of vital functions. It would be their duty (as-sisted by CBO) to maintain the scorekeeping reports that monitor the actions of the appropriations, authorization, and tax committees. The Budget Committees could also report reconciliation bills needed to control entitlements, devise better methods of controlling federal credit programs, and address other problems that cut across the jurisdictional lines of congressional committees. The informal, decentralized system of Congress worked in the past. It can work in the future. If tried, it would place a premium on the leadership ability of legislators, but that is why they are elected.

Relying on Committee Controls

Congress is often criticized for being "decentralized" and "fragmented." In fact, those quantities are a major source of strength and explain why Congress remains effective in protecting legislative prerogatives. Committees and subcommittees play a vital role in checking the executive branch. A few examples will drive this home.

During the Carter years, John Gilligan was appointed to head the Agency for International Development (AID). Senator Daniel Inouye (D-Hawaii), who chaired the Senate appropriations subcommittee with jurisdiction over AID, told Gilligan that agency-legislative relationships had deteriorated because of AID's penchant for diverting economic aid to military purposes without ever consulting Congress. Inouye said that whenever AID wanted to spend funds for purposes not previously justified to Congress, it would have to seek the approval of the House and Senate appropriations subcommittees responsible for foreign operations. Gilligan agreed. When Inouye asked to have the agreement drawn up as a letter, Gilligan consented to that as well.

After Gilligan had the draft letter routed through the agency's general counsel office, questions were raised about the constitutionality of allowing congressional committees to share in administrative decisions. The Justice Department specifically disapproved the arrangement. When Gilligan told Inouye what was happening, Inouye countered by placing the agreement in a public law. The foreign assistance appropriations bill for fiscal 1978 contained this language: "None of the funds made available by this Act may be obligated under an appropriation account to which they were not appropriated without the written prior approval of the Appropriations Committees of both Houses of the Congress."[46]

Carter signed the bill into law without expressing any constitutional objections to the committee-clearance procedure. But on that very day he wrote to Secretary of State Cyrus Vance, stating that Attorney General Griffin Bell had objected to the procedure. Consequently, Vance was to treat the section not as a legally binding requirement for prior approval but rather as a request by the appropriations subcommittees to be notified, after which Vance and AID could do as they liked. The Appropriations Committees did not learn of Carter's letter until almost two years later.

The Senate Appropriations Committee held hearings in 1980 to receive testimony from agency officials. The Senate legal counsel and I testified.[47] The administration's legal position was strained. The subcommittees were not trying to dictate the execution of a law, which would have intruded upon administrative responsibilities. They were concerned about executive *departures* from the law. The committees were included, and properly so, whenever the agency wanted to use funds for a purpose for which Congress had not appropriated.

Carter's letter to Vance suggests that the president had successfully repelled a congressional effort to intervene in administrative details. So it was, on the surface. But at the agency level, far below the lofty constitutional principles identified by the White House and the Justice Department, matters were handled differently. Gilligan consistently sought the prior approval of the appropriations subcommittees before diverting funds. This type of clearance process is commonplace. It helps build trust and good faith. It makes government workable.

In *INS v. Chadha* (1983), the Supreme Court struck down what had come to be known as the "legislative veto": efforts by Congress to control the executive branch by resolutions (one-House or two-House) that did not go to the president for his signature. The Court said that whenever congressional action has the "purpose and effect of altering the legal rights, duties, and relations" of persons outside the legislative branch, Congress must act through both Houses in a bill presented to the president.[48] The breadth of this ruling would have invalidated every type of legislative control, including committee and subcommittee vetoes.

Following the Court's ruling, Congress amended a number of statutes by deleting legislative vetoes and replacing them with joint resolutions (which do go to the president).[49] Yet Congress continues to add committee vetoes to bills and presidents continue to sign them into law. In the years following *Chadha,* Congress enacted over four hundred of these statutory provisions. When committee-veto provisions came to President Reagan in 1984, he signed the bills but announced that he would implement the statutes "in a manner consistent with the *Chadha* decision."[50] The clear implication: committee vetoes would have no legal effect. After notifying the committees, agencies could do as they liked without obtaining committee approval.

The House Appropriations Committee lost little time in deciding how to finesse this presidential threat. It reviewed a procedure that had worked well with the National Aeronautics and Space Administration (NASA) for about four years. Statutory ceilings ("caps") were placed on various NASA programs, usually at the level requested in the president's budget. NASA could exceed those caps only if it received permission from the Appropriations Committees. Because the administration now threatened to ignore the committee controls, the House Appropriations Committee said that it would repeal both the committee veto *and* NASA's authority to exceed the caps.[51] If NASA wanted to spend more than the caps allowed, it would have to do what the Court mandated in *Chadha:* pass a bill through both Houses and have it presented to the president.

NASA was aghast. It did not want to obtain a new public law every time it needed to exceed spending caps. To avoid that kind of administrative rigidity, NASA Administrator James M. Beggs wrote to the Appropriations Committees and suggested a compromise. Instead of putting the caps in a public law, he recommended that they be placed in a conference report that explained how Congress expected a public law to be carried out. He then pledged that NASA would not exceed any ceiling identified in the conference report without first obtaining the prior approval of the Appropriations Committees.[52] Imaginative remedies like this allow government to function.

Another example of informal legislative vetoes came to light in 1987 when OMB Director James C. Miller III objected to a statutory provision that required the administration to obtain "written prior approval" from the Appropriations Committees before transferring foreign assistance funds from one account to another. The provision, he claimed, violated *Chadha*.[53] The House Appropriations Committee gave a familiar reply: it would repeal the committee veto and, at the same time, repeal the administration's authority to transfer foreign assistance funds. Congressman Obey, chairman of the House appropriations subcommittee handling foreign assistance, remarked: "To me, that [OMB letter] means we don't have an accommodation any more, so the hell with it, spend the money like we appropriated it. It's just dumb on their part."[54]

OMB beat a hasty retreat. The regular legislative language, including the committee veto, was enacted into law.[55] When Miller repeated the challenge the next year, Congress followed through on its threat and deleted both the committee veto and the transfer authority. The two branches reached a compromise in 1989. Congress removed the committee veto from the public law but required the administration to follow "the regular notification procedures of the Committee on Appropriations" before transferring funds.[56] While not articulated in public law, those procedures require the administration to notify the committees of each transfer. If no objection is raised during a fifteen-day review period, the administration may exercise the authority. If the committees object, the administration could proceed but only at great peril. By ignoring committee objections, the agency would most likely lose transfer authority the next year.

For the most part, agencies find it in their interests to adhere closely to nonstatutory controls. Nonetheless, OMB Director Miller decided in 1988 to challenge Congress on its use of report language to control agency activities. The continuing resolution signed by President Reagan the previous December was accompanied by committee reports that earmarked a number of projects favored by legislators. Miller announced that the reports had "no force of law" because they had not been approved by Congress and signed by the president. In a memo to cabinet officers and agency heads, he said they could "redirect funds not legally required to be used for a particular wasteful, unnecessary, or low priority project to a legally authorized and higher priority project."[57]

Miller was asking for big-time trouble and got it. Congressman Jamie Whitten, chairman of the House Appropriations Committee, warned the administration that Miller's views were "unsound and must not be followed."[58] The congressional protest spread to become both bipartisan and bicameral. The Democratic chairmen of both Appropriations Committees, together with the ranking Republicans on those panels, wrote to Reagan and reminded him that the continuing resolution he signed contained this language in Section 107: "Amounts and authorities provided by this resolution shall be in accordance with the reports accompanying the bills as passed by or reported to the House and the Senate and in the Joint Explanatory Statement of the Conference accompanying this Joint Resolution." The four leaders asked Reagan to withdraw Miller's memo.[59]

Miller did not accept this interpretation of Section 107, but did write a conciliatory letter to the four legislators, explaining that it was not the intention of the administration to ignore the committee reports. Later, Miller backed away even more by telling federal agencies to follow report language. He said that legislators had "relied on what they perceived to be a formal practice" of using report language to fund projects, and that compliance with those understandings would be in the interest of "comity between the branches."[60] This type of committee and subcommittee control continues to be practiced and honored by executive agencies.

Rediscovering Institutional Values

Members of Congress need to reeducate themselves on their institutional duties and constitutional prerogatives. In town meetings or other contacts with constituents, they can help educate citizens about the structure of government and the importance of maintaining healthy checks on executive power. They need to be willing to explain why it is not only unconstitutional but unwise to allow presidents to engage the country in war singlehandedly, and why it is unnecessary and unwise to transfer item-veto powers to the president. If legislators fail to take the lead, citizens can challenge them at town-hall meetings and ask why they tolerate unilateral presidential action. Citizens need to remind lawmakers of their constitutional duties.

The remedy does not lie solely with Congress; it lies outside. Are courts likely to redress the imbalance? The record is fairly clear that if Congress wants to continue deferring to the president in the areas of foreign policy and war powers, judges are not likely to return abdicated power to Congress. Even when the Court does strike down a transfer of legislative power to the president, as it did in 1998 with the item veto case of *Clinton v. City of New York,* the result is discouraging. Legislators gave away power, perhaps hoping that the judiciary might give it back. That is not what the framers expected.

Thus, the answer depends heavily on increased public awareness. Citizens need to understand the impact they have on government. If they want to continue bashing Congress, the result will be a stronger and unchecked president with greater governmental capacity to abuse power and endanger individual freedoms. Many reform proposals in recent years—including term limits, the item veto, and the balanced budget amendment—would shift power to the executive branch. A deeper appreciation of institutional and constitutional interests is needed. Citizens should realize that their own interests coincide with a vigorous system of checks and balances, including a Congress able and willing to challenge the president.

A more informed and objective media would help. Reporters should not take White House announcements ("The President does not need congressional authority to send troops into battle.") as constitutional law. They are announcements, not legal doctrine. When a legislator acquiesces to executive initiatives, that is not the time for journalists to praise the lawmaker as a patriot and hero. Such stories tilt power toward the president and away from representative government. The press needs an independent and strong Congress. We all do.

Over the past decade I have advised a number of countries from Eastern Europe and the former Soviet Union and Yugoslavia. I worked with legislators, executive officials, judges, and constitutional experts from Albania, Armenia, Belarus, Bosnia-Herzegovina, Bulgaria, the Czech Republic, Hungary, Lithuania, Macedonia, Romania, Russia, Slovenia, and Ukraine. What impressed them (with their history of executive dominance) was the capacity of Congress to participate as a coequal branch and provide effective checks on the president. They saw the value of a vigorous system of checks and balances. So should we. The framers knew what monarchy looked like and rejected it. Yet especially in matters of the war power, the United States is recreating a system of monarchy while it professes to champion democracy and the rule of law abroad. When presidents act unilaterally to use military force ostensibly to further those values, they undermine democracy and the rule of law at home. That is the reality. What will citizens, voters, and opinion leaders do about it?

Notes

Preface

1. E.g., Arthur M. Schlesinger, Jr., *The Imperial Presidency;* Charles Roberts, ed., *Has the President Too Much Power?;* Theodore S. Sorensen, *Watchmen in the Night: Presidential Accountability After Watergate.*
2. Gordon S. Jones and John A. Marini, eds., *The Imperial Congress: Crisis in the Separation of Powers;* L. Gordon Crovitz and Jeremy A. Rabkin, eds., *The Fettered Presidency: Legal Constraints on the Executive Branch.*

Chapter 1. The Framers' Design

1. *The Federalist,* edited by Benjamin Fletcher Wright, p. 356.
2. Ibid., p. 355.
3. Ibid., p. 356.
4. Louis Fisher, *President and Congress,* pp. 243–51.
5. Oliver Wendell Holmes, *Collected Legal Papers,* p. 263.
6. Montesquieu, *The Spirit of the Laws,* vol. 1, p. 158.
7. Ibid., p. 156.
8. Ibid., pp. 159–60.
9. "It is necessary that, by the nature of things, that power check power." The French is taken from Montesquieu's collected works, *Oeuvres Complète,* vol. 2, p. 395.
10. Francis Newton Thorpe, ed., *The Federal and State Constitutions, Colonial Charters, and Other Organic Laws 1893, 1897, 1902, 1904, 1905,* vol. 3.
11. Thorpe, vol. 4, p. 2457 (art. XXXVII).
12. *The Writings of James Madison,* ed. by Gaillard Hunt, vol. 2, p. 328.
13. Max Farrand, ed., *The Records of the Federal Convention of 1787,* vol. 2, p. 35.
14. *The Federalist,* at p. 343 (*Federalist 48*).
15. *Writings of James Madison,* vol. 5, p. 26.
16. *The Federalist,* p. 269.
17. Ibid., pp. 336–37.
18. Ibid., p. 337.
19. Ibid., p. 338 (emphasis in original).
20. M. J. C. Vile, *Constitutionalism and the Separation of Powers,* p. 153.
21. Jonathan Elliot, ed., *The Debates in the Several State Conventions, on the Adoption of the Federal Constitution,* vol. 3, p. 280.

22. Ibid., vol. 4, p. 116.

23. John Bach McMaster and Frederick D. Stone, eds., *Pennsylvania and the Federal Constitution, 1787–1788*, pp. 475–77.

24. Edward Dumbauld, *The Bill of Rights and What It Means Today*, pp. 174–75, 183, 199.

25. *Annals of Congress* 453 (June 8, 1789).

26. Senate Journals, 1788–94, vol. 1, pp. 64, 73–74 (1820).

27. Kenneth Culp Davis, *Administrative Law and Government*, p. 54.

28. Paul Einzig, *The Control of the Purse: Progress and Decline of Parliament's Financial Control*, pp. 57–62, 100–106.

29. *The Federalist*, p. 345.

30. Ibid., p. 391.

31. Ibid., p. 446 (emphasis in original).

32. *The Writings of Thomas Jefferson*, ed. by Paul Leicester Ford, vol. 5, p. 123.

33. *Writings of James Madison*, vol. 6, p. 148 (emphasis in original).

34. Farrand, *Records of the Federal Convention of 1787*, vol. 1, pp. 139–40.

35. Ibid., pp. 64–65.

36. Ibid., pp. 65–66.

37. Ibid.

38. *The Collected Papers of John Bassett Moore*, vol. 5, p. 196.

39. William Michael Treanor, "Fame, the Founding, and the Power to Declare War," *Cornell Law Review* 82 (1997): 695.

40. *The Federalist*, p. 101.

41. *The Writings of James Madison*, vol. 6, p. 174.

42. Elliot, *Debates in the Several State Conventions*, vol. 2, p. 528.

43. Ibid., vol. 4, pp. 107, 287 (statements by James Iredell and Charles Pinckney).

44. *Writings of Thomas Jefferson*, vol. 6, p. 259.

45. *The Papers of Alexander Hamilton*, ed. by Harold C. Syrett, vol. 21, pp. 461–62 (emphasis in original).

46. *Blackstone's Commentaries*, vol. 1, p. 43.

47. Farrand, *Records of the Federal Convention of 1787*, vol. 1, p. 316.

48. 1 Stat. 117–18, §§ 25–28 (1790).

49. James Kent, *Commentaries on American Law*, vol. 1, p. 170.

50. *Dellums v. Smith*, 577 F.Supp. 1449, 1453 (D. Cal. 1984).

51. W. Taylor Reveley III, *War Powers of the President and Congress: Who Holds the Arrows and Olive Branches?*, p. 29.

52. Charles A. Lofgren, *"Government From Reflection and Choice": Constitutional Essays on War, Foreign Relations, and Federalism*, p. 36.

53. Ibid., p. 38.

54. John Hart Ely, *War and Responsibility: Constitutional Lessons of Vietnam and Its Aftermath*, p. 3.

55. David Gray Adler, "Court, Constitution, and Foreign Affairs," in *The Constitution and the Conduct of American Foreign Policy*, ed. by David Gray Adler and Larry N. George, p. 19.

56. Michael J. Glennon, *Constitutional Diplomacy*, p. 72.

57. Ibid., p. 81.

58. Harold Hongju Koh, *The National Security Constitution: Sharing Power after the Iran-Contra Affair*, p. 75 (emphasis in original).

59. Ibid., p. 76.

60. John C. Yoo, "The Continuation of Politics by Other Means: The Original Understanding of War Powers," *California Law Review* 84 (1996): 167.

Chapter 2. The Record from 1789 to 1945

1. Louis Fisher, *Presidential War Power*, pp. 13–17.

2. Clarence Edwin Carter, ed., *The Territorial Papers of the United States*, vol. 4, p. 195.

3. Ibid., pp. 220–21.

4. *The Writings of George Washington*, vol. 33, p. 73. In one of his messages on Indian affairs, Washington referred to military operations "offensive or defensive," but the full text of his message is designed to avoid any initiative in warmaking and to limit military actions to defensive measures (*American State Papers: Indian Affairs*, vol. 1, p. 97 [1832]).

5. Carter, ed., *Territorial Papers*, 4:387.

6. 1 Stat. 264, sec. 2 (1792).

7. James D. Richardson, ed., *A Compilation of the Messages and Papers of the Presidents*, vol. 1, pp. 150–52.

8. Homer Cummings and Carl McFarland, *Federal Justice: Chapters in the History of Justice and the Federal Executive*, pp. 43–45.

9. 1 Stat. 547–611 (1798).

10. Richardson, *A Compilation*, vol. 1, p. 315.

11. Fisher, *Presidential War Power*, p. 26.

12. Abraham D. Sofaer, *War, Foreign Affairs and Constitutional Power: The Origins*, pp. 209–14.

13. *Annals of Cong.*, 9th Cong., 1st Sess. 19 (1805).

14. 9 Stat. 9 (1846); Fisher, *Presidential War Power*, pp. 29–34.

15. John Locke, *Second Treatise on Civil Government*, ch. 14.

16. Richardson, *A Compilation*, vol. 7, p. 3225.

17. Ibid.

18. *Cong. Globe*, 37th Cong., 1st sess., 393 (1861) (Sen. Howe).

19. 12 Stat. 326 (1861).

20. *The Prize Cases*, 67 U.S. 635, 660, 668 (1863).

21. Martin S. Sheffer, *The Judicial Development of Presidential War Powers*, pp. x–xi.

22. *Bas v. Tingy*, 4 Dall. (4 U.S.) 37, 40 (1800).

23. Ibid., p. 43.

24. Ibid., p. 45.

25. *Little v. Barreme*, 2 Cr. (6 U.S.) 170, 179 (1804).

26. Francis Wharton, *State Trials of the United States during the Administrations of Washington and Adams*, pp. 84–85, 88.

27. *United States v. Smith*, 27 Fed. Cas. 1192, 1229 (C.C.N.Y. 1806) (No. 16,342).

28. Ibid., p. 1230.

29. Ibid.

30. *The Prize Cases*, 67 U.S. 635, 660, 668 (1863).

31. Ibid., p. 660 (emphasis in original).

32. Edward S. Corwin, "The President's Power," *New Republic,* Jan. 29, 1951, p. 16.

33. Richard F. Grimmett, "Instances of Use of United States Armed Forces Abroad, 1798–1998," Congressional Research Service Report No. 98–881 F, Oct. 27, 1998.

34. Fisher, *Presidential War Power,* pp. 35–37.

35. Louis Fisher, *Presidential Spending Power,* pp. 13–14, 20.

36. Richardson, *A Compilation,* vol. 3, pp. 1288–1312.

37. Register of Debates, 24th Cong., 2d sess., 379–418, 427–506 (1837); S. Journal, 24th Cong., 2d sess., 123–24 (1837).

38. Fisher, *Presidential Spending Power,* pp. 14–21.

39. Ibid., pp. 99–104, 123–27.

40. 7 *Congressional Record* 2713–17 (1878). See also 7 *Cong. Rec.* 18–26, 28–35 (1877), 9 *Cong. Rec.* 326–38 (1879), and 10 *Cong. Rec.* 200, 663, 1261 (1880).

41. 17 *Cong. Rec.* 286 (1885).

42. Thomas B. Reed, "Spending Public Money: Appropriations for the Nation," *North American Review* 424 (1892): 319, 321.

43. *Harper's Weekly,* Aug. 12, 1882, p. 497.

44. "History of the Committee of Finance," S. Doc. 91–57, 91st Cong., 2d sess., 78 (1970).

45. Talcott Powell, *Tattered Banners,* p. 130.

46. Henry F. Pringle, *The Life and Times of William Howard Taft,* vol. 2, p. 641.

47. "Presidential Vetoes, 1789–1988," S. Pub. 102–12 (Feb., 1992), pp. 65–137.

48. Richardson, *A Compilation,* vol. 5, pp. 5001–5002 (May 8, 1886).

49. Ibid., pp. 5028 (June 23, 1886) and 5033–34 (June 23, 1886).

50. *Harper's Weekly,* July 3, 1886, p. 421. For discussion of the Arthur and Cleveland vetoes, see Fisher, *Presidential Spending Power,* pp. 25–27.

51. John J. Fitzgerald, "Budget Systems," Municipal Research, No. 62 (June, 1915), pp. 312, 322, 327, 340.

52. Charles Wallace Collins, "Constitutional Aspects of a National Budget System," *Yale Law Journal* 25 (1916): 376.

53. Ibid., pp. 382–83.

54. H. Doc. No. 1006, 65th Cong., 2d sess. (1918).

55. Annual Report of the Secretary of the Treasury, 1918–19, p. 121 (from his testimony of Oct. 4, 1919, to the House Select Committee on the Budget).

56. Ibid., p. 117.

57. David Houston, *Eight Years with Wilson's Cabinet,* p. 88.

58. Joseph G. Cannon, "The National Budget," H. Doc. No. 264, 66th Cong., 1st sess., 28–29 (1919).

59. Edward Fitzpatrick, *Budget Making in a Democracy,* pp. viii–ix, 117.

60. 42 Stat. 20 (1921).

61. Fisher, *Presidential Spending Power,* pp. 40–44.

62. Louis Fisher, *President and Congress,* pp. 133–44.

63. Raymond P. Bauer, et al., *American Business and Public Policy,* p. 37.

64. *Public Papers of the Presidents,* 1929, p. 432.

65. 47 Stat. 413–15, Title IV (1932).

66. 48 Stat. 351 (1934).

67. 49 Stat. 115 (1935).

68. 79 *Cong. Rec.* 2014 (1935).

69. *Panama Refining Co. v. Ryan,* 293 U.S. 388 (1935); *Schechter Corp. v. United States,* 295 U.S. 495 (1935).

70. *United States v. Curtiss-Wright Export Corp.,* 14 F.Supp. 230 (S.D. N.Y. 1936).

71. Brief for the United States, *United States v. Curtiss-Wright Export Corp.; Landmark Briefs,* vol. 32, pp. 901–30.

72. S. Doc. No. 417, 61st Cong., 2d sess. (1910).

73. Joel Francis Paschal, *Mr. Justice Sutherland: A Man Against the State,* p. 93.

74. 299 U.S. 304, 315–16 (1936).

75. Charles Lofgren, "*United States v. Curtiss-Wright Export Corporation:* An Historical Reassessment," *Yale Law Journal* 83 (1973): 1; David M. Levitan, "The Foreign Relations Power: An Analysis of Mr. Justice Sutherland's Theory," *Yale Law Journal* 55 (1946): 467; Claude H. Van Tyne, "Sovereignty in the American Revolution: An Historical Study," *American History Review* 12 (1907): 529.

76. 299 U.S. at 319, 320.

77. Ibid., p. 320.

78. E.g., *Little v. Barreme,* 6 U.S. (2 Cr.) 169 (1804); *Talbot v. Seeman,* 5 U.S. 1, 28 (1801).

79. *Youngstown Co. v. Sawyer,* 343 U.S. 579, 636 n.2 (1952).

80. *American Intern. Group v. Islamic Republic of Iran,* 657 F.2d 430, 438 n.6 (D.C. Cir. 1981).

81. Delegation: Ex parte Endo, 323 U.S. 283, 298 n.21 (1944); *Zemel v. Rusk,* 381 U.S. 1, 17 (1965); *Goldwater v. Carter,* 444 U.S. 996, 1000 n.1 (1979). Inherent powers: *United States v. Pink,* 315 U.S. 203, 229 (1942); *Knauff v. Shaughnessy,* 338 U.S. 537, 542 (1950); *United States v. Mazurie,* 419 U.S. 544, 566–67 (1975); *Dames & Moore v. Regan,* 453 U.S. 654, 661 (1981).

Chapter 3. War Powers after World War II

1. S. Doc. No. 36, 79th Cong., 1st sess., 2 (1945).

2. S. Report No. 1011, 79th Cong., 2d sess., 1 (1946).

3. 60 Stat. 832, sec. 136 (1946).

4. 57 Stat. 163 (1943); *Public Papers of the Presidents,* 1946, p. 514.

5. *The Papers of Woodrow Wilson,* ed. by Arthur S. Link, vol. 63, p. 451, and vol. 64, pp. 47, 51.

6. 89 *Cong. Rec.* 7646–47, 7728–29 (1943); 89 *Cong. Rec.* 9187, 9222 (1943).

7. 91 *Cong. Rec.* 8185 (1945).

8. Ibid., p. 8190.

9. "Participation by the United States in United Nations Organization," hearings before the House Committee on Foreign Affairs, 79th Cong., 1st sess., 23 (1945).

10. Ibid.

11. S. Report No. 717, 79th Cong., 1st sess., 5, 8 (1945); H. Report No. 1383, 79th Cong., 1st scss., 7 (1945); 91 *Cong. Rec.* 12267 (1945) (Cong. Sol Bloom).

12. 63 Stat. 735–36, sec. 5 (1949).

13. 63 Stat. 2244, Art. 5 (1949).

14. Ibid., p. 2246.

15. 62 Stat. 1703, Art. 20 (1947).
16. "North Atlantic Treaty (Part 1)," hearings Before the Senate Committee on Foreign Relations, 81st Cong., 1st sess., 11 (1949).
17. Ibid., p. 21.
18. S. Exec. Report No. 8, 81st Cong., 1st sess., 8 (1949).
19. 145 *Cong. Rec.* E462 (daily ed. Mar. 17, 1999).
20. Richard H. Heindel, et al., "The North Atlantic Treaty in the United States Senate," *American Journal of International Law* 43 (1949): 633, 649.
21. Ibid., p. 650. Mutual security treaties are carefully analyzed in Glennon, *Constitutional Diplomacy,* pp. 192–228.
22. Robert H. Bork, "Comments on the Articles on the Legality of the United States Action in Cambodia," *American Journal of International Law* 65 (1971): 79, 81.
23. *Department of State Bulletin* 23 (1950): 43
24. Ibid., p. 46.
25. *Public Papers of the Presidents,* 1950, p. 529.
26. Glenn D. Paige, *The Korean Decision,* p. 188.
27. Dean Acheson, *Present at the Creation,* p. 408.
28. Merle Miller, *Plain Speaking: An Oral Biography of Harry S Truman,* p. 276.
29. *Foreign Relations of the United States,* 1950, Korea, vol. 7, p. 182.
30. Ibid., pp. 200–202.
31. Ibid., p. 257.
32. Ibid., pp. 282–83, nn. 1–2, 287–91.
33. 96 *Cong. Rec.* 9156 (1950).
34. Ibid., pp. 9228–29.
35. Ibid., p. 9229.
36. Ibid.
37. Ibid., p. 9233.
38. Ibid.
39. Ibid.
40. Ibid., p. 9234.
41. Ibid., p. 9240.
42. Ibid.
43. Ibid., p. 9268.
44. Robert F. Turner, "Truman, Korea, and the Constitution: Debunking the 'Imperial President' Myth," *Harvard Journal of Law & Public Policy* 19 (1996): 533, 567.
45. E.g., 91 *Cong. Rec.* 10974, 11296, 11301, 11303 (1945).
46. Turner, "Truman, Korea, and the Constitution," p. 574.
47. *Public Papers of the Presidents,* 1951, 4 (question 18).
48. Ibid., p. 19.
49. Ibid., p. 21.
50. "Assignment of Ground Forces of the United States to Duty in the European Area," hearings before the Senate Committees on Foreign Relations and Armed Services, 82d Cong., 1st sess., 93 (1951).
51. "Background Information on the Use of United States Armed Forces in Foreign Coun-

tries," printed for the use of the House Committee on Foreign Affairs, 82d Cong., 1st sess., 1 (Committee Print 1951).

52. *Public Papers of the Presidents, 1950,* p. 504.

53. Ibid.

54. Ibid., p. 522.

55. *Weissman v. Metropolitan Life Ins. Co.,* 112 F.Supp. 420, 425 (S.D. Cal. 1953); see also *Gagliormella v. Metropolitan Life Ins. Co.,* 122 F.Supp. 246 (D. Mass. 1954); *Carius v. New York Life Ins. Co.,* 124 F.Supp. 388 (D. Ill. 1954); and A. Kenneth Pye, "The Legal Status of the Korean Hostilities," *Georgetown Law Journal* 45 (1956): 45.

56. Executive Order 10340, 17 *Federal Register* 3139 (1952).

57. 98 *Cong. Rec.* 3956 (1952).

58. Ibid., pp. 4029–30, 4033–34.

59. H. Doc. No. 534, 82d Cong., 2d sess., 371–72 (1952).

60. *Youngstown Sheet & Tube Co. v. Sawyer,* 103 F.Supp. 569, 577 (D.D.C. 1952).

61. *Youngstown Co. v. Sawyer,* 343 U.S. 579 (1952).

62. Henry Steele Commager, "Presidential Power: The Issue Analyzed," *New York Times Magazine,* Jan. 14, 1951, p. 11.

63. Ibid., p. 24.

64. Arthur Schlesinger, Jr., "Presidential Powers: Taft Statement on Troops Opposed, Actions of Past Presidents Cited," *New York Times,* Jan. 9, 1951, p. 28.

65. Richardson, *A Compilation,* vol. 1, p. 315.

66. Edward S. Corwin, "The President's Power," *New Republic,* Jan. 29, 1951, p. 15.

67. Edward S. Corwin, "Who Has the Power to Make War?," *New York Times Magazine,* July 31, 1949, p. 14.

68. Ibid.

69. Arthur M. Schlesinger, Jr., and Alfred de Grazia, *Congress and the Presidency: Their Role in Modern Times,* pp. 27–28.

70. Arthur M. Schlesinger, Jr., *The Imperial Presidency,* p. 9. Emphasis in original.

71. Ibid., p. 139.

72. "Changing American Attitudes Towards Foreign Policy," hearings before the Senate Committee on Foreign Relations, 90th Cong., 1st sess., 21 (1967).

73. "War Powers Legislation," hearings before the Senate Committee on Foreign Relations, 92d Cong., 1st sess., 62 (1971).

74. Fisher, *Presidential War Power,* pp. 104–11.

75. Dwight D. Eisenhower, *Waging Peace,* p. 179.

76. *Public Papers of the Presidents, 1954,* p. 306.

77. *Foreign Relations of the United States, 1952–54,* Indochina, vol. 13, part 1, p. 1242 (1982).

78. Ibid., p. 1224.

79. Chalmers M. Roberts, "The Day We Didn't Go to War," *The Reporter,* Sept. 14, 1954, pp. 31–32.

80. Fisher, *Presidential War Power,* pp. 111–13.

81. Gary R. Hess, "Commitment in the Age of Counterinsurgency: Kennedy's Vietnam Options and Decisions, 1961–1963," in *Shadow on the White House: Presidents and the Vietnam War, 1945–1975,* ed. by David L. Anderson, pp. 67–68.

82. Stanley Karnow, *Vietnam: A History,* p. 276.

83. Michael Beschloss, *Taking Charge: The Johnson White House Tapes, 1963–64,* pp. 213–14.

84. Ibid., p. 88 (emphasis in original).

85. 110 *Cong. Rec.* 18399 (1964); Fisher, *Presidential War Power,* p. 117.

86. Edwin E. Moïse, *Tonkin Gulf and the Escalation of the Vietnam War.*

87. Keith B. Richburg, "Mission to Hanoi," *Washington Post,* Nov. 11, 1995, pp. A21, A25.

88. 110 *Cong. Rec.* 18459 (1964).

89. Ibid.

90. 112 *Cong. Rec.* 4378 (1966).

91. 110 *Cong. Rec.* 18421 (1964).

92. Ibid.

93. *Public Papers of the Presidents,* 1963–64, p. 927.

94. Beschloss, *Taking Charge,* p. 493.

95. Ibid., p. 509.

96. 110 *Cong. Rec.* 18457 (1964).

97. Ibid., pp. 18457–58.

98. Ibid., p. 18462.

99. Ibid.

100. Ibid., p. 18542.

101. Ibid.

102. Ibid., p. 18543.

103. Ezra Y. Siff, *Why the Senate Slept: The Gulf of Tonkin Resolution and the Beginning of America's Vietnam War,* pp. 2, 7–10, 40, 52–57, 100.

104. Ibid., p. 56.

105. "The Gulf of Tonkin, the 1964 Incidents," hearing before the Senate Committee on Foreign Relations, 90th Cong., 2d sess., 80 (1968). See also "The Gulf of Tonkin, the 1964 Incidents (Part II)," Senate Committee on Foreign Relations, 90th Cong., 2d sess. (Dec. 16, 1968, Committee Print).

106. S. Report No. 129, 91st Cong., 1st sess., 16 (1969).

107. Townsend Hoopes and Douglas Brinkley, *FDR and the Creation of the U.N.,* p. 6.

108. Ibid., p. 4.

109. S. Report No. 129, pp. 22–23 (emphasis in original).

110. Ibid., p. 32.

111. 115 *Cong. Rec.* 17214 (1969).

112. 115 *Cong. Rec.* 17245 (1969).

113. 119 *Cong. Rec.* 33555 (1973).

114. Representatives Bella Abzug, Robert Drinan, John Duncan, John James Flynt, Jr., William Harsha, Ken Hechler, Elizabeth Holtzman, William Hungate, Phillip Landrum, Trent Lott, Joseph Maraziti, Dale Milford, William Natcher, Frank Stubblefield, and Jamie Whitten.

115. 119 *Cong. Rec.* 36220 (1973) (Rep. Holtzman).

116. Ibid., p. 33870.

117. Ibid., p. 36221.

118. Thomas F. Eagleton, *War and Presidential Power: A Chronicle of Presidential Surrender,* pp. 213–20.

119. 119 *Cong. Rec.* at 36204.

120. Ibid., p. 36207.

121. Ibid., p. 36208.

122. Ibid., p. 36220.

123. Ibid., p. 35953.

124. Ibid., p. 36178.

125. Fisher, *Presidential War Power*, pp. 134–40.

126. *Public Papers of the Presidents, 1982*, II, p. 1063.

127. Ibid., p. 1079.

128. Ibid., p. 1188.

129. 97 Stat. 805 (1983).

130. *Public Papers of the Presidents, 1984*, I, p. 444.

131. *Public Papers of the Presidents, 1983*, II, p. 1513.

132. "U.S. Vetoes U.N. Resolution, 'Deploring' Grenada Invasion," *The New York Times*, Oct. 29, 1983, p. A1.

133. 129 *Cong. Rec.* 29994–99, 30285, 30600 (1983).

134. *The New York Times*, Nov. 17, 1983, p. 3.

135. *Public Papers of the Presidents, 1983*, II, p. 1674.

136. *Public Papers of the Presidents, 1986*, I, pp. 406–407.

137. Ibid., p. 468.

138. Ibid., p. 469.

139. Ibid., p. 478.

140. William L. Ball, III, letter to assistant to the president, Mar. 26, 1986, responding to Congressman Fascell's letter of Mar. 24, 1986, to President Reagan.

141. 98 Stat. 1935, § 8066(a) (1984).

142. "Security and Development Assistance," hearings before the Senate Committee on Foreign Relations, 99th Cong., 1st sess., 908–10 (1985); "Department of Defense Appropriations for 1986" (Part 2), hearings before the House Committee on Appropriations, 99th Cong., 1st sess., 1092 (1985).

143. H. Report No. 433 and S. Report No. 216, 100th Cong., 1st sess., 86–103 (1987).

144. Ibid., pp. 38–39, 45, 63, 69–70.

145. "Iran-Contra Investigation" (vol. 100-7, part 2), joint hearings before the Senate Select Committee on Secret Military Assistance to Iran and the Nicaraguan Opposition and the House Select Committee to Investigate Covert Arms Transactions with Iran, 100th Cong., 1st sess., 37 (1987). See also vol. 100–7, part 1, at p. 207.

146. Iran-Contra hearings, vol. 100–8, p. 158.

147. Ibid., vol. 100–2, pp. 25, 201, 279–80. See also Alex Whiting, "Controlling Tin Cup Diplomacy," *Yale Law Journal* 99 (1990): 2043, 2044–47.

148. 103 Stat. 1251, § 582(a) (1989). See Koh, *The National Security Constitution* and Theodore Draper, *A Very Thin Line: The Iran-Contra Affairs*.

149. *Crockett v. Reagan*, 558 F.Supp. 893 (D.D.C. 1982), affirmed, *Crockett v. Reagan*, 720 F.2d 1355 (D.C. Cir. 1983).

150. *Conyers v. Reagan*, 578 F.Supp. 324 (D.D.C. 1984), dismissed as moot, *Conyers v. Reagan*, 765 F.2d 1124 (D.C. Cir. 1985).

151. *Sanchez-Espinoza v. Reagan*, 568 F.Supp. 596, 600 (D.D.C. 1983).

152. *Sanchez-Espinoza v. Reagan,* 770 F.2d 202, 211 (D.C. Cir. 1985).

153. *Lowry v. Reagan,* 676 F.Supp. 333 (D.D.C. 1987), affirmed, No. 87–5426 (D.C. Cir. 1988).

Chapter 4. Military Operations by Bush and Clinton

1. *Public Papers of the Presidents,* 1990, I, p. 130.

2. *Public Papers of the Presidents,* 1989, II, p. 1723.

3. Ibid., pp. 1722–23.

4. U.S. Department of State, Bureau of Public Affairs, "Panama: A Just Cause," Current Policy No. 1240, p. 2.

5. 136 *Cong. Rec.* 1507 (1990).

6. James A. Baker, III, *The Politics of Diplomacy,* p. 304.

7. H. Doc. No. 101-237, 101st Cong., 2d sess. (1990).

8. 136 *Cong. Rec.* 25067–68 (1990).

9. "U.N. Vote Authorizes Use of Force Against Iraq," *Washington Post,* Nov. 30, 1990, p. A1.

10. Ibid.

11. Matthew D. Berger, "Implementing a United Nations Security Council Resolution: The President's Power to Use Force Without the Authorization of Congress," *Hastings International & Comparative Law Review* 15 (1991): 83, 88–89.

12. Jane E. Stromseth, "Understanding Constitutional War Powers Today: Why Methodology Matters," *Yale Law Journal* 106 (1996): 845, 896.

13. Thomas M. Franck, "Declare War? Congress Can't," *The New York Times,* Dec. 11, 1990, p. A27.

14. Thomas M. Franck and Faiza Patel, "UN Police Action in Lieu of War: 'The Old Order Changeth,'" *American Journal of International Law* 85 (1991): 74.

15. "Crisis in the Persian Gulf Region: U.S. Policy Options and Implications," hearings before the Senate Committee on Armed Services, 101st Cong., 2d sess., 701 (1990).

16. Congressional Quarterly Almanac, 1990, p. 742.

17. *Dellums v. Bush,* 752 F.Supp. 1141, 1151 (D.D.C. 1990).

18. *Public Papers of the Presidents,* 1991, I, pp. 13–14.

19. Ibid., p. 20.

20. George Bush and Brent Scowcroft, *A World Transformed,* p. 441.

21. 137 *Cong. Rec.* 1034, 1049 (1991).

22. *Public Papers of the Presidents,* 1991, I, p. 40.

23. Bush and Scowcroft, *A World Transformed,* p. 446.

24. Louis Fisher, "President Clinton as Commander in Chief," in *Rivals for Power,* ed. by James A. Thurber, p. 215.

25. *Public Papers of the Presidents,* 1993, I, p. 337.

26. Ibid., p. 938.

27. Ibid., p. 940.

28. "Show of Strength Offers Benefits for Clinton," *Washington Post,* June 28, 1993, pp. A1, A14.

29. *Public Papers of the Presidents,* 1993, I, pp. 938–39.

30. Michael Ratner and Jules Lobel, "Bombing Baghdad: Illegal Reprisal or Self-Defense?" *Legal Times,* July 5, 1993, p. 24.

31. *Public Papers of the Presidents,* 1992, II, pp. 2176, 2180.
32. *Public Papers of the Presidents,* 1993, I, p. 870.
33. 139 *Cong. Rec.* 22748 (1993).
34. Ibid., p. 22754.
35. *Public Papers of the Presidents,* 1993, II, p. 1705.
36. Ibid., p. 1740.
37. *Public Papers of the Presidents,* 1993, II, p. 1755.
38. *Washington Post,* Oct. 18, 1993, p. A16.
39. 139 *Cong. Rec.* 25729 (1993).
40. Ibid.
41. *Public Papers of the Presidents,* 1994, I, p. 823.
42. 140 *Cong. Rec.* 11632–33 (1994).
43. Ibid., pp. 12420–21.
44. *Congressional Quarterly Weekly Report,* May 28, 1994, p. 1420, and June 11, 1994, p. 1560.
45. 140 *Cong. Rec.* 12418 (1994).
46. "Clinton Ratchets Up Sanctions Against Haiti Military Regime," *Washington Post,* June 11, 1994, p. A1; "Escalating U.S. Pressure on Haiti is Two-Edged Sword," *Washington Post,* June 12, 1994, p. A9.
47. 140 *Cong. Rec.* 15016 (1994).
48. Ibid.
49. Ibid., p. 15018.
50. Ibid., p. 15019.
51. Ibid., p. 15023.
52. Ibid., p. 15031.
53. Ibid., p. 15032.
54. Fisher, *Presidential War Power,* pp. 24–28.
55. Ibid., pp. 15047, 15052.
56. "U.N. Authorizes Invasion of Haiti," *Washington Post,* Aug. 1, 1994, p. A1.
57. 140 *Cong. Rec.* 19324 (1994).
58. Ibid., p. 19320.
59. *Public Papers of the Presidents,* 1994, II, p. 1419.
60. Ibid., p. 1559.
61. Ibid., p. 1551.
62. Ibid., p. 1549.
63. "Clinton Halts Invasion as Haiti Leaders Agree to Quit; U.S. Forces Land Today," *Washington Post,* Sept. 19, 1994, p. A1.
64. 140 *Cong. Rec.* H10972–73 (daily ed. Oct. 5, 1994); 140 *Cong. Rec.* H11121–22 (daily ed. Oct. 6, 1994); 108 Stat. 4358, sec. 1(b) (1994).
65. 140 *Cong. Rec.* 28236 (1994).
66. *Public Papers of the Presidents,* 1993, I, p. 594.
67. *Public Papers of the Presidents,* 1993, II, at 1455.
68. Ibid., p. 1781.
69. bid., p. 1620.
70. 139 *Cong. Rec.* 22304–305 (1993).
71. *Public Papers of the Presidents,* 1993, II, p. 1763.

72. Ibid., p. 1764.
73. Ibid., p. 1768.
74. Ibid., p. 1770.
75. 139 *Cong. Rec.* 25479, 25485 (1993).
76. Ibid., p. 25483.
77. Ibid.
78. 107 Stat. 1474, sec. 8146 (1993).
79. *Public Papers of the Presidents,* 1994, I, p. 186.
80. Ibid., p. 355.
81. Ibid., p. 661.
82. U.S. Department of State, The Clinton Administration's Policy on Reforming Multilateral Peace Operations, May, 1994, p. 3.
83. 140 *Cong. Rec.* 15482–84 (1994).
84. Ibid., pp. 12391–408.
85. "NATO Bombs Serbs in War's Biggest Air Raid," *Washington Post,* Aug. 30, 1995, p. A1.
86. *Public Papers of the Presidents,* 1995, II, p. 1280.
87. Ibid.
88. Ibid., p. 1353.
89. 141 *Cong. Rec.* S14634 (daily ed. Sept. 29, 1995).
90. Ibid.
91. Ibid.
92. Ibid., p. S14636.
93. Ibid.
94. Ibid., p. S14640.
95. "President Not 'Bound' by Hill on Deploying Troops, Christopher Says," *Washington Post,* Oct. 18, 1995, p. A27.
96. *Public Papers of the Presidents,* 1995, II, p. 1630.
97. 141 *Cong. Rec.* H11398–422 (daily ed. Oct. 30, 1995).
98. Ibid., p. H11403.
99. Ibid., pp. H11404, H11407–408.
100. Ibid., p. H13248 (daily ed. Nov. 17, 1995).
101. Ibid., p. H13224.
102. Ibid., p. H13229.
103. Ibid., p. H13230.
104. Ibid., p. H13239.
105. 141 *Cong. Rec.* S15394 (daily ed. Oct. 20, 1995).
106. *Public Papers of the Presidents,* 1995, II, p. 1702.
107. 141 *Cong. Rec.* H13228 (daily ed. Nov. 17, 1995).
108. *Public Papers of the Presidents,* 1995, II, p. 1784.
109. Ibid., p. 1857.
110. 141 *Cong. Rec.* S17529 (daily ed. Nov. 27, 1995).
111. "As Dole Equivocates on Troop Deployment, Most GOP Rivals Oppose Plan," *Washington Post,* Nov. 28, 1995, p. A9.
112. Ibid.
113. Ibid., p. S17584 (daily ed. Nov. 28, 1995).

114. Ibid., p. S17543.

115. Ibid., pp. S18506–12 (daily ed. Dec. 13, 1995).

116. Ibid., pp. S18403–405 (daily ed. Dec. 12, 1995).

117. Ibid., pp. S18458–59 (daily ed. Dec. 13, 1995).

118. Ibid., pp. S18398–401 (daily ed. Dec. 12, 1995); S18465–66 (daily ed. Dec. 13, 1995).

119. Ibid., p. S18512.

120. Ibid., p. S18470.

121. Ibid., p. S18552.

122. Ibid., p. S18549.

123. Ibid., p. S18550.

124. Ibid.

125. Ibid., pp. H14796–872 (daily ed. Dec. 13, 1995).

126. *Public Papers of the Presidents,* 1995, II, p. 1917.

127. *Public Papers of the Presidents,* 1996, II, p. 2221.

128. Ibid., p. 2220 (emphasis added).

129. 34 *Weekly Compilation of Presidential Documents* 374 (Mar. 3, 1998).

130. 144 *Cong. Rec.* S2506–32 (daily ed. Mar. 25, 1998); 144 *Cong. Rec.* S3810–17, S3840, S3843 (Apr. 30, 1998).

131. "White House to Ask $1 Billion for Bosnia Troop Deployment," *Washington Post,* Sept. 28, 1995, p. A24.

132. "Cost of U.S. Bosnia Force Put at $1.5 Billion," *Washington Post,* Nov. 11, 1995, p. A21.

133. *Public Papers of the Presidents,* 1995, II, p. 1813.

134. "Clinton Accepts Hill's Defense Spending Bill," *Washington Post,* Dec. 1, 1995, p. A6.

135. U.S. Department of Defense, Bosnia FY 1996 Funding and Financing, Jan. 22, 1996. See also "Funding Proposal Altered for Bosnia Deployment," *Washington Post,* Jan. 20, 1996, p. A4.

136. Alice M. Rivlin, director of the Office of Management and Budget, letter to President Clinton, undated (probably late January, 1996). See "A Secret Agency's Secret Budgets Yield 'Lost' Billions, Officials Say," *The New York Times,* Jan. 30, 1996, p. A1. For further details on the funding of the Bosnia commitment, see William C. Banks and Jeffrey D. Straussman, "A New Imperial Presidency? Insights from U.S. Involvement in Bosnia," *Political Science Quarterly* 114 (1999): 203–208.

137. 34 *Weekly Compilation of Presidential Documents,* 2008 (Oct. 8, 1998).

138. "Hill Signals Support for Airstrikes," *Washington Post,* Oct. 2, 1998, p. A35.

139. "Italy's Center-Left Government is Toppled by One Vote," *The New York Times,* Oct. 10, 1998, p. A3.

140. "Allies Grim, Milosevic Defiant Amid Kosovo Uncertainty," *Washington Post,* Oct. 8, 1998, p. A32.

141. 145 *Cong. Rec.* H1249–50 (daily ed. Mar. 11, 1999).

142. Ibid., p. S3118.

143. James A. Leach, "A War Vote," *Washington Post,* Apr. 15, 1999, p. A31.

144. 145 *Cong. Rec.* H2419 (daily ed. Apr. 28, 1999).

145. 145 *Cong. Rec.* S4531 (daily ed. May 3, 1999). Letter of Apr. 28, 1999.

146. 145 *Cong. Rec.* S4616 (daily ed. May 4, 1999). Most of the debate occurred on May 3 (pp. S4514–70).

147. Ibid., p. S4553 (daily ed. May 3, 1999).

148. Ibid., p. S5809 (daily ed. May 24, 1999).

149. Ibid., p. S5920.

150. Ibid., p. S5939.

151. Ibid., pp. S6034–40 (daily ed. May 26, 1999).

152. *Campbell v. Clinton,* 52 F.Supp. 2d 34, 43 (D.D.C. 1999), affirmed Feb. 18, 2000.

153. 34 *Weekly Compilation of Presidential Documents,* 1643 (1998).

154. Ibid., p. 1644.

155. "Possible Benign Use Is Seen for Chemical At Factory in Sudan," *The New York Times,* Aug. 27, 1998, p. A1.

156. "Flaws in U.S. Account Raise Questions of Strike in Sudan," *The New York Times,* Aug. 29, 1998, pp. A1, A4. See also "U.S. Notes Gaps in Data About Drug Plant," *The New York Times,* Sept. 3, 1998, p. A6.

157. "Saudi Demands Compensation for Destroyed Plant," *Washington Post,* Feb. 4, 1999, p. A9.

158. "U.S. Unfreezes $24 Million in Assets of Saudi Who Owned El Shifa Plant," *Washington Post,* May 4, 1999, p. A11.

159. "U.S. Wasn't Sure Plant Had Nerve Gas Role," *Washington Post,* Aug. 21, 1999, p. A1; "To Bomb Sudan Plant, or Not: A Year Later, Debates Rankle," *The New York Times,* Oct 27, 1999, p. A12.

160. *Public Papers of the Presidents,* 1996, II, p. 1469.

161. "Cleland Warns against Repeating Tonkin Gulf Mistake," *Congressional Quarterly Weekly Report,* Jan. 31, 1998, p. 247; "Iraq Resolution Sends Chills through Some in Congress," *Washington Post,* Feb. 3, 1998, p. A13.

162. 105 Stat. 3, sec. 2(a) (1991).

163. *Congressional Quarterly Weekly Report,* Dec. 1, 1990, p. 4007.

164. "Students Receive Albright Politely," *Washington Post,* Feb. 20, 1998, p. A19.

165. 34 *Weekly Compilation of Presidential Documents,* 2494–97 (Dec. 16, 1998).

166. Ibid., p. 2496.

167. "Jets Said to Avoid Poison Gas Sites," *The New York Times,* Dec. 18, 1998, p. A1.

168. 34 *Weekly Compilation of Presidential Documents,* 2513 (Dec. 18, 1998).

169. "U.S. Warns Iraq of More Raids," *Washington Post,* Dec. 21, 1998, p. A1.

170. "In Intense but Little-Noticed Fight, Allies Have Bombed Iraq All Year," *The New York Times,* Aug. 13, 1999, p. A1.

171. 137 *Cong. Rec.* 408 (1991).

172. 139 *Cong. Rec.* 25483 (1993).

173. Ibid.

174. "U.S. Troops Vital to Bosnia Peace, Clinton Says," *Washington Post,* Nov. 28, 1995, p. A1.

175. 145 *Cong. Rec.* S960 (daily ed. Jan. 23, 1999).

176. 141 *Cong. Rec.* S17863 (daily ed. Nov. 30, 1995).

177. 90 Stat. 757, sec. 404 (1976).

178. 100 Stat. 3341–307, sec. 216 (1986). See also Louis Fisher, "Presidential Independence and the Power of the Purse," *U.C. Davis Journal of International Law & Politics* 3 (1997): 107; Louis Fisher, "How Tightly Can Congress Draw the Purse Strings?," *American Journal of International Law* 83 (1989): 758.

179. 141 *Cong. Rec.* H5672 (daily ed. June 7, 1995).

180. Ibid., p. H5763.

181. 144 *Cong. Rec.* H11722 (daily ed. Dec. 17, 1998).

182. Ibid.

183. Ibid.

184. Ibid., pp. H11726 (Cong. Sanders), H11727 (Cong. Skaggs and Traficant), H11729 (Cong. Paul), H11733 (Cong. DeFazio), H11734 (Cong. Gekas).

185. "Sen. Lott's Statement on Iraq," *Washington Post,* Dec. 17, 1998, p. A34.

186. Ibid.

187. "Lott Retreats From Criticism of Airstrikes," *Washington Post,* Dec. 18, 1998, p. A42.

188. "Legislators Get Plea by Clinton on Bosnia Force," *The New York Times,* Nov. 29, 1995, p. A1. The same reporter a week later stated that "President Clinton does not need the support of Congress for the mission." "Congress and the White House Barter Over Support for U.S. Mission," *The New York Times,* Dec. 5, 1995, p. A7. The following day, this reporter wrote: "President Clinton does not need a resolution from Congress to deploy the troops." "G.O.P. Opposition Forces Dole to Delay Vote on Bosnia," *The New York Times,* Dec. 6, 1995, p. A14.

189. Louis Fisher, letter to Katharine Q. Seelye, *The New York Times,* Dec. 7, 1995.

190. "Clinton Gives Republicans Pledge on Arming Bosnians," *The New York Times,* Dec. 13, 1995, p. A16. The following day the reporter wrote: "Mr. Clinton said he did not need Congressional approval to send 20,000 troops as part of a 60,000-member NATO force." "Senate and House Won't Stop Funds on Bosnia Mission," *The New York Times,* Dec. 14, 1995, p. A1.

191. "Bosnia and Congress," *The Hill,* Oct. 25, 1995, p. 32.

192. "Say 'no' to the Dayton Deal," *The Hill,* Nov. 29, 1995, p. 24.

193. *Washington Post,* Nov. 29, 1995, p. A24.

194. "As Dole Equivocates on Troop Deployment, Most GOP Rivals Oppose Plan," *Washington Post,* Nov. 28, 1995, p. A9.

195. "Dole Supports U.S. Troop Plan for Bosnia Peace," *Washington Post,* Dec. 1, 1995, p. A1.

196. "Dole's 'Old Values' Emerge on Bosnia," *Washington Post,* Dec. 12, 1995, p. A1.

197. Ibid., p. A6.

198. Ibid.

199. David S. Broder, "Dole: Clear and Consistent on Bosnia," *Washington Post,* Dec. 3, 1995, p. C7.

200. "Ireland Sends Home a Chief," *Washington Post,* Dec. 5, 1995, p. A2.

201. "Fewer Doubts about Clinton as Commander," *Washington Post,* Sept. 6, 1996, p. A28.

202. Ibid.

203. Louis Fisher, "Sidestepping Congress: Presidents Acting under the UN and NATO," *Case Western Reserve Law Review* 47 (1997): 1237.

Chapter 5. Spending Powers after World War II

1. Louis Fisher, *Presidential Spending Power,* pp. 147–74.

2. "Executive Impoundment of Funds," hearings before the Senate Committee on the Judiciary, 92d Cong., 1st sess., p. 1 (1971).

3. Ibid., pp. 2–3.

4. Ibid., p. 3.

5. Ibid., p. 94.

6. Ibid., p. 97.

7. Ibid., p. 135.

8. *Public Papers of the Presidents,* 1972, pp. 965–66.

9. Ibid., p. 742.

10. "Nixon Message Warns Congress against Voting 'Excessive' Money Bills," *Wall Street Journal,* July 27, 1972, p. 3.

11. Richard D. Fenno, Jr., "If, as Ralph Nader Says, Congress is 'The Broken Branch,' How Come We Love Our Congressmen So Much?," paper presented to the Harvard Club, Boston, Mass., Dec. 12, 1972, reprinted at 119 *Cong. Rec.* 7174 (1973). The quoted material appears in the third column, last full paragraph, on p. 7174.

12. H. Report No. 147, 93d Cong., 1st sess., 39 (1973).

13. H. Report No. 90, 93d Cong., 1st sess., 7 (1973); S. Report No. 731, 94th Cong., 2d sess., 3 (1976).

14. "$465 Billion Debt Limit," hearing before the Senate Committee on Finance, 92d Cong., 2d sess., 42 (1972).

15. 8 *Weekly Compilation of Presidential Documents,* 1752 (Dec. 11, 1972).

16. Fisher, *Presidential Spending Power,* pp. 147–74, 177–97; James P. Pfiffner, *The President, the Budget, and Congress: Impoundment and the 1974 Budget Act,* pp. 40–44.

17. 119 *Cong. Rec.* 11873 (1973).

18. Ibid., pp. 14483–85.

19. *Public Citizen, Inc., v. Clawson,* Civil Action No. 759–73 (D.D.C. July 30, 1973).

20. "Impoundment of Appropriated Funds by the President," joint hearings before the Committees on Government Operations and the Judiciary, 93d Cong., 1st sess., 1 (1973).

21. Ibid., pp. 1–2.

22. Ibid., p. 4.

23. Ibid., p. 25.

24. Ibid., pp. 26–27.

25. Ibid., pp. 269–72 (statement by Roy L. Ash, director-designate of the Office of Management and Budget).

26. Ibid., p. 269.

27. Ibid., p. 270.

28. Ibid., p. 362.

29. Ibid., p. 363.

30. Ibid.

31. Ibid.

32. 120 *Cong. Rec.* 19674 (1974).

33. 119 *Cong. Rec.* 15236 (1973).

34. "The Deferral Process After *Chadha,*" hearing the House Committee on Rules, 96th Cong., 2d sess., 1 (1986).

35. Ibid., pp. 21–22.

36. *City of New Haven, Conn., v. United States,* 809 F.2d 900 (D.C. Cir. 1987); 101 Stat. 785, sec. 206 (1987).

37. H. Report No. 147, 93d Cong., 1st sess., 1 (1973).

38. John B. Gilmour, *Reconcilable Differences? Congress, the Budget Process, and the Deficit,* p. 229.

39. Ibid., p. 230.

40. Allen Schick, *Congress and Money,* p. 313. See also Joel Havemann, *Congress and the Budget,* pp. 152–53.

41. Schick, *Congress and Money,* pp. 469–70, 474–81.

42. 122 *Cong. Rec.* 17843 (1976).

43. 124 *Cong. Rec.* 12077 (1978).

44. Ibid.

45. Ibid., p. 12082.

46. 125 *Cong. Rec.* 9028 (1979).

47. Rudolph G. Penner, "An Appraisal of the Congressional Budget Process," in *Crisis in the Budget Process,* ed. by Allen Schick, p. 69.

48. David A. Stockman, *The Triumph of Politics,* p. 59.

49. Ibid., p. 200.

50. Ibid., p. 91.

51. Ibid., p. 245.

52. Richard Darman, *Who's In Control? Polar Politics and the Sensible Center,* pp. 95–97. A similar account appears in Stockman, *The Triumph of Politics,* p. 291.

53. Trent Lott, "The Need to Improve the Budget Process: A Republican's View," in *Crisis in the Budget Process,* ed. by Schick, p. 72.

54. "Budget Reform Proposals," joint hearings before the Senate Committees on Governmental Affairs and the Budget, 101st Cong., 1st sess., 3 (1989).

55. Allen Schick, *The Capacity to Budget,* p. 204.

56. Ibid., p. 205.

57. 134 *Cong. Rec.* 587 (1988).

58. Raphael Thelwell, "Gramm-Rudman-Hollings Four Years Later: A Dangerous Illusion," *Public Administration Review* 50 (1990): 190, 197.

59. "Budget Process Reform," hearings before the House Committee on the Budget, 101st Cong., 2d sess., 1 (1990).

60. Louis Fisher, *The Politics of Shared Power,* p. 240.

61. Ibid.

62. "The Balanced Budget and Emergency Deficit Control Act of 1985," hearing Before the House Committee on Government Operations, 99th Cong., 1st sess., 26–27 (1985).

63. Ibid., p. 200; see also pp. 198–200, 207–12.

64. Ibid., p. 200.

65. Ibid., p. 221.

66. 131 *Cong. Rec.* 26197 (1985).

67. Ibid., p. 26198.

68. Ibid., p. 30160.

69. Ibid., p. 30274.

70. 99 Stat. 1098, sec. 274 (1985).

71. 131 *Cong. Rec.* 36079 (1985).

72. Ibid., p. 36079.

73. Ibid., p. 36080.
74. Ibid., p. 35915.
75. Ibid., pp. 36102–103, 35916.
76. *Synar v. United States,* 626 F.Supp. 1374, 1391–93 (D.D.C. 1986) (three-judge court).
77. *Bowsher v. Synar,* 478 U.S. 714 (1986).
78. See Timothy J. Muris, "The Uses and Abuses of Budget Baselines," in John F. Cogan, Timothy J. Muris, and Allen Schick, *The Budget Puzzle,* pp. 41–78; Allen Schick, "The Study of Microbudgeting," in Cogan, et al., *The Budget Puzzle,* pp. 116–17.
79. 130 *Cong. Rec.* 10844 (1984).
80. Ibid., pp. 10851–52.
81. Ibid., pp. 10857–59.
82. Ibid., pp. 10851, 10859–70.
83. Ibid., p. 10860.
84. Ibid., p. 10861.
85. Ibid.
86. Ibid., p. 10870.
87. E.g., *Public Papers of the Presidents,* 1984, I, p. 89; *Public Papers of the Presidents,* 1985, I, p. 105; *Public Papers of the Presidents,* 1986, I, p. 127; *Public Papers of the Presidents,* 1987, I, p. 58.
88. *Public Papers of the Presidents,* 1988, I, p. 86.
89. Stephen Glazier, "Reagan Already Has Line-Item Veto," The *Wall Street Journal,* Dec. 4, 1987, reprinted at 133 *Cong. Rec.* 34208 (1987).
90. 1 Stat. 95, ch. XXIII (1789).
91. 1 Stat. 104 (1790).
92. *The Writings of George Washington,* ed. by John Clement Fitzpatrick, vol. 33, p. 96.
93. 1 Stat. 342, 346 (1794).
94. 1 Stat. 542, 547, 563.
95. Farrand, *Records of the Federal Convention of 1787,* vol. 2, p. 273.
96. H. Doc. No. 104–272, 104th Cong., 2d sess., 233 (1997).
97. *Congressional Quarterly Weekly Report,* May 14, 1988, p. 1284.
98. Ibid.
99. *Pork Barrels and Principles: The Politics of the Presidential Veto,* published by the National Legal Center for the Public Interest in 1988. The sponsors of this conference were the National Tax Limitation Foundation and Citizens for America.
100. *Opinions of the Office of Legal Counsel,* Department of Justice, vol. 12, p. 128 (1988).
101. "Resolution Urges President to Try Line-Item Veto as a Test of Power," Roll Call, May 20, 1991, p. 3.
102. *Public Papers of the Presidents,* 1992, II, p. 479.
103. "Line Item Veto: The President's Constitutional Authority," hearing before the Senate Committee on the Judiciary, 103rd Cong., 2d sess., 197 (1994).
104. Ibid., p. 190.
105. For further analysis of the varied claims for an inherent item veto, see my statement for the Senate Judiciary Committee in "Line Item Veto: The President's Constitutional Authority," 103d Cong., 2d sess., 200–205 (1994).
106. U.S. General Accounting Office, Line Item Veto: Estimating Potential Savings (GAO/AFMD-92-7, Jan., 1992).

107. 138 *Cong. Rec.* 3562 (1992).

108. Ibid.

109. 138 *Cong. Rec.* 9981–82 (1992).

110. 142 *Cong. Rec.* S2942 (daily ed. Mar. 27, 1996). The letter was dated July 23, 1992.

111. 138 *Cong. Rec.* 30600–11, 31015–16 (1992); 139 *Cong. Rec.* 8502–12, 8519–40, 8617–43 (1993); 140 *Cong. Rec.* 16551–82 (1994).

112. 139 *Cong. Rec.* 8628 (1993).

113. 138 *Cong. Rec.* 30607 (1992).

114. 139 *Cong. Rec.* 8622–23 (1993).

115. 138 *Cong. Rec.* 3530–31 (1992).

116. Ibid., pp. 3534, 3535, 3538.

117. Ibid., p. 3534.

118. Ibid., pp. 3539–73.

119. Ibid., pp. 3861–62.

120. 139 *Cong. Rec.* 4504 (1993).

121. *Public Papers of the Presidents,* 1992 93, I, p. 479; *Congressional Quarterly Weekly Report,* Mar. 28, 1992, pp. 792–93.

122. 138 *Cong. Rec.* 6807 (1992).

123. "House Rearranges Bush's Budget Cuts," *Washington Post,* May 8, 1992, p. A8.

124. S. Report No. 102–274, 102d Cong., 2d sess., 47 (1992).

125. Contract with America 24–25 (1994).

126. "Line-Item Veto," joint hearing before the House Committee on Government Reform and Oversight and the Senate Committee on Governmental Affairs, 104th Cong., 1st sess., 22 (1995).

127. Ibid., pp. 57–58.

128. Ibid., p. 60.

129. Ibid., p. 62.

130. 141 *Cong. Rec.* H1264 (daily ed. Feb. 6, 1995).

131. 141 *Cong. Rec.* H1081 (daily ed. Feb. 2, 1995) [Cong. Gerald Solomon (R-N.Y.)].

132. Ibid., p. H1097 [Cong. Randy Tate (R-Wash.)].

133. Ibid., p. H1098 [Cong. Mike Parker (D-Miss.)].

134. S. Report No. 9, 104th Cong., 1st sess. (1995); S. Report No. 10, 104th Cong., 1st sess. (1995); S. Report No. 13, 104th Cong., 1st sess. (1995); S. Report No. 14, 104th Cong., 1st sess. (1995).

135. "Senate GOP Delays Line-Item Veto Debate," *Washington Post,* Mar. 13, 1995, p. A4.

136. S. Report No. 104-13, 104th Cong., 1st sess., 3–4 (1995).

137. 141 *Cong. Rec.* S4484 (daily ed. Mar. 23, 1995).

138. Elizabeth Drew, *Showdown: The Struggle Between the Gingrich Congress and the Clinton White House,* pp. 169–70.

139. H. Report No. 104-491, 104th Cong., 2d sess., 15 (1996).

140. 142 *Cong. Rec.* S2931 (daily ed. Mar. 27, 1996); 142 *Cong. Rec.* H2981 (daily ed. Mar. 28, 1996).

141. 142 *Cong. Rec.* S2955 (daily ed. Mar. 27, 1996).

142. 110 Stat. 1200 (1996).

143. "The Line Item Veto," hearing before the House Committee on Rules, 105th Cong., 2d sess., 13 (1998).

144. 33 *Weekly Compilation of Presidential Documents,* 1501–1502 (1997).

145. 143 *Cong. Rec.* S10800 (daily ed. Oct. 9, 1997) (statement by Sen. Stevens).

146. 143 *Cong. Rec.* S12570–72 (daily ed. Nov. 13, 1997).

147. "Clinton Recants on Item Veto of Pension Switch," *Washington Post,* Dec. 20, 1997, p. A1.

148. 33 *Weekly Compilation of Presidential Documents,* 1226 (Aug. 11, 1997).

149. Ibid., p. 1209 (Aug. 6, 1997).

150. 110 Stat. at 1211, sec. 3.

151. 142 *Cong. Rec.* H3010 (daily ed. Mar. 28, 1996).

152. Ibid.

153. *Byrd v. Raines,* 956 F.Supp. 25 (D.D.C. 1997). The court argued that presidential cancellations were equivalent to repeal, and that repeal could be accomplished only through the regular legislative process: passage by both Houses and presentment of a bill to the President.

154. *Raines v. Byrd,* 117 S.Ct. 2312 (1997).

155. *Clinton v. City of New York,* 118 S.Ct. 2091 (1998), affirming, *City of New York v. Clinton,* 985 F.Supp. 168 (D.D.C. 1998).

156. *Clinton v. City of New York,* 118 S.Ct. at 2116–17.

157. Ibid., p. 2118.

158. Ibid., p. 2121.

159. *Annals of Congress,* 14th Cong., 1st sess. (1816), p. 1161 (Cong. Benjamin Huger).

160. *Annals of Congress,* 14th Cong., 2d sess. (1816), p. 237 (Cong. Richard Johnson).

161. 2 *Cong. Rec.* 110 (1873).

162. 18 Stat. 4 (1874). For more on these legislative travails, see Louis Fisher, "History of Pay Adjustments for Members of Congress," in Robert W. Hartman and Arnold R. Weber, eds., *The Rewards of Public Service: Compensating Top Federal Officials,* pp. 25–52.

163. 81 Stat. 644 (1967); 84 Stat. 1946 (1970).

164. *National Treasury Employees Union v. Nixon,* 492 F.2d 587 (D.C. Cir. 1974).

165. *Pressler v. Simon,* 428 F.Supp. 302 (D.D.C. 1976), vacated and remanded in light of intervening amendment to the Salary Act, 431 U.S. 169 (1977), but later affirmed, 434 U.S. 1028 (1978).

166. 135 *Cong. Rec.* 1725–26, 1754 (1989).

167. 103 Stat. 1765 (1989); 2 U.S.C. § 359 (1994).

168. 141 *Cong. Rec.* 2361 (1995).

169. *Public Papers of the Presidents,* 1984, II, p. 1228.

170. *Dieck v. Unified School Dist. of Antigo,* 477 N.W.2d 613, 617–18 (Wis. 1991).

171. For example, *Dwyer v. Omaha-Douglas Public Bldg. Comm'n,* 195 N.W.2d 236 (Neb. 1972).

172. See Louis Fisher, "The Effects of a Balanced Budget Amendment on Political Institutions," *Journal of Law & Politics* 9 (1992): 96–100.

173. 141 *Cong. Rec.* H3833 (daily ed. Mar. 28, 1995).

174. 143 *Cong. Rec.* H470 (daily ed. Feb. 12, 1997).

Chapter 6. What Might Be Done?

1. David S. Friedman, "Waging War Against Checks and Balances—The Claim of an Unlimited Presidential War Power," *St. John's Law Review* 57 (1983): 213, 228.

2. 145 *Cong. Rec.* S959 (daily ed. Jan. 23, 1999).

3. Cong. Lee H. Hamilton, "The Role of the Congress in U.S. Foreign Policy," delivered to the Center for Strategic and International Studies, Nov. 19, 1998, at p. 1.

4. Joseph A. Califano, Jr., "When There's No Draft," *Washington Post,* Apr. 6, 1999, p. A23.

5. "Iraq Remains Defiant as U.S. Ends Attacks," *Washington Post,* Dec. 20, 1998, p. A48.

6. 144 *Cong. Rec.* E1668 (daily ed. Sept. 9, 1998).

7. For compilations of these incidents, see Richard F. Grimmett, "Instances of Use of United States Armed Forces Abroad, 1798–1998," Congressional Research Service Report No. 98–881 F, Oct. 27, 1998; R. Ernest Dupuy and William H. Baumer, *The Little Wars of the United States;* James Grafton Rogers, *World Policing and the Constitution;* and Milton Offutt, "The Protection of Citizens Abroad by the Armed Forces of the United States," *Johns Hopkins University Studies in Historical and Political Science,* Series XLIV, No. 4 (1928).

8. "No Reservoir of Credibility: Politics Stop No More At the Water's Edge," *The New York Times,* Dec. 17, 1998, p. A1.

9. Ibid., p. A15.

10. 35 *Weekly Compilation of Presidential Documents,* 760 (Apr. 28, 1999).

11. *Schenck v. United States,* 249 U.S. 47 (1919).

12. *Frohwerk v. United States,* 249 U.S. 204 (1919); *Debs v. United States,* 249 U.S. 211 (1919).

13. Zechariah Chafee, Jr., "Freedom of Speech in War Time," *Harvard Law Review* 32 (1919): 932.

14. James M. Lindsay, *Congress and the Politics of U.S. Foreign Policy,* p. 183.

15. "Students Receive Albright Politely," *Washington Post,* Feb. 20, 1998, p. A19.

16. Louis Fisher and David Gray Adler, "The War Powers Resolution: Time to Say Goodbye," *Political Science Quarterly* 113 (1998): 1.

17. H. Report No. 104–101, 104th Cong., 1st sess., 25 (1995).

18. 144 *Cong. Rec.* H5247 (daily ed. June 24, 1998).

19. Ibid., pp. S9386–92 (daily ed. July 30, 1998).

20. 144 *Cong. Rec.* H5217 (daily ed. June 24, 1998).

21. "Executive Privilege: Legal Opinions Regarding Claim of President Ronald Reagan in Response to a Subpoena Issued to James G. Watt, Secretary of the Interior," prepared for the House Committee on Energy and Commerce, 97th Cong., 1st sess., 2 (Comm. Print Nov. 1981).

22. "Contempt of Congress," hearings before the House Committee on Energy and Commerce, 97th Cong., 2d sess., 385–94 (1982); H. Report No. 898, 97th Cong., 2d sess. (1982).

23. "Disclosure of Classified Information to Congress," hearings before the Senate Select Committee on Intelligence, 105th Cong., 2d sess., 6 (1998).

24. Ibid., pp. 4–61.

25. S. Report No. 105–165, 105th Cong., 2d sess., 2 (1998).

26. Ibid., p. 5.

27. 144 *Cong. Rec.* S1561–64 (daily ed. Mar. 9, 1998).

28. "Record of Proceedings on H.R. 3829, The Intelligence Community Whistleblower Protection Act," hearings before the House Permanent Select Committee on Intelligence, 106th Cong., 1st sess., 32–53 (1998).

29. H. Report No. 105–747, Part 1, 105th Cong., 2d sess., 15 (1998).

30. 112 Stat. 2413, sec. 701(b) (1998). See H. Report No. 105–780, 105th Cong., 2d sess., 19 (1998).

31. "Lawmakers' Spending Plans Could Turn Surplus to Deficit," *New York Times,* Sept. 9, 1999, p. A18.

32. "Lott Says Veto Is Likely to Kill Tax Cut in '99," *New York Times,* Sept. 9, 1999, p. A1.

33. "House Narrowly Passes Foreign Aid Measures," *Washington Post,* Oct. 6, 1999, pp. A6, A7.

34. "Spending Agreement Eludes Negotiators," *Washington Post,* Nov. 13, 1999, p. A4.

35. 145 *Cong. Rec.* H259–63 (daily ed. Jan. 19, 1999).

36. Daniel J. Palazzolo, *Done Deal? The Politics of the 1997 Budget Agreement,* p. 37.

37. Jackie Koszczuk, "Gingrich Under Fire as Discord Simmers From Rank to Top," *Congressional Quarterly Weekly Report,* June 21, 1997, pp. 1415–18.

38. Andrew Taylor, "Clinton Gains Ground in Struggle Over Catchall Spending Bill," *Congressional Quarterly Weekly Report,* Oct. 10, 1998, pp. 2723–26.

39. Jeffrey L. Katz, "Shakeup in the House," *Congressional Quarterly Weekly Report,* Nov. 7, 1998, pp. 2989–92.

40. 144 *Cong. Rec.* H11584 (daily ed. Oct. 20, 1998).

41. 129 *Cong. Rec.* 25417 (1983).

42. *Public Papers of the Presidents,* 1985, II, p. 1401.

43. "Congressional Budget Process," hearings before the House Committee on Rules, 97th Cong., 2d sess., 239 (1982).

44. "Congressional Budget Process" (Part 3), hearings before the House Committee on Rules, 98th Cong., 2d sess., 161 (1984).

45. House Committee on Rules web site, hearing on "Points of Order That Guarantee Spending Levels," July 21, 1999.

46. 91 Stat. 1235, sec. 115 (1977).

47. President Carter, letter to Secretary Vance, Oct. 31, 1977, is reprinted in these hearings. "Foreign Assistance and Related Programs Appropriations, Fiscal Year 1981 (Part 1), hearings before the Senate Committee on Appropriations, 96th Cong., 2d sess., 53–170 (1980).

48. 462 U.S. 919, 952 (1983).

49. Louis Fisher, "The Legislative Veto: Invalidated, It Survives," *Law & Contemporary Problems* 56 (1993): 286–87.

50. *Public Papers of the Presidents,* 1984, II, p. 1057.

51. H. Report No. 916, 98th Cong., 2d sess., 48 (1984).

52. Letter is reproduced in Fisher, "The Legislative Veto: Invalidated, It Survives," p. 289.

53. "OMB Objection Raises House Panel's Hackles," *Washington Post,* Aug. 13, 1987, p. A13.

54. Ibid.

55. 101 Stat. 1329–155, sec. 514 (1987).

56. 103 Stat. 1219, sec. 514 (1989).

57. "Review of 'Pork' Projects Ordered by Budget Chief," *Washington Post,* Mar. 19, 1988, p. A4; James C. Miller III, Memorandum for Cabinet Officers and Agency Heads, Mar. 15, 1988.

58. Jamie L. Whitten, chairman of the House Appropriations Committee, letter to James C. Miller, OMB Director, Mar. 23, 1988.

59. John Stennis, chairman of the Senate Appropriations Committee, Jamie L. Whitten, chairman of the House Appropriations Committee, Mark O. Hatfield, ranking Republican of

the Senate Appropriations Committee, and Silvio O. Conte, ranking Republican of the House Appropriations Committee, letter to President Reagan, Mar. 23, 1988.

60. OMB Director Miller, letter to Representatives Whitten and Conte and Senators Stennis and Hatfield, Apr. 19, 1988; OMB Director Miller, memorandum for Cabinet Officers and Agency Heads, July 8, 1988, M-88-25; "Miller Acts to End Feud with Hill over Funding," *Washington Post,* July 12, 1988, p. A20.

Bibliography

Acheson, Dean. *Present at the Creation: My Years in the State Department.* New York: Norton, 1969.

Adler, David Gray, and Larry N. George, eds. *The Constitution and the Conduct of American Foreign Policy.* Lawrence: University Press of Kansas, 1996.

Anderson, David L., ed. *Shadow on the White House: Presidents and the Vietnam War, 1945–1975.* Lawrence: University Press of Kansas, 1993.

Baker, James A., III. *The Politics of Diplomacy: Revolution, War, and Peace, 1989–1992.* New York: G. P. Putnam's Sons, 1995.

Banks, William C., and Peter Raven-Hansen. *National Security Law and the Power of the Purse.* New York: Oxford University Press, 1994.

Bauer, Raymond A., Ithiel de Sola Pool, and Lewis Anthony Dexter. *American Business and Public Policy: The Politics of Foreign Trade.* New York: Atherton Press, 1963.

Beschloss, Michael. *Taking Charge: The Johnson White House Tapes, 1963–64.* New York: Simon & Schuster, 1997.

Blackstone, William. *Commentaries.* 5 vols. Philadelphia: William Young Birch, and Abraham Small, 1803.

Bush, George, and Brent Scowcroft. *A World Transformed.* New York: Knopf, 1998.

Carter, Clarence Edwin, ed. *The Territorial Papers of the United States.* 26 vols. Washington, D.C.: National Archives and Records Service, 1934–62.

Cogan, John F., Timothy J. Muris, and Allen Schick. *The Budget Puzzle: Understanding Federal Spending.* Stanford, Calif.: Stanford University Press, 1994.

Crovitz, L. Gordon, and Jeremy A. Rabkin, eds. *The Fettered Presidency: Legal Constraints on the Executive Branch.* Washington, D.C.: American Enterprise Institute, 1989.

Cummings, Homer, and Carl McFarland. *Federal Justice: Chapters in the History of Justice and the Federal Executive.* New York: Macmillan, 1937.

Darman, Richard. *Who's in Control? Polar Politics and the Sensible Center.* New York: Simon & Schuster, 1996.

Davis, Kenneth Culp. *Administrative Law and Government.* St. Paul, Minn.: West, 1960.

Draper, Theodore. *A Very Thin Line: The Iran Contra Affairs.* New York: Hill and Wang, 1991.

Drew, Elizabeth. *Showdown: The Struggle between the Gingrich Congress and the Clinton White House.* Touchstone Books, 1997.

Dumbauld, Edward. *The Bill of Rights and What It Means Today.* Norman: University of Oklahoma Press, 1957.

Dupuy, R. Ernest, and William H. Baumer. *The Little Wars of the United States.* New York: Hawthorn Books, 1968.

Eagleton, Thomas F. *War and Presidential Power: A Chronicle of Presidential Surrender.* New York: Liveright, 1974.

Einzig, Paul. *The Control of the Purse: Progress and Decline of Parliament's Financial Control.* London: Secker & Warburg, 1959.

Eisenhower, Dwight D. *Waging Peace.* Garden City, N.Y.: Doubleday, 1965.

Elliot, Jonathan, ed. *The Debates in the Several State Conventions, on the Adoption of the Federal Constitution.* 5 vols. Washington, D.C., 1836–45.

Ely, John Hart. *War and Responsibility: Constitutional Lessons of Vietnam and Its Aftermath.* Princeton, N.J.: Princeton University Press, 1993.

Farrand, Max, ed., *The Records of the Federal Convention of 1787.* 4 vols. New Haven, Conn.: Yale University Press, 1937.

Federalist, The, ed. Benjamin Fletcher Wright. Cambridge, Mass.: Belknap Press of Harvard University Press, 1961.

Fisher, Louis. *The Politics of Shared Power.* College Station: Texas A&M University Press, 1998.

———. *President and Congress: Power and Policy.* New York: Free Press, 1972.

———. *Presidential Spending Power.* Princeton, N.J.: Princeton University Press, 1975.

———. *Presidential War Power.* Lawrence: University Press of Kansas, 1995.

Fitzpatrick, Edward. *Budget Making in a Democracy.* New York: Macmillan, 1918.

Gilmour, John B. *Reconcilable Differences? Congress, the Budget Process, and the Deficit.* Berkeley: University of California Press, 1990.

Glennon, Michael J. *Constitutional Diplomacy.* Princeton, N.J.: Princeton University Press, 1990.

Hamilton, Alexander. *The Papers of Alexander Hamilton,* ed. Harold C. Syrett. New York: Columbia University Press, 1974.

Hartman, Robert W., and Arnold R. Weber, eds. *The Rewards of Public Service: Compensating Top Federal Officials.* Washington, D.C.: Brookings Institution, 1980.

Havemann, Joel. *Congress and the Budget.* Bloomington: Indiana University Press, 1978.

Holmes, Oliver Wendell. *Collected Legal Papers.* New York: Harcourt, Brace, and Howe, 1920.

Hoopes, Townsend, and Douglas Brinkley. *FDR and the Creation of the U.N.* New Haven, Conn.: Yale University Press, 1997.

Houston, David F. *Eight Years with Wilson's Cabinet.* Garden City, N.Y.: Doubleday, Page, and Company, 1926.

Jefferson, Thomas. *The Writings of Thomas Jefferson,* ed. Paul Leicester Ford. 10 vols. New York: G. P. Putnam's Sons, 1892–99.

Jones, Gordon S., and John A. Marini, eds. *The Imperial Congress: Crisis in the Separation of Powers.* New York: Pharos Books, 1988.

Karnow, Stanley. *Vietnam: A History.* New York: Viking, 1991.

Kent, James. *Commentaries on American Law.* 4 vols. New York: O. Halsted, 1830.

Koh, Harold Hongju. *The National Security Constitution: Sharing Power after the Iran-Contra Affair.* New Haven, Conn.: Yale University Press, 1990.

Landmark Briefs and Arguments of the Supreme Court of the United States: Constitutional Law (Philip B. Kurland and Gerhard Casper, eds.). Bethesda, Md.: University Publications of America, 1978–99.

Lindsay, James M. *Congress and the Politics of U.S. Foreign Policy.* Baltimore, Md.: Johns Hopkins University Press, 1994.

Locke, John. *Two Treatises of Civil Government.* London: J. M. Dent & Sons, 1962.

Lofgren, Charles A. *"Government from Reflection and Choice": Constitutional Essays on War, Foreign Relations, and Federalism.* New York: Oxford University Press, 1986.

McMaster, John Bach, and Frederick D. Stone, eds. *Pennsylvania and the Federal Constitution, 1787–1788.* Philadelphia: Historical Society of Pennsylvania, 1888.

Madison, James. *The Writings of James Madison,* ed. Gaillard Hunt. 9 vols. New York: G. P. Putnam's Sons, 1900–10.

Miller, Merle. *Plain Speaking: An Oral Biography of Harry S Truman.* New York: Berkley Medallion Books, 1974.

Moïse, Edwin E. *Tonkin Gulf and the Escalation of the Vietnam War.* Chapel Hill: University of North Carolina Press, 1996.

Montesquieu. *Oeuvres Complète.* Paris: Librairie Gallimard, 1951.

———. *The Spirit of the Laws,* New York: Hafner Publishing, 1949.

Moore, John Bassett. *The Collected Papers of John Bassett Moore.* New Haven: Yale University Press, 1944.

Ornstein, Norman J., ed. *President and Congress: Assessing Reagan's First Year.* Washington, D.C.: American Enterprise Institute, 1982.

Paige, Glenn D. *The Korean Decision.* New York: Free Press, 1968.

Palazzolo, Daniel J. *Done Deal? The Politics of the 1997 Budget Agreement.* Seven Bridges Press, 1999.

Paschal, Joel Francis. *Mr. Justice Sutherland: A Man against the State.* Princeton, N.J.: Princeton University Press, 1951.

Pfiffner, James P. *The President, the Budget, and Congress: Impoundment and the 1974 Budget Act.* Boulder, Colo.: Westview Press, 1979.

Pork Barrels and Principles: The Politics of the Presidential Veto. National Legal Center for the Public Interest, 1988.

Powell, Talcott. *Tattered Banners.* New York: Harcourt, Brace, and Company, 1933.

Pringle, Henry F. *The Life and Times of William Howard Taft.* 2 vols. New York: Farrar and Rinehart, 1939.

Reveley, W. Taylor, III. *War Powers of the President and Congress: Who Holds the Arrows and Olive Branches?* Charlottesville: University Press of Virginia, 1981.

Richardson, James D., ed. *A Compilation of the Messages and Papers of the Presidents.* 20 vols. New York: Bureau of National Literature, 1897–1925.

Roberts, Charles, ed. *Has the President Too Much Power?* New York: Harper's Magazine Press, 1974.

Rogers, James Grafton. *World Policing and the Constitution.* Boston: World Peace Foundation, 1945.

Schick, Allen. *The Capacity to Budget.* Washington, D.C.: Urban Institute Press, 1990.

———. *Congress and Money: Budgeting, Spending, and Taxing.* Washington, D.C.: Urban Institute Press, 1980.

———, ed. *Crisis in the Budget Process: Exercising Political Choice.* Washington, D.C.: American Enterprise Institute for Public Policy Research, 1986.

Schlesinger, Arthur M., Jr. *The Imperial Presidency.* Boston: Houghton Mifflin, 1973.

———, and Alfred de Grazia. *Congress and the Presidency: Their Role in Modern Times.* Washington, D.C.: American Enterprise Institute for Public Policy Research, 1967.

Sheffer, Martin S. *The Judicial Development of Presidential War Powers.* Westport, Conn.: Praeger, 1999.

Siff, Ezra Y. *Why the Senate Slept: The Gulf of Tonkin Resolution and the Beginning of America's Vietnam War.* Westport, Conn.: Praeger, 1999.

Sofaer, Abraham D. *War, Foreign Affairs and Constitutional Power: The Origins.* Cambridge, Mass.: Ballinger Publishing Co., 1976.

Sorensen, Theodore S. *Watchmen in the Night: Presidential Accountability after Watergate.* Cambridge, Mass.: MIT Press, 1975.

Stockman, David A. *The Triumph of Politics: How the Reagan Revolution Failed.* New York: Harper & Row, 1986.

Story, Joseph. *Commentaries on the Constitution of the United States.* Vol. 3. 1833.

Thorpe, Francis Newton, ed. *The Federal and State Constitutions, Colonial Charters, and Other Organic Laws 1893, 1897, 1902, 1904, 1905.* Washington, D.C.: Government Printing Office, 1909.

Thurber, James A., ed. *Rivals for Power.* Washington, D.C.: Congressional Quarterly Books, 1996.

Tiefer, Charles. *The Semi-Sovereign Presidency: The Bush Administration's Strategy for Governing without Congress.* Boulder, Colo.: Westview Press, 1994.

Vile, M. J. C. *Constitutionalism and the Separation of Powers.* Oxford: Clarendon Press, 1967.

Washington, George. *The Writings of George Washington,* ed. John C. Fitzpatrick. Washington, D.C.: U.S. Printing Office, 1940.

Weissman, Stephen R. *A Culture of Deference: Congress's Failure of Leadership in Foreign Policy.* New York: Basic Books, 1996.

Wharton, Francis. *State Trials of the United States during the Administrations of Washington and Adams.* 1849.

Wilson, Woodrow. *The Papers of Woodrow Wilson,* ed. Arthur S. Link. 69 vols. Princeton, N.J.: Princeton University Press, 1974–94.

Index of Cases

Index

Joseph V. Hughes, Jr., and Holly O. Hughes Series in the Presidency and Leadership Studies

Bose, Meena. *Shaping and Signaling Presidential Policy: The National Security Decision Making of Eisenhower and Kennedy.* 1998.

Califano, Joseph A., Jr. *The Triumph and Tragedy of Lyndon Johnson: The White House Years.* 2000.

Campbell, James E. *The American Campaign: U.S. Presidential Campaigns and the National Vote.* 2000.

Fisher, Louis. *The Politics of Shared Power: Congress and the Executive.* 4th ed. 1998.

Garrison, Jean A. *Games Advisors Play: Foreign Policy in the Nixon and Carter Administrations.* 1999.

Pfiffner, James P., ed. *The Managerial Presidency.* 2d ed. 1999.

Ponder, Daniel E. *Good Advice: Information and Policy Making in the White House.* 2000.